BIG BOOK OF
HOME COOKING

Cheesy Beef
& Bacon Burger
Meatloaf (page 80)

BIG BOOK OF
HOME COOKING

Favorite family recipes, tips & ideas for delicious, comforting food at its best

BIG BOOK OF
HOME COOKING

©2013 by Gooseberry Patch
2500 Farmers Dr., #110, Columbus, Ohio 43235
1-800-854-6673, **gooseberrypatch.com**

©2013 by Time Home Entertainment Inc.
135 West 50th Street, New York, NY 10020

ISBN-13: 978-0-8487-4225-6
ISBN-10: 0-8487-4225-7
Library of Congress Control Number: 2011933435
Printed in the United States of America
Fourth Printing 2013

Oxmoor House
VP, Publishing Director: Jim Childs
Editorial Director: Susan Payne Dobbs
Brand Manager: Vanessa Tiongson
Senior Editor: Rebecca Brennan
Managing Editor: Laurie S. Herr

Gooseberry Patch Big Book of Home Cooking
Editor: Ashley T. Strickland
Project Editor: Sarah H. Doss
Designer: Melissa Clark
Assistant Designer: Allison Sperando Potter
Director, Test Kitchens: Elizabeth Tyler Austin
Assistant Directors, Test Kitchens: Julie Christopher,
    Julie Gunter
Test Kitchens Professionals: Wendy Ball, Allison E. Cox,
    Victoria E. Cox, Margaret Monroe Dickey,
    Alyson Moreland Haynes, Stefanie Maloney,
    Callie Nash, Catherine Crowell Steele, Leah Van Deren
Photography Director: Jim Bathie
Senior Photo Stylist: Kay E. Clarke
Associate Photo Stylist: Katherine Eckert Coyne

Assistant Photo Stylist: Mary Louise Menendez
Production Manager: Theresa Beste-Farley

Contributors
Compositor: Cathy Robbins
Copy Editors: Donna Baldone, Norma McKittrick
Proofreader: Lauren Brooks
Indexer: Nanette Cardon
Interns: Erin Bishop, Blair Gillespie, Alison Loughman,
    Lindsay A. Rozier, Caitlin Watzke
Test Kitchens Professional: Kathleen Royal Phillips
Photographer: Mary Britton Senseney
Photo Stylist: Mindi Shapiro Levine

Time Home Entertainment Inc.
Publisher: Richard Fraiman
General Manager: Steven Sandonato
Executive Director, Marketing Services: Carol Pittard
Executive Director, Retail & Special Sales: Tom Mifsud
Director, New Product Development: Peter Harper
Director, Bookazine Development & Marketing: Laura Adam
Assistant Director, Brand Marketing: Joy Butts
Associate Counsel: Helen Wan

To order additional publications, call 1-800-765-6400 or 1-800-491-0551.

To search, savor, and share thousands of recipes, visit **myrecipes.com**

Front Cover (from left to right, top to bottom): Red Velvet Cake *(page 325)*, Gruyère Rolls *(page 310)*, Three-Cheese
Pasta Bake *(page 188)*, Easy Chicken Pot Pie *(page 302)*, Raisin-Oatmeal Cookies *(page 246)*, Pork & Raspberry Sauce *(page 82)*

Page 1: Fresh Strawberry Shortcake *(page 214)*

Back Cover (from left to right, top to bottom): Sour Cherry Pie *(page 231)*, Chocolate Bread *(page 272)*,
Sweet & Spicy Baby Back Ribs *(page 83)*, Mom's Everything Waffles *(page 52)*, Parmesan-Onion Soup *(page 158)*

Dear Friend,

What better way to show your love for family and friends than a home-cooked meal? Whether it's a comforting casserole to welcome a new baby, a cozy bowl of soup to enjoy in front of the fire, or a fresh-baked pie using the fruit you've gathered from the local farmers' market, this brand-new recipe collection from Gooseberry Patch will provide countless new memories as well as honor those from the past.

Create memorable weeknight family meals with favorites like Ultimate Cheeseburger Pizza (page 78). Start your day off right with a slice of Farm-house Quiche (page 40) and Sugar Plum Bacon (page 51). Or, impress your friends at the neighborhood potluck with Chicken Tex-Mex Bake (page 302).

We're also sharing sensational slow cooker recipes, our best bread recipes, and heartwarming soups and sandwiches. And, to satisfy your sweet tooth, we've included our best cookie and candy recipes and prize winning cakes and pies such as Mocha Pecan Mud Pie (page 236).

So flip through the pages…you'll find lots of helpful tips and clever menu planning ideas as well as mouthwatering recipes. Whether you need a birthday cake for someone special or a quick weeknight dinner solution, we hope this cookbook will be your guide.

From our kitchen to yours,

Vickie & JoAnn

Black Beans & Vegetable
Chili (page 153)

Sweet & Spicy
Baby Back Ribs (page 83)

Sesame Chicken
(page 136)

Old-Fashioned Jam Cake
(page 216)

contents

Vickie's Gazpacho Dip (page 28)

Marinated Olives (page 35)

Patchwork Wheel of Brie (page 32)

Spiced Chocolate Coffee (page 12)

MUNCHIES & MORE

Scrumptious ways to begin your meal

Refreshing
Mint Punch

Refreshing Mint Punch

With only four ingredients, this crowd-pleasing punch is easy to mix up.

2 c. fresh mint leaves, packed
2 c. water
12-oz. can frozen lemonade concentrate,
    thawed
1 qt. ginger ale

Bring mint and water to boil; bruise mint with potato masher. Set aside overnight; strain and discard solids. Add lemonade, 3 lemonade cans of water and ginger ale to mint mixture; mix well and serve. Serves 10 to 12.

Mary Murray
Mt. Vernon, OH

Summer Sparkle

Enjoy the tangy flavor of this cool, crisp and refreshing sipper.

48-oz. bottle ruby red grapefruit juice
12-oz. can frozen orange juice concentrate,
    thawed
6-oz. can frozen lemonade concentrate,
    thawed
2-ltr. bottle lemon-lime soda
Garnish: orange and lemon slices

Combine grapefruit juice, orange juice concentrate and lemonade concentrate in a gallon pitcher. Stir ingredients; cover and refrigerate until chilled. When ready to serve, add soda to pitcher; stir. Pour into tall glasses with ice; garnish. Makes 20 cups.

Eleanor Bamford
Boonton, NJ

Daffodil Banana Crush Punch

My grandmother sent me off to college with this recipe…it was always a hit at every gathering!

6 c. water
4 c. sugar
32-oz. can pineapple juice
6-oz. can frozen orange juice concentrate,
    thawed
½ c. lemon juice
6 bananas, mashed
3 qts. ginger ale, chilled

Combine all ingredients except ginger ale; mix well. Divide into 8 large plastic zipping freezer bags; freeze. Remove bags from freezer 3 to 4 hours before serving. Pour into punch bowl; add 3 quarts of chilled ginger ale. Serves 40.

Christi Perry
Gainesville, TX

Cinnamon Tea

Serve this tea in a crystal punch bowl with floating lemon and orange slices; add a rosemary wreath around the punch bowl base.

14 c. water, divided
12 cinnamon herb teabags
2 c. sugar
6-oz. can frozen pineapple juice concentrate
6-oz. can frozen lemonade concentrate
6-oz. can frozen orange juice concentrate
6 3-inch cinnamon sticks

Bring 12 cups water to a boil, add teabags and steep for 5 minutes. Discard teabags. Add remaining water, sugar, juice concentrates and cinnamon sticks. Heat through, stirring well. Serves 30.

Spiced Chocolate Coffee

This sweet sipper is conveniently made in a slow cooker. Top with sweetened whipped cream for a special treat.

8 c. brewed coffee
⅓ c. sugar
¼ c. chocolate syrup
4 4-inch cinnamon sticks, broken
1½ t. whole cloves
Garnish: cinnamon sticks, sweetened
   whipped cream

Combine first 3 ingredients in a 3-quart slow cooker; set aside.
Wrap spices in a coffee filter or cheesecloth and tie with kitchen string; add to slow cooker. Cover and cook on low setting for 2 to 3 hours. Remove and discard spices. Ladle coffee into mugs and garnish. Makes about 8 cups.

Regina Vining
Warwick, RI

Spiced
Chocolate
Coffee

(Note: The recipe for
Peppery Molasses Cookies
is on page 245.)

Old-Fashioned Eggnog

Old-Fashioned Eggnog

This creamy holiday favorite is a definite crowd-pleaser.

6 eggs
1 c. sugar
½ t. salt
1 qt. light cream, divided
1 c. golden rum or 1 T. rum extract
    plus 1 c. water
nutmeg, to taste
Garnish: cinnamon sticks

Beat eggs until light and foamy. Add sugar and salt, beating until thick. Combine egg mixture and 2 cups light cream in a large saucepan. Stirring constantly, cook over low heat until mixture coats the back of a metal spoon and reaches 160 degrees on a candy thermometer. Remove from heat. Stir in remaining light cream; add rum or extract and water. Chill several hours. Sprinkle with nutmeg and garnish before serving. Makes 6 cups.

Frosty Orange Creamsicle

So cool and refreshing!

6-oz. can frozen orange juice concentrate
1 c. milk
1 c. water
1 c. ice cubes
¼ c. sugar
½ t. vanilla extract

Combine all ingredients in a blender until smooth. Serve immediately or freeze until ready to serve. Serves 6.

Molly Bordonaro
Worthington, OH

Brown Cow

This is a twist on a traditional root beer float.

¼ c. evaporated milk
¼ c. chocolate syrup
crushed ice
root beer
chocolate sprinkles

Shake milk and syrup together; add ice and pour in a soda glass. Fill glass with root beer; top with sprinkles. Serves one.

Carol Sheets
Delaware, OH

milkshake memories

Years ago, soda fountains were always found in drugstores. Many young children and teenagers saved their allowance to enjoy milkshakes, malts or Brown Cows!

Citrus Mimosa

This fruity drink makes the Champagne go a little further!

1 c. prepared strawberry daiquiri mix
6-oz. can frozen orange juice concentrate, thawed
6 oz. cold water
¾ c. fresh grapefruit juice
⅓ c. frozen lemonade concentrate, thawed
3 T. frozen limeade concentrate, thawed
1 bottle Champagne or sparkling white wine, chilled
Garnish: thin orange slices, halved

Combine prepared daiquiri mix, orange juice concentrate, water, grapefruit juice, lemonade and limeade concentrate in a pitcher or bowl. Stir until well combined. Cover and chill. To serve, pour the chilled juice mixture into 8 ice-filled glasses, filling each glass half-full. Pour an equal amount of the chilled Champagne into each glass. Garnish with orange slice halves. Serves 8.

NOTE: *For a non-alcoholic drink, substitute chilled carbonated water for the Champagne.*

Sonia's Holiday Sangria

Use your favorite fresh fruit in this holiday treat.

1 qt. Burgundy wine or grape juice
2 c. lemon-lime soda
⅔ c. strawberry nectar
6-oz. can frozen orange juice concentrate
6-oz. can peach nectar
⅛ t. cinnamon
1 c. fruit, sliced
Garnish: orange, lemon and lime slices

Combine first 7 ingredients in a large container. Cover and refrigerate for 24 hours. Serve chilled. Garnish with orange, lemon and lime slices. Makes about 9 cups.

Sonia Bracamonte

Tomato Cocktail

A great beverage to serve while you're putting the finishing touches on brunch.

46-oz. can tomato juice
juice of ½ lemon
⅛ t. hot pepper sauce
1 t. sweet onion, grated
1 t. Worcestershire sauce
Optional: celery sticks

Combine all ingredients except celery sticks; chill. Garnish, if desired. Serves 6.

Sonia's Holiday Sangria

Fresh Salsa

Fresh Salsa

This garden-fresh favorite can be made ahead.
The flavors only improve over time.

1 jalapeño pepper, seeded and minced
1 cucumber, peeled and diced
4 plum tomatoes, chopped
½ c. fresh cilantro, finely chopped
2 T. vinegar
2 T. olive oil
1 t. sugar
1 t. ground cumin
½ t. salt
tortilla chips

Stir together all ingredients except tortilla chips in a small bowl. Cover and chill at least one hour. Serve with tortilla chips. Makes about 3½ cups.

summertime splendor
Take advantage of warm summer evenings and enjoy a frosty drink and appetizer on the porch swing.

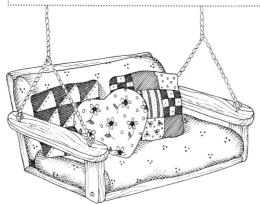

Healthy Hummus

A popular taste from the Mediterranean.

3 green onions, sliced
4 cloves garlic, chopped
15½-oz. can chickpeas
2 T. vegetable broth
2 T. lemon juice
1 t. olive oil
½ t. pepper
⅛ t. hot pepper sauce
carrot sticks or toasted pita wedges

Combine all ingredients except carrots and pita wedges in a food processor; process until smooth. Serve with carrot sticks or toasted pita wedges. Serves 2 to 4.

Terri Webber
Miami, FL

Apple Dip

This is also great served with baked cinnamon pita chips.

8-oz. pkg. cream cheese, softened
2 T. milk
1 t. vanilla extract
2 T. brown sugar
1 t. cinnamon
¼ t. nutmeg
apple wedges

Blend all ingredients except apple wedges together until smooth. Chill until ready to serve. Serve with apple wedges. Makes about 1¼ cups.

Caramelized Vidalia Onion Dip

Here's a new take on an old favorite appetizer. Look for sturdy sweet potato chips for scooping up this mega-cheesy family favorite. (Pictured on page 357)

2 T. butter
3 Vidalia or other sweet onions, thinly sliced
8-oz. pkg. cream cheese, softened
8-oz. pkg. shredded Swiss cheese
1 c. grated Parmesan cheese
1 c. mayonnaise
sweet potato chips

Melt butter in a large skillet over medium heat; add sliced onions. Cook, stirring often, 30 to 40 minutes or until onions are caramel colored. Combine onions, cheeses and mayonnaise, stirring well. Spoon dip into a lightly greased 1½ to 2-quart casserole dish. Bake, uncovered, at 375 degrees for 30 minutes or until golden and bubbly. Serve with sweet potato chips. Makes 4 cups.

Festive Chicken Enchilada Dip

Terrific served with crispy corn tortilla chips.

2 8-oz. pkgs. cream cheese, softened
1⅓ c. shredded Cheddar cheese
1 t. minced garlic
1½ T. chili powder
1 t. ground cumin
1 t. dried oregano
1 t. paprika
cayenne pepper, to taste
3 boneless, skinless chicken breasts, cooked
   and chopped
1 bunch fresh cilantro, chopped
4 green onions, chopped
10-oz. can diced tomatoes with green chiles

Mix cheeses together until well blended; add garlic, chili powder, cumin, oregano, paprika and cayenne pepper. Mix well; stir in remaining ingredients. Cover and refrigerate overnight. Serves 12.

Jeannine English
Wylie, TX

Baked Spinach & Artichoke Dip

This creamy dip is sure to be a hit at any tailgating party. You may even want to double the recipe!

2 6-oz. pkgs. baby spinach
1 T. butter
8-oz. pkg. Neufchâtel cheese
1 clove garlic, chopped
14-oz. can artichoke hearts, drained and chopped
½ c. light sour cream
½ c. shredded mozzarella cheese, divided
pita wedges or pita chips

Microwave spinach in a large microwave-safe bowl on high 3 minutes or until wilted; drain well. Press spinach between paper towels to remove excess moisture. Chop spinach.

Melt butter in a non-stick skillet over medium-high heat. Add Neufchâtel cheese and garlic; cook 3 to 4 minutes, stirring constantly, until cream cheese melts. Fold in spinach, artichokes, sour cream and ¼ cup mozzarella cheese; stir until mozzarella cheese melts.

Transfer mixture to a shallow one-quart casserole dish. Sprinkle with remaining mozzarella cheese. Bake at 350 degrees for 15 minutes or until hot and bubbly. Serve immediately with pita wedges or pita chips. Serves 11.

Baked Spinach & Artichoke Dip

Spicy Crawfish Spread

Spicy Crawfish Spread

Serve this sassy Cajun spread with corn chips, vegetable crudités or crackers.

3 T. butter
¾ c. onion, finely diced
¾ c. celery, finely diced
4 cloves garlic, minced
2 T. salt-free seasoning
½ t. cayenne pepper
8 oz. peeled, cooked crawfish tails, chopped
8-oz. pkg. cream cheese, softened
Optional: celery leaf

Melt butter in a small skillet over medium-high heat. Add onion, celery and garlic; sauté 5 minutes or until onion and celery are tender. Add seasonings; sauté 30 seconds.

Combine sautéed vegetables and crawfish tails in a bowl. Add cream cheese and stir gently to combine. Garnish with a celery leaf, if desired. Makes about 2 cups.

Curried Chutney Spread

8-oz. pkg. cream cheese, softened
2 T. sour cream
1 t. curry powder
½ c. green onions, sliced
½ c. chopped peanuts
9-oz. jar chutney
crackers

In a small bowl, beat together cream cheese, sour cream and curry powder until smooth. Fold in onions and peanuts. Spread about ½-inch thick on a serving plate. Chill until ready to serve. Just before serving, spread chutney on top. Serve with crackers. Serves 12.

Lynda Robson
Boston, MA

Crabby Artichoke Spread

Your guests will just love this creamy, spicy dip!

1 jalapeño pepper, seeded and chopped
1 t. oil
14-oz. can artichokes, drained and chopped
2 6-oz. cans crabmeat, drained
1 c. mayonnaise
½ red pepper, chopped
¼ c. grated Parmesan cheese
2 green onions, chopped
2 t. lemon juice
2 t. Worcestershire sauce
½ t. celery seed
toasted bread rounds or crackers

Sauté jalapeño in oil until tender. Combine jalapeño and remaining ingredients except bread rounds in a slow cooker. Cover and cook on low setting for 4 hours. Serve with bread rounds or crackers. Makes 3 to 4 cups.

Kathy Grashoff
Fort Wayne, IN

Crabby Artichoke Spread

Stuffed Mushrooms

Easy to make ahead…just chop, sauté, stuff and then cover with plastic wrap and refrigerate for up to two hours. Bake them just before guests arrive.

20 mushrooms
¼ c. onion, chopped
2 cloves garlic, minced
1 T. butter
10-oz. pkg. frozen chopped spinach,
    thawed and drained
¼ c. grated Parmesan cheese
¼ c. bread crumbs
¼ c. minced pimento
½ t. dried basil
½ t. dried oregano
salt and pepper to taste

Remove stems from mushrooms; set aside caps. Chop stems; sauté with onion and garlic in butter until tender. Add spinach; heat on low until liquid is evaporated. Remove from heat; stir in remaining ingredients, except mushroom caps. Spoon mixture into mushroom caps; arrange in a 15"x10" jelly-roll pan sprayed with non-stick vegetable spray. Bake at 425 degrees until golden, about 10 to 15 minutes; serve warm. Makes 20.

Jo Ann
Gooseberry Patch

fresh idea
Hollow out small cabbages, bell peppers, melons or pineapples to fill with savory and sweet dips instead of using a bowl.

Festive Cheese Ball

Make ahead of time to allow the flavors to blend.

2 8-oz. pkgs. cream cheese, softened
2 c. shredded Cheddar cheese
1 T. onion, finely chopped
1 T. pimento, finely chopped
1 T. green pepper, finely chopped
2 t. Worcestershire sauce
1 t. lemon juice
⅛ t. salt
⅛ t. cayenne pepper
½ c. chopped walnuts, toasted
crackers or red and green pepper strips

In a medium bowl, combine cheeses. Mix in remaining ingredients except walnuts and crackers. Place mixture on plastic wrap and shape into a ball; wrap tightly and chill thoroughly. Roll in chopped walnuts and serve with assorted crackers or strips of red and green peppers. Makes 4 cups.

Green Olive-Cheese Puffs

These cheesy bites with a surprise inside are sure to go fast!

8-oz. pkg. shredded sharp Cheddar cheese
½ c. butter, softened
1 c. all-purpose flour
7-oz. jar green olives with pimentos, drained

Combine cheese and butter in a blender or food processor; blend until smooth. Place in a mixing bowl; add flour and mix well. Roll out to ¼-inch thickness; cut into 48, 2-inch by 2-inch squares. Wrap each square around an olive, sealing seams. Arrange on an ungreased baking sheet; bake at 400 degrees for 10 to 15 minutes, until golden. Makes 4 dozen.

Staci Meyers
Cocoa, FL

Festive Cheese Ball

Ultimate Nachos

This crowd-pleaser is loaded with ooey-gooey cheese and all your favorite toppings.

⅓ c. onion, finely chopped
1 clove garlic, minced
1 T. olive oil
16-oz. can refried beans
½ c. salsa
13-oz. pkg. restaurant-style tortilla chips
1½ c. shredded Monterey Jack cheese
1½ c. shredded Cheddar cheese
pickled jalapeño slices, well drained
Optional: 1 c. guacamole, ½ c. sour cream
Optional: chopped fresh cilantro, sliced ripe olives,
  shredded lettuce, additional salsa

Sauté onion and garlic in oil in a skillet over medium heat 4 to 5 minutes or until onion is tender. Add beans and salsa to skillet, stirring until beans are creamy. Cook one minute or until heated through.

Scatter most of chips on a parchment paper-lined large baking sheet or an oven-proof platter. Top with bean mixture, cheeses and desired amount of jalapeños.

Bake at 450 degrees for 8 minutes or until cheeses melt and edges are golden.

Garnish with small dollops of guacamole and sour cream, if desired. Garnish with cilantro, olives, lettuce and salsa, if desired. Serve hot. Serves 6 to 8.

Fried Dill Pickles

This county fair recipe is always well-received.

1 egg, beaten
1 c. milk
1 T. Worcestershire sauce
3½ c. plus 1 T. all-purpose flour, divided
6 drops hot pepper sauce
¾ t. salt
¾ t. pepper
1 qt. dill pickles, sliced
oil for deep frying

Combine egg, milk, Worcestershire sauce, one tablespoon flour and hot sauce; set aside. Mix together salt, pepper and remaining flour. Dip pickles in milk mixture, then in flour mixture. Pour oil to a depth of 3 inches in a Dutch oven. Heat oil to 350 degrees. Fry pickles until golden; drain. Serves 4 to 6.

Sheila Williams
Mayodan, NC

BLT Bites

A favorite sandwich becomes an appetizer!

16 to 20 cherry tomatoes
8 slices bacon, crisply cooked and crumbled
½ c. mayonnaise
⅓ c. green onion, chopped
3 T. grated Parmesan cheese
2 T. fresh parsley, finely chopped

Cut a thin slice off the top of each tomato; scoop out and discard pulp. Invert tomatoes onto a paper towel to drain. Combine the remaining ingredients in a small bowl; mix well. Spoon mixture into each tomato; refrigerate for several hours before serving. Serves 6.

Deanna Smith
Huntington, WV

Cucumber & Salmon Slices

The salmon mixture also makes a great sandwich spread.

3-oz. pkg. smoked salmon, flaked
1 t. lemon juice
1 t. fresh dill, chopped
½ c. sour cream
cucumbers
Garnish: fresh dill or parsley sprigs

Blend salmon, lemon juice, dill and sour cream. Place in a covered container and chill one hour. Place a design on the outside of whole cucumbers by slicing several thin strips of peel from the length of the cucumber, or scoring the peel with the tines of a fork. Cut into ½-inch slices. Spread with chilled salmon mixture and garnish with dill or parsley. Makes about 48.

picnic place setting
Make your picnic more festive by wrapping plastic forks, spoons and knives with a decorative paper napkin. Place in a flower pot and insert fresh blooms if you'd like.

Tangy Deviled Eggs

No family reunion is complete without deviled eggs!

4 eggs, hard-boiled and peeled
1 t. prepared horseradish
1 t. onion, minced
⅓ c. mayonnaise
¼ t. celery salt

Slice eggs in half lengthwise and remove yolks. Mince yolks in a small mixing bowl; combine with horseradish, onion, mayonnaise and salt. Spoon mixture into egg white halves; keep chilled. Serves 8.

Jo Ann
Gooseberry Patch

Veggie-dillas

¾ c. broccoli, chopped
¼ c. carrots, peeled and shredded
¼ c. green onion, sliced
2 T. water
6 6-inch flour tortillas
1 t. oil
2 c. shredded Cheddar cheese
Garnish: sour cream, salsa, sliced olives,
    sliced green onion

Combine broccoli, carrots, onions and water in a saucepan; cook until vegetables are crisp-tender. Drain; set aside. Brush one side of each tortilla with oil; place 3 tortillas oil-side down in an ungreased 15"x10" jelly-roll pan. Top with cheese; spread with vegetable mixture. Place remaining tortillas on top oil-side up; bake, uncovered, at 450 degrees until golden, about 6 minutes. Slice into wedges to serve; garnish. Serves 12.

Glena Steele
Richfield, OH

Vickie's Gazpacho Dip

Serve multicolored tortilla chips with this Tex-Mex dip to make it even more festive.

3 tomatoes, diced
3 avocados, peeled, pitted and diced
4 green onions, thinly sliced
4.5-oz. can diced green chiles, undrained
3 T. olive oil
1½ T. cider vinegar
1 t. garlic salt
½ t. salt
¼ t. pepper

Combine tomatoes, avocados, onions and chiles in a large bowl; set aside. Whisk together olive oil and remaining ingredients; drizzle over vegetables and toss well. Cover and chill. Makes 5 cups.

Vickie
Gooseberry Patch

"Fresh summer flavors burst from each scoop of this chunky dip." —Vickie

Vickie's Gazpacho Dip

Bacon & Greens Salsa

Bacon & Greens Salsa

We also loved this salsa over cream cheese (a great idea for leftovers). You can prepare the recipe up to a day ahead...just reheat the salsa before serving.

8 slices bacon
16-oz. pkg. frozen mixed greens,
    thawed and drained
½ sweet onion, chopped
1 t. minced garlic
1½ c. frozen corn, thawed
1 serrano chile pepper, minced
¼ t. salt
¼ t. pepper
2 T. cider vinegar
pork rinds and sweet potato chips
hot pepper sauce

Cook bacon in a large skillet over medium-high heat 7 to 9 minutes or until crisp; remove bacon and drain on paper towels, reserving 2 tablespoons drippings in skillet. Crumble bacon; set aside.

Sauté greens, onion and garlic in hot drippings 7 to 10 minutes or until tender. Stir in corn and next 3 ingredients, and cook 3 minutes or until thoroughly heated. Remove from heat, and stir in vinegar. Sprinkle with bacon. Serve warm with pork rinds, sweet potato chips, and hot pepper sauce. Makes 4 cups.

The Best-Yet Buffalo Wings

These wings are sweet, but the sauce is hot. Reduce the hot pepper sauce if you're sensitive to spice.

3 lbs. chicken wings
seasoned salt to taste
2-oz. bottle hot pepper sauce
1 c. water
1 c. brown sugar, packed
1 T. mustard seed

Arrange chicken wings on a 15"x10" jelly-roll pan sprayed with non-stick vegetable spray. Bake at 400 degrees for 20 minutes; turn wings. Bake 20 to 30 more minutes, until golden and juices run clear; drain. Sprinkle with seasoned salt; arrange on serving platter. Combine hot pepper sauce, water, brown sugar and mustard seed in saucepan; bring to a boil over medium heat. Reduce heat to low; cook until mixture caramelizes and becomes a dark burgundy color, stirring occasionally. Pour sauce over wings before serving, or serve on the side for dipping. Makes about 3 dozen.

Kristen Taylor
Fort Smith, AR

Hot Smoky Pecans

This is the perfect appetizer to munch on before dinner.

¼ c. butter, melted
2 T. soy sauce
1 T. Worcestershire sauce
½ t. hot pepper sauce
2 c. pecan halves

Stir together all ingredients; spread pecans in a single layer in a 15"x10" jelly-roll pan. Bake at 300 degrees for 25 minutes or until toasted, stirring 3 times. Makes 2 cups.

Hot Smoky Pecans

Patchwork Wheel of Brie

A festive centerpiece for your appetizer table.

5-lb. round of Brie
½ c. sweetened dried cranberries
 or dried currants
½ c. walnuts, finely chopped
½ c. fresh dill or chives, chopped
¼ c. poppy seed
1 c. sliced almonds, toasted
bread rounds

Remove the rind from the top of the cheese by cutting carefully with a sharp knife. Lightly score the top of the cheese into 10 equal pie-shaped sections. Sprinkle half of each of the toppings onto each wedge and press gently until you have decorated all 10 sections. Allow to stand at room temperature for at least 40 minutes before serving. Serve with bread rounds. Serves 20 to 25.

Cranberry Cocktail Sausages

These sausages are so simple to make!

14-oz. can whole-berry cranberry sauce
⅓ c. seedless raspberry jam
1 t. cornstarch
½ t. hot pepper sauce
2 1-lb. pkgs. mini smoked sausages
Optional: sliced green onions

Mix together all ingredients except onions in a large saucepan over medium-high heat; stir frequently until simmering. Reduce heat to low. Cook, uncovered, for 15 minutes, stirring occasionally, until sausages are heated through. Place in a serving dish and sprinkle with green onions, if desired. Serves 4 to 6.

Janice Woods
Northern Cambria, PA

Patchwork Wheel of Brie

Marinated
Olives

Marinated Olives

These olives are quite spicy & will please anyone who loves to nibble on fiery foods!

6-oz. can pitted ripe olives, drained
6-oz. jar pitted green olives, drained
1 hot chili pepper, minced
3 cloves garlic, minced
1 t. dried oregano
1 c. olive oil

Combine olives, chili pepper, garlic and oregano in a jar with a lid. Cover with olive oil. Shake olives gently and let stand at room temperature overnight. Store in refrigerator and use within one week. Makes 2½ cups.

Karen's Cayenne Pretzels

Serve these to munch on while watching the ball game. Just be sure to have a cold beverage nearby to tame the flames.

1 c. oil
1-oz. pkg. ranch salad dressing mix
1 t. garlic salt
1½ t. cayenne pepper
2 10-oz. pkgs. pretzel twists

Mix together first 4 ingredients; pour over pretzels in a large bowl. Stir until well coated; spread onto ungreased baking sheets. Bake at 200 degrees for one hour and 15 minutes to 1½ hours. Makes 8 to 10 cups.

Karen Boehme
Greensburg, PA

"These spicy-hot pretzels are always a hit!"
—*Karen*

Everyone's Favorite Party Mix

I like to package this mix in tins to hand out to family & friends…the empty tins often make their way back to me to be refilled!

5 c. doughnut-shaped oat cereal
5 c. bite-size crispy corn or rice cereal squares
9.4-oz. pkg. candy-coated chocolates
12-oz. jar peanuts
15-oz. pkg. mini pretzels
2 12-oz. pkgs. white chocolate chips
3 T. oil

Combine first 5 ingredients in a large roasting pan; set aside. Place chocolate chips and oil in a microwave-safe bowl; heat until melted, stirring often. Pour over cereal mixture; toss to coat. Spread mixture on wax paper; let dry until firm. Break into pieces; store in an airtight container. Serves 20.

Jennie Wiseman
Coshocton, OH

snack swap
Host a party where everyone brings enough bags of their favorite homemade goodies for each person attending. Everyone will leave with a plethora of scrumptious treats!

Buttermilk Pancakes (page 56)

Apple & Berry Breakfast
Crisp (page 64)

Herbed
Salmon Omelets
(page 44)

Mom's Everything
Waffles
(page 52)

BREAKFAST ANYTIME

*Enjoy these sunny sensations,
morning, noon or night*

Laura's Eggs
Benedict

Laura's Eggs Benedict

You can easily substitute split biscuits for the English muffins and even a sausage patty for the Canadian bacon…it's tasty either way.

4 English muffins, split and toasted
16 slices Canadian bacon
8 eggs
¼ c. plus 1 T. butter, divided
¼ c. all-purpose flour
1 t. paprika
⅛ t. nutmeg
2 c. milk
8-oz. pkg. shredded Swiss cheese
½ c. chicken broth
1 c. corn flake cereal, crushed

Arrange muffins split-side up in a lightly greased 13"x9" baking pan. Place 2 bacon slices on each muffin half. Fill a large skillet halfway with water; bring to just boiling. Break one egg into a dish; carefully slide into water. Repeat with 3 more eggs. Simmer, uncovered, 3 minutes or just until set. Remove eggs with a slotted spoon. Repeat with remaining eggs. Place one egg on each muffin half; set aside. In a saucepan over medium heat, melt ¼ cup butter; stir in flour, paprika and nutmeg. Add milk; cook and stir until thick and bubbly. Stir in cheese until melted; add broth. Carefully spoon sauce over eggs. Melt remaining butter; stir in cereal and sprinkle over top. Cover and refrigerate overnight. Bake, uncovered, at 375 degrees for 20 to 25 minutes, or until heated through. Serves 8.

Laura Fuller
Fort Wayne, IN

Rise & Shine Breakfast Pizza

Tasty layers of all your breakfast favorites!

2-lb. pkg. frozen shredded hashbrowns
1½ c. shredded Cheddar cheese, divided
7 eggs
½ c. milk
salt and pepper to taste
10 to 12 sausage patties, cooked

Prepare hashbrowns according to package directions; spread on an ungreased baking sheet or pizza pan. Top with ½ cup cheese; set aside. Whisk eggs and milk together in a microwave-safe bowl; microwave on high for 3 minutes, then scramble eggs well with a whisk. Return to microwave and cook 3 more minutes; whisk well to scramble. Layer eggs on top of cheese; add salt and pepper to taste. Top with remaining cheese. Arrange sausage patties on top. Bake at 400 degrees for 10 minutes or until cheese is melted. Cut into wedges to serve. Serves 8 to 10.

Micki Stephens
Marion, OH

flea market find
Use an old-fashioned pitcher to hold kitchen utensils or fresh-cut flowers.

Western-Style Quiche

Serve with a side of hashbrowns for a stick-to-your-ribs dish!

12-oz. tube refrigerated buttermilk biscuits
8-oz. pkg. ground pork sausage
½ c. green pepper, chopped
½ c. onion, chopped
6 eggs, beaten
2 c. shredded Cheddar cheese
salt and pepper to taste

Arrange biscuits in an ungreased 13"x9" baking pan; set aside. Brown sausage with green pepper and onion in a skillet; drain and transfer to a large mixing bowl. Stir in eggs, cheese, salt and pepper; mix well. Pour over biscuits; bake at 350 degrees for 30 minutes. Serves 8.

Jennifer Upchurch
Junction City, IL

breakfast for dinner
Paired with a green salad, quiches are a hearty choice to serve your family as a simple supper.

Farmhouse Quiche

Salsa and sour cream make great toppings for this veggie-packed quiche.

9-inch pie crust
2 T. olive oil
½ red pepper, diced
½ green pepper, diced
2 cloves garlic, minced
¼ c. zucchini, diced
2 T. fresh basil, chopped
4 eggs, beaten
1 c. half-and-half
1 t. salt
½ t. pepper
8-oz. pkg. shredded Pepper Jack cheese
⅓ c. grated Parmesan cheese
3 plum tomatoes, sliced

Place crust in a 9" pie plate; pierce bottom and sides with a fork. Bake at 425 degrees for 10 minutes; set aside. Heat oil in a large skillet over medium heat; sauté peppers, garlic, zucchini and basil until tender. Whisk together eggs, half-and-half, salt and pepper in a large bowl. Stir in pepper mixture and cheeses. Pour into pie crust and top with sliced tomatoes. Bake at 375 degrees for 45 minutes. Let stand 5 minutes before slicing. Serves 6.

Jo Ann
Gooseberry Patch

Fresh tasting and packed with flavor, this is one recipe I make for our whole family all summer long. —Jo Ann

Farmhouse
Quiche

Garden-Fresh
Egg Casserole

Garden-Fresh Egg Casserole

18 eggs, beaten
1½ c. shredded Monterey Jack cheese
1 c. buttermilk
1 c. cottage cheese
1 c. spinach, chopped
1 c. tomatoes, chopped
½ c. butter, melted
½ c. onion, grated

Combine all ingredients; pour into a greased 13"x9" baking dish. Cover and refrigerate overnight. Bake, uncovered, at 350 degrees for 50 minutes to one hour. Serves 8 to 10.

Anne Muns
Scottsdale, AZ

Southern Country Casserole

2 c. water
½ c. quick-cooking grits, uncooked
3½ c. shredded Cheddar cheese, divided
4 eggs, beaten
1 c. milk
½ t. salt
½ t. pepper
1 lb. ground pork sausage, browned and drained
1 T. fresh parsley, chopped

Bring water to a boil in a large saucepan; add grits. Return to a boil; reduce heat and simmer for 4 minutes. Mix in 2 cups cheese; stir until melted. Remove from heat; add eggs, milk, salt, pepper and sausage, mixing well. Pour into a greased 13"x9" baking pan; bake at 350 degrees for 45 to 50 minutes. Sprinkle with remaining cheese and parsley; return to oven until cheese melts, about 5 minutes. Serves 6 to 8.

Michelle Garner
Tampa, FL

Pesto & Green Onion Omelet

Preserve the fresh herb flavors of summer…make your own pesto sauce. It's easy!

2 T. butter
2 T. canola oil
6 eggs
salt and pepper
2 T. water
¼ c. green onions, chopped
¼ c. Pesto Sauce
Garnish: garlic chives, cherry tomatoes, parsley

Melt butter with oil in a skillet over medium heat, coating sides and bottom well. Separate eggs into 2 small mixing bowls. Beat whites until they form soft peaks; beat yolks until frothy. Add salt, pepper and water to yolks, blending well; blend in whites. Add onions. Add mixture to hot skillet, and cook without stirring, lifting edges to allow uncooked egg to flow underneath. When almost set, spoon Pesto Sauce on half of omelet. Fold other half over, slide onto a plate and garnish with chives, tomatoes and parsley. Serves 2.

Pesto Sauce:

2 c. fresh basil, washed and dried
3 cloves garlic
4 T. walnuts
½ c. olive oil
½ c. Parmesan cheese, grated

Place basil, garlic, walnuts and oil in a food processor until mixture forms a paste; add cheese and blend. Remove from processor and blend again with a spoon.

Herbed Salmon
Omelets

Mini Spinach & Bacon Quiches

These are an elegant addition to a holiday brunch buffet and can be assembled the night before and refrigerated.

¼ c. onion, diced
3 slices bacon, crisply cooked and crumbled, drippings reserved
10-oz. pkg. frozen chopped spinach, thawed and drained
⅛ t. salt
½ t. pepper
⅛ t. nutmeg
15-oz. container ricotta cheese
8-oz. pkg. shredded mozzarella cheese
1 c. grated Parmesan cheese
3 eggs, beaten

In a skillet over medium heat, cook onion in reserved drippings until tender. Add spinach and seasonings; stir over medium heat about 3 minutes or until liquid evaporates. Remove from heat; stir in bacon and cool.

Combine cheeses in a large bowl. Add eggs; stir until well blended. Add cooled spinach mixture; stir until well blended. Divide mixture evenly among 12 lightly greased muffin cups. Bake at 350 degrees for 40 minutes or until filling is set. Let stand 10 minutes; run a thin knife around edges to release. Serve warm. Makes 12.

Vickie
Gooseberry Patch

Herbed Salmon Omelets

To make this dish even healthier, add some sautéed veggies like onions or green peppers.

¼ c. sour cream
2 T. fresh dill, chopped
2 T. fresh chives, chopped
2 T. butter, divided
¼ lb. smoked salmon, chopped and divided
6 eggs, beaten and divided

Mix together sour cream and herbs in a small bowl; set aside. Heat one tablespoon butter in a skillet over low heat. Add half the salmon; cook one minute, stirring constantly. Add half the eggs to skillet and cook, lifting edges to allow uncooked egg to flow underneath. When almost set, spoon half of sour cream mixture over half of omelet. Fold other half over and slide onto plate. Keep warm. Repeat procedure with remaining ingredients. Serves 2.

Carrie O'Shea
Marina Del Ray, CA

personal panache
Change up the flavor of these handheld bites by substituting other veggies for the spinach or a different cheese for the Parmesan. The possibilities are endless!

Mini Spinach
& Bacon Quiches

Make-Ahead
Scrambled
Eggs

Make-Ahead Scrambled Eggs

These eggs are so easy to make!

3 T. butter, divided
2 doz. eggs, beaten and divided
½ c. milk
10¾-oz. can cream of mushroom soup
4-oz. can sliced mushrooms, drained
½ c. green pepper, chopped
½ c. onion, chopped
1 c. pasteurized process cheese spread, cubed

    Melt half the butter in a large skillet over medium heat. Add half the eggs; cook until lightly set. Place in a lightly greased 13"x9" baking pan. Melt remaining butter in skillet; cook remaining eggs. Add to eggs already in baking pan. Combine milk and soup; pour over eggs. Top with mushrooms, pepper, onion and cheese. Refrigerate overnight. Bake, covered, at 300 degrees for one hour. Serves 10 to 12.

Vickie
Gooseberry Patch

super secret
For the fluffiest scrambled eggs, add a pinch of baking powder.

Sausage & Red Pepper Strata

Serve this hearty breakfast favorite with fresh fruit to round out your meal.

6-oz. pkg. ground pork sausage
½ t. dried oregano
¼ t. red pepper flakes
4 slices French bread, cubed
½ red pepper, chopped
1 t. dried parsley
4 eggs
1 c. evaporated milk
1 t. Dijon mustard
¼ t. pepper
½ c. shredded sharp Cheddar cheese

    Brown sausage with oregano and red pepper flakes in a skillet; drain and set aside. Line bottom of a greased 8"x8" baking pan with bread; top with sausage mixture, red pepper and parsley. Set aside. Combine eggs, milk, mustard and pepper; whisk until well blended. Pour evenly over sausage mixture; cover tightly with aluminum foil and refrigerate overnight. Bake, covered, at 350 degrees for 55 minutes. Remove aluminum foil; sprinkle with cheese. Bake 5 more minutes or until cheese is melted. Serves 4 to 6.

Lynette Mull
Newton, KS

This breakfast casserole is delicious, and best of all, you can make it the night before!

—Lynette

Garden-Fresh Denver Omelet

You can add any of your favorite vegetables to this hearty omelet.

1 slice bacon, cut into ½-inch pieces
2 T. red pepper, diced
2 T. green pepper, diced
2 T. red onion, diced
1 slice baked ham, shredded
2 eggs, beaten
¼ c. milk
salt and pepper to taste
1 t. fresh chives, chopped
2 t. unsalted butter
Garnish: sour cream, salsa

Place bacon in a non-stick skillet and cook over medium-low heat until just crisp, about 5 minutes. Using a slotted spoon, transfer bacon to a paper towel to drain. Discard all but one tablespoon of drippings. Add peppers and onion to skillet and cook over low heat, stirring until just wilted, about 5 minutes. Transfer vegetables to a bowl and add bacon and ham.

In a separate bowl, beat eggs with milk. Season with salt and pepper and whisk in chives. Stir in vegetable mixture. Melt butter in a non-stick skillet over medium heat until it foams. Add egg mixture to skillet and cook without stirring, lifting edges to allow uncooked egg to flow underneath. Cover and cook 30 to 45 more seconds, or until eggs are cooked to desired doneness. Gently fold omelet in half, slide onto a plate and garnish with sour cream and salsa. Serves one.

Donna Dye
Ray, OH

Betty's Hot Cheese Toast

1 c. mayonnaise
2 t. Worcestershire sauce
½ t. ranch salad dressing mix
¼ t. paprika
2 green onions, chopped
2½-oz. pkg. chopped almonds
8-oz. pkg. shredded Cheddar cheese
2 T. bacon bits
15 bread slices, halved

Combine all ingredients except bread slices; mix well. Spread on half-slices of bread; arrange slices on a lightly greased baking sheet. Bake at 400 degrees for 10 minutes, until golden. Serve hot. Serves 12 to 15.

Connie Chambers
Colorado City, TX

Fluffy Baked Eggs

14 eggs, beaten
1 lb. sliced bacon, crisply cooked and crumbled, 2 T. drippings reserved
1⅓ c. cottage cheese
8-oz. can crushed pineapple, drained
1 t. vanilla extract
Garnish: fresh parsley, chopped

Blend together eggs, bacon, drippings, cottage cheese, pineapple and vanilla; spoon into a greased 11"x7" casserole dish. Bake, uncovered, at 350 degrees for 40 to 45 minutes or until center is set and a toothpick inserted in center comes out clean. Allow casserole dish to stand 5 minutes before slicing. Garnish with parsley and cut into squares. Serves 8.

Amy Butcher
Columbus, GA

Sausage Gravy & Biscuits

Enjoy these light and fluffy biscuits topped with hot sausage gravy any time of the day.

½ c. all-purpose flour
2 lbs. ground pork sausage, browned and
  drained
4 c. milk
salt and pepper to taste

In a medium saucepan over medium heat, sprinkle flour in with sausage, stirring until flour is dissolved. Gradually stir in milk and cook over medium heat until thick and bubbly. Season with salt and pepper; serve over warm Biscuits. Serves 10 to 12.

Biscuits:

4 c. self-rising flour
3 T. baking powder
2 T. sugar
7 T. shortening
2 c. buttermilk

Sift together flour, baking powder and sugar; cut in shortening. Mix in buttermilk with a fork, just until dough is moistened. Shape dough into a ball and knead a few times on a lightly floured surface. Roll out to ¾-inch thickness and cut with a 3-inch biscuit cutter. Place biscuits on a greased baking sheet. Bake at 450 degrees for about 15 minutes or until golden. Makes 2 dozen.

Vickie
Gooseberry Patch

Sausage Gravy
& Biscuits

Smoked Gouda Grits

These smoky and creamy grits are the perfect addition to scrambled eggs and breakfast sausage...yum!

6 c. chicken broth
2 c. milk
1 t. salt
½ t. white pepper
2 c. quick-cooking grits, uncooked
1⅔ c. shredded smoked Gouda cheese
3 T. butter, softened

Bring broth, milk, salt and pepper to a boil in a large saucepan over medium heat. Gradually whisk in grits. Reduce heat; cover and simmer, stirring occasionally, about 5 minutes or until thickened. Add cheese and butter; stir until melted. Serves 6 to 8.

Becky Woods
Ballwin, MO

Smoked Gouda Grits

Sunrise Granola

Carry this with you on an early morning hike!

1 c. long-cooking oats, uncooked
¼ c. sweetened flaked coconut
2 T. sunflower seeds
¼ c. wheat germ
¼ t. cinnamon
2 T. honey
¼ t. vanilla extract
1 T. oil

In a large mixing bowl, combine oats, coconut, sunflower seeds, wheat germ and cinnamon. In a separate bowl, combine honey, vanilla and oil; blend well. Pour honey mixture into oat mixture; blend well. Spread on a baking sheet and bake at 350 degrees for 20 to 25 minutes, stirring every 5 minutes. Let cool, then store in an airtight jar. Makes 1½ cups.

Jennifer Hansen
Escanaba, MI

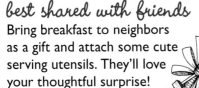

best shared with friends
Bring breakfast to neighbors as a gift and attach some cute serving utensils. They'll love your thoughtful surprise!

Maple-Raisin-Walnut Spread

Spread this flavorful cream cheese on warm toasted bagels.

8-oz. pkg. cream cheese, softened
1 T. chopped walnuts
1 T. raisins
1 t. water
3½ T. dark brown sugar, packed
⅛ t. maple extract
⅛ t. cinnamon

Whip cream cheese until smooth; set aside. Grind walnuts coarsely in a food processor or blender; set aside. Place raisins and water in food processor; chop into small pieces. Combine raisin mixture and one teaspoon walnuts with cream cheese; mix well. Add remaining walnuts, brown sugar, extract and cinnamon; mix well, cover and chill until firm. Makes about one cup.

Cora Baker
La Rue, OH

Sugar Plum Bacon

Crunchy and sweet...your guests will love it!

½ c. brown sugar, packed
1 t. cinnamon
½ lb. sliced bacon

Combine brown sugar and cinnamon. Cut each bacon slice in half crosswise and coat each slice with brown sugar mixture. Twist bacon slices and place in a 13"x9" baking pan. Bake at 350 degrees for 15 to 20 minutes or until bacon is crisp and sugar is bubbly. Place cooked bacon on aluminum foil to cool. Serve at room temperature. Serves 8.

Beth Burgmeier
East Dubuque, IL

Strawberry Cheesecake French Toast

Mom's Everything Waffles

The delicious flavors of peanut butter, pecans, blueberries and even chocolate come together in this one-of-a-kind breakfast favorite.

2 c. biscuit baking mix
1½ c. quick-cooking oats, uncooked
¼ c. wheat germ
½ c. chopped pecans or walnuts
2 eggs, beaten
¼ c. peanut butter
½ c. vanilla yogurt
3½ c. low-fat milk, divided
1 c. blueberries
Optional: ¼ c. mini chocolate chips
Garnish: maple syrup, fruit topping,
   whipped cream

Combine baking mix, oats, wheat germ and nuts in a large bowl; set aside. In a separate bowl, whisk together eggs, peanut butter, yogurt and 3 cups milk. Add to dry ingredients and stir. Add remaining milk as needed to get the consistency of applesauce. Fold in berries and chocolate chips, if desired. Pour by ½ cupfuls onto a preheated waffle iron that has been sprayed with non-stick vegetable spray. Bake until crisp, according to manufacturer's directions. Serve with maple syrup or fruit topping and a dollop of whipped cream. Serves 4 to 6.

Tamara Ahrens
Sparta, MI

Strawberry Cheesecake French Toast

Two favorite foods in one dish...strawberries and cheesecake. Now that's something to wake up to!

4-oz. cream cheese, softened
2 T. powdered sugar
2 T. strawberry preserves
8 slices country white bread
2 eggs
½ c. half-and-half
2 T. sugar
4 T. butter, divided

Combine cream cheese and powdered sugar in a small bowl; mix well. Stir in preserves. Spread cream cheese mixture evenly over 4 slices of bread; top with remaining slices to form sandwiches. Whisk together eggs, half-and-half and sugar in a medium bowl; set aside.

Melt 2 tablespoons butter in a large skillet over medium heat. Dip each sandwich into egg mixture, completely covering both sides. Cook 2 sandwiches at a time for one to 2 minutes per side or until golden. Melt remaining butter and cook remaining sandwiches as instructed. Serves 4.

Kris Coburn
Dansville, NY

These waffles have been a Saturday morning tradition in our family since our children were very little. If a week goes by without our waffles, we try to slip them in for a weeknight meal. They have developed over time with the addition of many tasty ingredients...even chocolate chips for birthdays and Christmas! –Tamara

Mom's Everything Waffles

Holiday Morning French Toast

A sweet breakfast treat that's sure to have family and friends asking for the recipe.

1 c. brown sugar, packed
½ c. butter, melted
1 T. cinnamon, divided
3 to 4 Granny Smith apples, peeled, cored
   and thinly sliced
½ c. raisins
1 loaf French or Italian bread, sliced 1-inch thick
8 to 9 eggs, beaten
2 c. milk
1 T. vanilla extract
Optional: syrup

Combine brown sugar, butter and one teaspoon cinnamon in a lightly greased 13"x9" baking pan. Add apples and raisins; toss to coat well. Spread apple mixture evenly over bottom of baking pan. Arrange slices of bread on top; set aside. Blend together eggs, milk, vanilla and remaining cinnamon until well mixed. Pour mixture over bread, soaking bread completely. Cover with aluminum foil and refrigerate for 4 to 24 hours.

Bake, covered, at 375 degrees for 40 minutes. Uncover and bake 15 more minutes. Let stand 5 minutes. Serve warm with syrup, if desired. Serves 12.

Coleen Lambert
Casco, WI

Holiday Morning
French Toast

Cocoa Waffles

Serve these chocolatey waffles with hot maple syrup and a dollop of sweetened whipped cream.

2 eggs, beaten
¾ c. whipping cream
1¼ c. cake flour
½ t. salt
3 t. baking powder
6 T. baking cocoa
½ c. sugar
¼ c. butter, melted
¼ t. vanilla extract
2 egg whites, stiffly beaten

Blend eggs and cream. Sift together dry ingredients; stir into egg mixture. Add butter and vanilla; mix well. Fold in egg whites. Bake in waffle iron 1½ to 2 minutes or until crispy. Makes 8.

Chef's Baked Oatmeal

A yummy way to start an early morning. It's a wintertime favorite!

3 c. quick-cooking oats, uncooked
2 t. baking powder
1 t. salt
½ c. butter, softened
2 eggs, beaten
2 c. milk

Stir together oats, baking powder and salt in a mixing bowl; set aside. In a separate bowl, combine butter, eggs and milk; blend into dry ingredients. Pour into an ungreased 13"x9" baking pan; bake at 375 degrees for 25 minutes. Serves 6 to 8.

Laura Leeper
Altoona, IA

Grandma's Old-Fashioned Doughnuts

These are easier to make than you'd think, and they're so delicious! Fry up the doughnut holes as well.

4 c. all-purpose flour
4 t. baking powder
½ t. salt
1 c. sugar
1 c. cinnamon
2 eggs, beaten
1 c. milk
2 T. butter, softened
1 t. vanilla extract
oil for deep frying
Garnish: sugar

Sift together dry ingredients; set aside. In a separate bowl, combine remaining ingredients except oil and garnish; gradually add dry ingredients until well mixed. Turn dough out onto a floured surface; roll to ½-inch thickness. Cut dough with a doughnut or biscuit cutter or the top of a 3-inch diameter glass dipped in sugar. Pour oil to a depth of 1½ to 2 inches in a Dutch oven. Heat oil to 360 degrees. Fry 2 to 3 minutes or until golden. Roll in sugar while still warm. Makes about 2 dozen.

Cheri Emery
Quincy, IL

Graham Cracker Breakfast Cakes

A favorite that warms us up on those chilly fall mornings.

¾ c. all-purpose flour
¾ c. graham cracker crumbs
1 T. baking powder
¼ t. salt
1 c. milk
2 T. butter, melted
1 egg
½ c. chopped pecans

Combine first 4 ingredients; set aside. Whisk milk, butter and egg together; mix into flour mixture. Fold in pecans; pour by ¼ cupfuls onto a hot, greased griddle or skillet. Cook until bubbles form along edges; flip and cook until golden on both sides. Serves 8 to 10.

The Governor's Inn
Ludlow, VT

breakfast in bed
Surprise your sweetie with a breakfast tray filled with his or her favorite morning meal, a newspaper, and a hot cup of coffee.

Buttermilk Pancakes

1¾ c. all-purpose flour
2 T. sugar
2 t. baking powder
1 t. baking soda
½ t. salt
2 eggs, beaten
2 c. buttermilk
¼ c. oil
½ t. vanilla extract

Combine dry ingredients in a large bowl; set aside. Combine eggs, buttermilk, oil and vanilla in a mixing bowl; stir into flour mixture just until moistened. Pour batter by ¼ cupfuls onto a greased hot griddle. Turn pancakes when bubbles appear on surface; cook until golden. Serves 6.

Rita Morgan
Pueblo, CO

Delicious Oatmeal Pancakes

2 c. milk
1½ c. quick-cooking oats, uncooked
1 c. all-purpose flour
2½ t. baking powder
1 t. salt
2 T. sugar
2 eggs, beaten
⅓ c. oil

Mix together milk and oats; let stand while sifting together flour, baking powder, salt and sugar in a separate bowl. Stir eggs into oat mixture; mix in dry ingredients and oil. Drop by ¼ cupfuls onto a hot, lightly greased griddle; flip over when bubbles appear around edges. Cook on each side until lightly golden. Makes 10 to 12.

June Eier
Forest, OH

Buttermilk
Pancakes

Cheddar & Bacon
Breakfast Sandwiches

Cheddar & Bacon Breakfast Sandwiches

Substitute Monterey Jack or Swiss cheese for a variety of flavor!

3 eggs, beaten
¼ c. milk
2 T. butter
8 thick slices bread
12 slices Cheddar cheese
½ T. chopped walnuts
4 slices bacon, crisply cooked and crumbled

In a large bowl, whisk together eggs and milk; set aside. Prepare a griddle or large skillet by melting butter over low heat. Dip only one side of 4 bread slices in egg mixture. Place 4 bread slices, coated side down, on griddle or in skillet. Top each bread slice with 3 cheese slices. Sprinkle cheese with an equal amount of walnuts and bacon. Dip only one side of the remaining 4 bread slices in egg mixture and place over walnuts and bacon, coated side up. Cook 5 minutes per side or until bread is golden and cheese is melted. Serves 4.

Vickie
Gooseberry Patch

patchwork potholder

Salvage an old worn-out quilt by sewing trim around a 4-inch square piece to create a homestyle potholder.

Homestyle Potato Pancakes

This golden and crispy side dish won't last long!

4 c. mashed potatoes
2 eggs, beaten
2 onions, finely chopped
1 t. salt
½ t. pepper
4 T. olive oil

Combine potatoes, eggs and onion in a medium mixing bowl; stir well to blend. Add salt and pepper. Heat oil in a large skillet over medium heat. Drop ¼ cupfuls potato mixture into oil, flatten each to ¾-inch thick. Cook each pancake until golden on both sides. Serves about 6.

Vickie
Gooseberry Patch

Mom's Red Flannel Hash

This down-home breakfast dish is a good way to use up leftover cooked potatoes.

12-oz. can corned beef, coarsely chopped
2 c. beets, peeled, cooked and chopped
2 c. potatoes, peeled, cooked and chopped
½ c. butter, melted

Toss together all ingredients. Pour into a greased 2-quart casserole dish. Bake, uncovered, at 350 degrees for 40 minutes. Serves 4 to 6.

Phyllis Peters
Three Rivers, MI

Strawberry Popover Pancake

A wonderful breakfast treat!

2 T. butter
½ c. all-purpose flour
½ c. milk
2 eggs, beaten
¼ c. mini chocolate chips
¼ c. sugar
1 pt. strawberries, sliced
Garnish: whipped topping

Place butter in a 9" glass pie plate; place in 200-degree oven until butter is melted. In a medium bowl, beat flour, milk and eggs until well blended. Pour mixture over melted butter; do not stir. Drop chocolate chips evenly over flour mixture. Bake at 400 degrees for 20 to 25 minutes or until edges of pancake are puffed and a deep golden brown. In a small bowl, sprinkle sugar on strawberries and spoon into center of pancake; cut into wedges. Garnish with whipped topping. Serves 6.

Marla Arbet
Burlington, WI

Cinnamon-Pumpkin Pancakes

A great way to enjoy the spicy taste of pumpkin year-round.

1 c. all-purpose flour
1 T. sugar
2 t. baking powder
½ t. salt
½ t. cinnamon
1 c. milk
½ c. canned pumpkin
2 eggs, separated and divided
2 T. oil

In a large mixing bowl, combine flour, sugar, baking powder, salt and cinnamon. In a separate bowl, blend together milk, pumpkin, beaten egg yolks and oil. Add pumpkin mixture to flour mixture all at once, stirring until just blended. Beat egg whites until stiff peaks form, then gently fold into pancake batter. Spoon ¼ cup batter onto a griddle sprayed with non-stick vegetable spray. Cook until bubbles begin to form around edges; turn and cook until second side is golden. Serve with Apple Cider Syrup. Serves 6.

Apple Cider Syrup:

¾ c. apple cider
½ c. brown sugar, packed
½ c. corn syrup
2 T. butter
½ t. lemon juice
⅛ t. cinnamon
⅛ t. nutmeg

In a medium saucepan, combine all ingredients. Cook, stirring often, over medium heat until sugar dissolves and mixture is bubbly. Simmer, stirring occasionally, for about 20 minutes or until mixture is reduced to one cup. Let stand for 30 minutes to thicken.

Paula Johnson
Center City, MN

Gingerbread Pancakes

These are oh-so scrumptious topped with tangy Lemon Sauce.

1½ c. all-purpose flour
1 t. baking powder
¼ t. baking soda
¼ t. salt
1 t. cinnamon
½ t. ground ginger
1¼ c. milk
1 egg, beaten
¼ c. molasses
3 T. oil
Garnish: lemon zest strips

Sift together dry ingredients in a medium bowl; set aside. In a large bowl, beat milk and egg until well blended; stir in molasses and oil. Add flour mixture to milk mixture, stirring just until moistened. Pour batter by ⅓ cupfuls onto a lightly greased hot griddle. Cook over medium heat until bubbly on top; flip and cook until golden. Serve with Lemon Sauce and garnish with lemon zest strips. Serves 4.

Lemon Sauce:

½ c. sugar
1 T. cornstarch
⅛ t. nutmeg
1 c. water
2 T. butter
½ t. lemon zest
2 T. lemon juice

Stir together sugar, cornstarch and nutmeg in a small saucepan; add water. Cook over medium heat until thick and bubbly; cook and stir 2 more minutes. Remove from heat; add remaining ingredients. Stir just until butter melts. Serve warm.

Kendall Hale
Lynn, MA

Gingerbread Pancakes

Gorilla Bread

Gorilla Bread

Don't let the cream cheese get too soft before you cut it into cubes...it's much easier to deal with when it's cold and right out of the refrigerator.

½ c. sugar
1 T. cinnamon
2 c. brown sugar, packed
1 c. butter
2 12-oz. tubes refrigerated biscuits
8-oz. pkg. cream cheese, cut into 20 cubes
1½ c. walnuts, coarsely chopped and divided

   Mix sugar and cinnamon; set aside. Melt brown sugar and butter in a saucepan over low heat, stirring well; set aside. Flatten biscuits; sprinkle each with ½ teaspoon sugar mixture.
   Place a cream cheese cube in center of each biscuit, wrapping and sealing dough around cream cheese. Set aside. Spray a 12-cup Bundt® pan with non-stick vegetable spray; sprinkle ½ cup nuts in bottom of pan. Arrange half the biscuits in pan. Sprinkle with half the sugar mixture; pour half the butter mixture over top and sprinkle with ½ cup nuts. Repeat layers with remaining biscuits, sugar mixture, butter mixture and nuts. Bake at 350 degrees for 30 minutes. Let cool 5 minutes; place a plate on top and invert. Serves 20.

Brenda Hughes
Houston, TX

Like monkey bread, but better...everyone will ask for second helpings and even thirds when you serve this recipe! –Brenda

Flaky Cheese Danish

Terrific served for a brunch buffet.

2 8-oz. tubes crescent rolls, divided
1¼ c. sugar, divided
1 egg, separated and divided
8-oz. pkg. cream cheese, softened
1 t. vanilla extract
1 t. cinnamon
½ c. chopped walnuts

   Unroll one package of crescent rolls, separate and place on bottom of a 13"x9" baking pan; press seams together. Beat one cup sugar, egg yolk, cream cheese and vanilla. Spread mixture evenly over crescent rolls. Unroll remaining tube of crescent rolls and place over top of cream cheese mixture. Beat egg white until frothy; brush over crescent rolls. Mix together cinnamon, remaining sugar and walnuts; sprinkle on top. Bake at 350 degrees for 30 minutes. Serves 16.

Jackie Overton
Mattoon, IL

egg-cellent tip
Did a little yolk escape when you separated your egg? Not to worry! Use the eggshell to fish it out...the yolk will naturally be attracted to it.

Apple & Berry Breakfast Crisp

Use sliced strawberries instead of blueberries and it's just as tasty…and a dollop of vanilla yogurt on top makes it perfect! (Pictured on page 36)

4 apples, cored, peeled and thinly sliced
2 c. blueberries
¼ c. brown sugar, packed
¼ c. frozen orange juice concentrate,
    thawed
2 T. all-purpose flour
1 t. cinnamon
Optional: vanilla yogurt

Combine all ingredients except yogurt in a large bowl; stir until fruit is evenly coated. Spoon into a lightly greased 8"x8" baking pan. Sprinkle Oat Topping evenly over fruit. Bake at 350 degrees for 30 to 35 minutes or until apples are tender. Serve warm with yogurt, if desired. Serves 9.

Oat Topping:
1 c. quick-cooking or long-cooking oats,
    uncooked
½ c. brown sugar, packed
⅓ c. butter, melted
2 T. all-purpose flour

Combine all ingredients; mix well.

Connie Herek
Bay City, MI

Tangy Cranberry Breakfast Cake

This yummy coffee cake has three fantastic layers!

2 c. all-purpose flour
1⅓ c. sugar, divided
1½ t. baking powder
½ t. baking soda
¼ t. salt
2 eggs, divided
¾ c. orange juice
¼ c. butter, melted
2 t. vanilla extract, divided
2 c. cranberries, coarsely chopped
Optional: 1 T. orange zest
8-oz. pkg. cream cheese, softened

Combine flour, one cup sugar, baking powder, baking soda and salt in a large bowl; mix well and set aside. Combine one egg, orange juice, butter and one teaspoon vanilla in a small bowl; mix well and stir into flour mixture until well combined. Fold in cranberries and zest, if desired. Pour into a greased 9" round springform pan and set aside.
Beat together cream cheese and remaining ⅓ cup sugar in a small bowl until smooth. Add remaining egg and one teaspoon vanilla; mix well. Spread over batter; sprinkle with Topping. Place pan on a baking sheet; bake at 350 degrees for one hour and 25 minutes or until golden. Let cool on wire rack for 15 minutes before removing sides of pan. Serves 12.

Topping:
6 T. all-purpose flour
¼ c. sugar
2 T. butter

Combine flour and sugar in a small bowl. Cut in butter with a fork until mixture resembles coarse crumbs.

Linda Hendrix
Moundville, MO

Tangy Cranberry
Breakfast Cake

Gran's Rosemary Roast Chicken (page 70)

Red Beans & Rice (page 85)

Santa Fe Grilled Veggie
Pizzas (page 93)

Garlicky Baked Shrimp
(page 90)

WEEKNIGHT FAVORITES

Main dish must-haves to please the whole family

Fried Chicken
& Milk Gravy

Fried Chicken & Milk Gravy

If you prefer, you can substitute chicken breasts, sliced in half lengthwise, so they'll cook quicker.

1¼ c. all-purpose flour, divided
1¼ t. dried thyme
¾ t. onion powder
¾ t. seasoning salt
¾ t. pepper, divided
8 chicken thighs or drumsticks
⅔ c. buttermilk
2 to 4 T. oil
1 t. chicken bouillon granules
1½ c. milk

Combine one cup flour, thyme, onion powder, salt and ½ teaspoon pepper in a large plastic zipping bag. Add chicken to bag, one or 2 pieces at a time; shake to coat well. Dip chicken into buttermilk; return to bag and shake to coat. Heat oil in a large skillet over medium heat. Add chicken and cook 15 minutes, turning to cook evenly until golden. Reduce heat to medium-low. Cook, uncovered, 35 to 40 more minutes or until chicken is tender and juices run clear when chicken is pierced with a fork. Remove chicken to paper towels, reserving drippings; cover chicken to keep warm. Stir bouillon, remaining flour and remaining pepper into skillet drippings, scraping up any browned bits. Add milk. Cook and stir over medium heat until thickened and bubbly; cook and stir one more minute. Serve hot gravy over chicken. Serves 4.

Darrell Lawry
Kissimmee, FL

Spinach & Cheese-Stuffed Chicken Breasts

Try this dish served over wild rice.

6 5-oz. skinless, boneless chicken breasts
¼ c. oil
2 T. dried thyme, crushed
2 T. butter
¼ c. sweet onion, diced
10-oz. pkg. frozen spinach, thawed and drained
¼ c. cottage cheese
¼ c. grated Parmesan cheese
½ t. basil

Place chicken breasts between 2 sheets of plastic wrap and flatten to ¼-inch thickness using a rolling pin or flat side of a meat mallet. Brush chicken breasts with oil, sprinkle with thyme and set aside. Melt butter in a saucepan over medium heat and sauté onion until tender. Remove from heat and set aside. Combine spinach in a large bowl with cottage cheese, Parmesan cheese and basil. Stir in sautéed onions and mix well. Place a portion of spinach mixture in center of each chicken breast and bring sides to center, overlapping. Secure with metal skewers and bake, uncovered, at 375 degrees for 30 minutes. Remove skewers before serving. Serves 6.

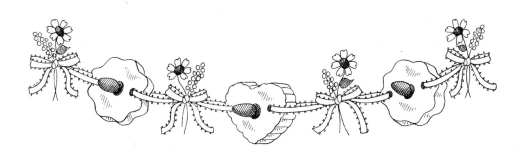

Chicken & Artichoke Pasta

This is one of our favorites…it's a great way to use leftovers.

4 cloves garlic, minced
¼ c. olive oil
1 c. asparagus, sliced
4 c. bowtie pasta, cooked
1 bunch fresh basil, chopped
1 c. sun-dried tomatoes in oil
1 c. deli roast chicken, chopped
1 c. canned artichokes, chopped
salt and pepper to taste
Garnish: shredded Parmesan cheese

Sauté garlic in oil in a large pan over medium heat. Add asparagus; cook until crisp-tender. Fold in remaining ingredients except salt, pepper and cheese; mix well and heat through. Sprinkle with salt and pepper; garnish with cheese. Serves 4.

Linda Behling
Cecil, PA

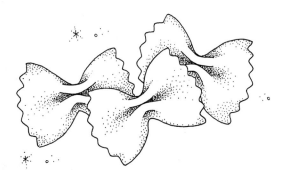

Gran's Rosemary Roast Chicken

Tuck some small new potatoes and baby carrots around the chicken for a complete meal…so simple and delicious!

4-lb. roasting chicken
1 t. salt
¼ t. pepper
1 onion, quartered
8 cloves garlic, pressed
¼ c. fresh rosemary, chopped
¼ c. butter, melted

Place chicken in a large greased roasting pan; sprinkle with salt and pepper. Place onion, garlic and rosemary inside chicken; brush butter over chicken. Bake, uncovered, at 400 degrees for 1½ hours, basting with pan juices, until golden and juices run clear when chicken is pierced with a fork. Serves 4 to 6.

Audrey Lett
Newark, DE

Chicken Cacciatore

1 lb. chicken breasts, cubed
2 T. oil
28-oz. jar spaghetti sauce
14½-oz. can diced tomatoes
1 green pepper, chopped
1 onion, chopped
2 cloves garlic, minced
1 t. Italian seasoning
salt and pepper to taste

Brown chicken in oil in a large skillet over medium heat. Add spaghetti sauce and stir in remaining ingredients. Simmer until vegetables are tender. Serves 2 to 4.

Jennifer Minekheim
Garden Grove, CA

Gran's Rosemary
Roast Chicken

Grilled Chicken with White BBQ Sauce

Aromatic herbs scent the air when you grill this chicken seasoned with a dry rub. The flavors go well with a creamy white barbecue sauce spiced with tangy brown mustard and a spoonful of horseradish.

3 lbs. chicken thighs and drumsticks
1 T. dried thyme
1 T. dried oregano
1 T. ground cumin
1 T. paprika
1 t. onion powder
½ t. salt
½ t. pepper

Rinse chicken and pat dry with paper towels. Combine remaining ingredients; rub mixture evenly over chicken. Place chicken in a large plastic zipping bag. Seal and chill 4 hours.

Remove chicken from bag, discarding bag. Grill chicken, covered with grill lid, over medium-high heat (350 to 400 degrees) for 8 to 10 minutes on each side until a meat thermometer inserted into thickest portion registers 165 degrees, or to desired doneness. Serve with White BBQ Sauce. Serves 5.

White BBQ Sauce:

1½ c. mayonnaise
¼ c. white wine vinegar
1 clove garlic, minced
1 T. coarsely ground pepper
1 T. spicy brown mustard
2 t. horseradish
1 t. sugar
1 t. salt

Stir together all ingredients until well blended. Store in an airtight container in refrigerator at least 2 hours and up to one week. Makes about 1¾ cups.

Grilled Chicken with White BBQ Sauce

Polynesian Chicken

Baked chicken pieces combine with pineapple and orange soy sauce...a delicious taste of the islands!

2 lbs. chicken, cut up
¼ c. soy sauce
1 t. ground ginger
¼ t. pepper
2 T. dried, minced onion
3 T. brown sugar, packed
8¾-oz. can pineapple chunks, drained
    and juice reserved
½ c. orange juice
2 t. cornstarch
¼ c. water
11-oz. can mandarin oranges, drained
4 c. hot cooked rice

Polynesian Chicken

Arrange chicken pieces in a single layer in an ungreased 13"x9" baking pan; set aside.

Combine soy sauce, ginger, pepper, onion, brown sugar, reserved pineapple juice and orange juice; pour over chicken. Cover and refrigerate one hour or overnight, turning once. Bake, covered, at 350 degrees for 30 minutes or until tender.

Uncover, and bake 20 to 25 more minutes or until golden and juices run clear when chicken is pierced with a fork. Remove chicken from baking pan; keep warm on a platter.

Skim off fat from pan drippings. In a medium saucepan, combine cornstarch and water with pan juices; heat until thickened and bubbly. Stir in pineapple and oranges and warm through; pour over chicken. Serve with cooked rice. Serves 8.

Norma Burton
Meridian, ID

As my children have grown and started their own families, this favorite recipe is always included in the cookbooks I make for them. –Norma

Chicken Chow Mein

Most of the ingredients are right in your pantry.

6-oz. can chicken, drained
4-oz. can sliced mushrooms, drained
10¾-oz. can cream of celery soup
5-oz. can evaporated milk
5-oz. can chow mein noodles
1 c. celery, chopped
1 c. cashews, chopped
Optional: hot cooked rice

Mix together all ingredients except rice. Bake, uncovered, at 350 degrees in a lightly greased 3 to 4-quart casserole dish until golden and bubbly, and celery is tender, about 25 to 30 minutes. Serve over cooked rice, if desired. Serves 3 to 4.

Linda Davidson
Lexington, KY

Chicken Cordon Bleu

A special dish I serve family and friends…it's delicious every time.

4 boneless, skinless chicken breasts
4 slices deli ham
4 slices Swiss cheese
8 slices bacon
2 eggs, beaten
½ c. milk
½ c. all-purpose flour
¾ c. bread crumbs
½ t. garlic powder
1 t. dried oregano
¼ c. grated Parmesan cheese

Flatten chicken breasts between 2 pieces of wax paper until ¼-inch thick. Top each piece with a slice of ham and cheese; roll up tightly. Wrap 2 slices of bacon around each bundle, securing with toothpicks. In a small bowl, beat eggs and milk together; set aside. Place flour in a separate bowl; set aside. In a third bowl, combine bread crumbs, garlic powder, oregano and Parmesan cheese. Dip each chicken bundle in egg mixture, then in flour. Dip in egg mixture again, and lastly in bread crumb mixture. Place on a greased baking sheet; bake at 350 degrees for 45 minutes. Serves 4.

Jen Sell
Farmington, MN

---

kids in the kitchen
Little ones will love to help pound out chicken breasts and make them into bundles for Chicken Cordon Bleu. For less mess, allow Mom and Dad to do the breading.

Chicken-Fried Steak & Gravy

Authentic chicken-fried steak is crunchy outside, tender inside and served with plenty of cream gravy!

2¼ t. salt, divided
1¾ t. pepper, divided
6 4-oz. cube steaks
1 sleeve saltine crackers, crushed
1¼ c. all-purpose flour, divided
½ t. baking powder
½ t. cayenne pepper
4¾ c. milk, divided
2 eggs, beaten
3½ c. peanut oil

Sprinkle ¼ teaspoon each salt and black pepper over steaks. Set aside.

Combine cracker crumbs, one cup flour, baking powder, one teaspoon salt, ½ teaspoon black pepper and cayenne pepper.

Whisk together ¾ cup milk and eggs. Dredge steaks in cracker crumb mixture; dip in milk mixture and dredge in cracker mixture again.

Pour oil into a large skillet; heat to 360 degrees. Do not use a non-stick skillet. Fry steaks, in batches, 10 minutes. Turn and fry each batch 4 to 5 more minutes or until golden brown. Remove to a wire rack on a 15"x10" jelly-roll pan. Keep steaks warm in a 225-degree oven. Carefully drain hot oil, reserving cooked bits and one tablespoon drippings in skillet.

Whisk together remaining ¼ cup flour, one teaspoon salt, one teaspoon black pepper and 4 cups milk. Pour mixture into reserved drippings in skillet; cook over medium-high heat, whisking constantly, 10 to 12 minutes or until thickened. Serve gravy with steaks. Serves 6.

Chicken-Fried Steak
& Gravy

Festive Cajun Pepper Steak

Festive Cajun Pepper Steak

Cajun seasoning kicks up the flavor of saucy sirloin beef tips spooned over yummy mashed potatoes.

1½ lbs. sirloin beef tips
1 t. salt-free Cajun seasoning
1 T. oil
1 green pepper, chopped
1 onion, chopped
3 cloves garlic, minced
14½-oz. can diced tomatoes
14½-oz. can beef broth
2 t. Worcestershire sauce
1 t. white wine vinegar
½ t. dried basil
¼ t. salt
⅛ t. pepper
22-oz. pkg. refrigerated or frozen mashed
    potatoes
2 T. cornstarch
2 T. cold water

Sprinkle beef tips with Cajun seasoning. Cook beef in hot oil in a large skillet over medium-high heat 10 minutes or until browned. Add green pepper, onion and garlic; sauté 3 minutes.

Stir in tomatoes with juice and next 6 ingredients. Bring to a boil; reduce heat, cover and simmer one hour or until meat is tender.

Prepare mashed potatoes according to package directions. Stir together cornstarch and water until smooth; stir into beef mixture. Bring to a boil; cook, stirring constantly, 2 minutes or until thickened. Serve over mashed potatoes. Serves 4 to 6.

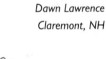

> ### marvelous menu
> For a special touch, write out your menu and attach it to a vase of fresh-cut flowers from the garden with a pretty ribbon.

Salisbury Steak & Onion Gravy

Serve this homestyle meal over mashed potatoes. It won't last long!

10½-oz. can French onion soup, divided
1½ lbs. ground beef
½ c. bread crumbs
1 egg, beaten
¼ t. salt
⅛ t. pepper
1 T. all-purpose flour
¼ c. catsup
¼ c. water
1 t. Worcestershire sauce
½ t. mustard

Combine ½ cup soup, beef, bread crumbs, egg, salt and pepper in a large mixing bowl; shape into 6 patties. Brown in a skillet over medium heat; drain and set aside. Gradually blend remaining soup with flour until smooth; add remaining ingredients. Pour into skillet; stir well. Return patties to skillet. Cover; return to low heat and simmer for 20 minutes, stirring occasionally. Serves 6.

*Dawn Lawrence
Claremont, NH*

Marinated Flank Steak

Refrigerating the steaks in a spicy marinade really adds to the flavor.

1 to 2-lb. beef flank steaks
½ c. soy sauce
2 T. honey
2 T. white vinegar
1½ T. ground ginger
1½ t. garlic powder
1½ t. cinnamon
1½ t. nutmeg
¾ c. oil
1 onion, chopped

Using a sharp knife, make shallow cuts in steaks; set aside. Mix remaining ingredients together in a large plastic zipping bag; add steaks. Refrigerate for at least 24 hours, turning several times. Grill or broil for 5 to 10 minutes on each side, or until desired doneness. Slice thinly on an angle to serve. Serves 4 to 6.

Irene Robinson
Cincinnati, OH

Ultimate Cheeseburger Pizza

½ lb. lean ground beef
14½-oz. can whole tomatoes, drained and chopped
1 t. garlic, minced
12-inch prebaked pizza crust
1½ c. shredded Cheddar cheese
¼ c. green onions, chopped
½ t. salt

Brown beef in a skillet over medium-high heat, stirring often, 4 minutes or until beef crumbles and is no longer pink; drain well.

Stir together tomatoes and garlic. Spread crust evenly with tomato mixture; sprinkle with beef, cheese, green onions and salt.

Bake at 450 degrees directly on oven rack for 12 to 14 minutes or until cheese is melted. Serves 4.

Now & Later Chili Mac

This chili freezes well...cool and freeze in a plastic zipping bag for a fast future dinner.

3 lbs. ground beef
2 T. ground cumin
salt and pepper to taste
2 c. water
4 15½-oz. cans mild chili beans
2 15½-oz. cans hot chili beans
2 15½-oz. cans dark red kidney beans, drained and rinsed
8-oz. pkg. angel hair pasta, cooked
Optional: shredded Cheddar cheese, diced onion

Brown beef over medium heat in a large stock-pot until no longer pink; drain. Stir in cumin, salt and pepper. Add water and beans; cover and simmer for one hour, stirring occasionally. Divide cooked pasta among 4 plates and ladle chili over each. Garnish with cheese and onion, if desired. Serves 4.

Peggy Donnally
Toledo, OH

Ultimate Cheeseburger Pizza

Cheesy Beef & Bacon Burger Meatloaf

Minimal prep and maximum flavor make this recipe perfect for busy weeknights or casual get-togethers.

1 lb. bacon, crisply cooked, crumbled and divided
1½ lbs. ground beef sirloin
1½ c. shredded Cheddar cheese
2 eggs, beaten
⅓ c. dry bread crumbs
⅓ c. mayonnaise
1 T. Worcestershire sauce
½ t. salt
½ t. pepper
½ c. catsup
¼ t. hot pepper sauce
3 T. Dijon mustard

Set aside ½ cup bacon for topping. Combine remaining bacon, ground beef, cheese, eggs, bread crumbs, mayonnaise, Worcestershire sauce, salt and pepper in a large bowl; set aside. Mix together catsup, hot pepper sauce and mustard; set aside 3 tablespoons of mixture. Add remaining catsup mixture to beef mixture; blend well. Press into an ungreased 9"x5" loaf pan; spread reserved catsup mixture over top and sprinkle with reserved bacon. Bake, uncovered, at 350 degrees for 50 to 60 minutes or until beef is no longer pink. Remove from oven; let stand 5 to 10 minutes before slicing. Serves 6 to 8.

Kelly Masten
Hudson, NY

Cheesy Beef & Bacon
Burger Meatloaf

Spice-Rubbed Steak

Pair with grilled fresh corn and herb butter for a memorable meal.

2 t. paprika
1 t. salt
1 t. pepper
½ t. garlic powder
½ t. onion powder
½ t. dried thyme
1 to 1½-lb. beef strip steak
2 T. butter
¼ c. shallots, minced
8-oz. pkg. sliced mushrooms
2 T. red wine or beef broth
1 T. oil

Mix together seasonings; sprinkle on both sides of steak and set aside. Melt butter in a large skillet over medium heat. Add shallots; cook for one minute. Add mushrooms and cook for 2 to 3 minutes, until tender. Stir in wine or broth; cook until most of liquid has evaporated. Remove from heat; keep warm. Heat oil in a separate skillet over medium-high heat. Add steak; cook for 5 to 7 minutes on each side or to desired doneness. Remove to a plate and let stand several minutes. Cut into serving-size portions and spoon mushroom mixture over top. Serves 3 to 4.

Samantha Starks
Madison, WI

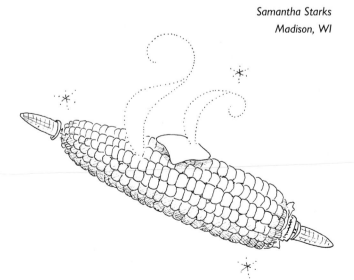

Tuscan Pork Loin

This is a delicious pork loin for holiday gatherings. Guests always ask for this recipe, and leftovers are delicious the next day. If you'd like, instead of cream cheese, try garlic and herb spreadable cheese.

4-lb. boneless pork loin roast
8-oz. pkg. cream cheese, softened
1 T. dried pesto seasoning
½ c. baby spinach
6 slices bacon, crisply cooked
12-oz. jar roasted red peppers, drained and divided
1 t. paprika
1 t. salt
½ t. pepper
baby spinach

Slice pork lengthwise, cutting down center, but not through other side. Open halves and cut down center of each half, cutting to, but not through other sides. Open into a rectangle. Place plastic wrap over pork and pound to an even thickness with a meat mallet or rolling pin. Spread cream cheese evenly over pork. Sprinkle with pesto seasoning; arrange ½ cup of spinach over cream cheese. Top with bacon and half the red peppers, reserving remaining peppers for another recipe. Roll up pork lengthwise; tie at 2-inch intervals with kitchen string. Rub pork with paprika, salt and pepper. Place seam-side down on a lightly greased rack on an aluminum foil-lined baking sheet. Bake at 425 degrees for 30 minutes or until a meat thermometer inserted into thickest portion registers 155 degrees. Remove from oven; let stand for 10 minutes until temperature reaches 160 degrees. Remove string from pork; slice ½-inch thick. Serve pork slices on a bed of spinach leaves. Serves 8 to 10.

Gina McClenning
Valrico, FL

Pork & Raspberry Sauce

A tender pork roast will make your family's holiday homecoming so memorable!

3 to 4-lb. boneless pork loin roast
1 t. salt
1 t. pepper
1 t. rubbed sage

Sprinkle roast with salt, pepper and sage. Place roast on rack in shallow roasting pan. Bake at 325 degrees for 1½ to 2 hours or until meat thermometer registers 150 degrees. Cover and let stand until thermometer registers 160 degrees. Place roast on platter; serve with Raspberry Sauce. Serves 10.

Raspberry Sauce:

12-oz. pkg. frozen raspberries, thawed
3 c. sugar
½ c. white vinegar
½ t. ground cloves
½ t. ground ginger
½ t. nutmeg
½ c. cornstarch
2 T. lemon juice
2 T. butter, melted
6 to 8 drops red food coloring

Drain raspberries and set aside, reserving juice. Add water to juice, if necessary, to make 1½ cups. Combine one cup of the raspberry liquid with sugar, vinegar, cloves, ginger and nutmeg in a saucepan. Bring to a boil. Reduce heat; simmer, uncovered, 10 minutes. Blend cornstarch and remaining raspberry liquid; add to saucepan. Cook over medium heat, stirring constantly, one minute or until thickened. Stir in raspberries, lemon juice, butter and food coloring.

Robbin Chamberlain
Worthington, OH

Pork & Raspberry Sauce

Sweet & Tangy Pork

Serve over cooked rice for a complete meal.

1 T. oil
4 boneless pork chops
10¾-oz. can tomato soup
2 T. vinegar
1 T. Worcestershire sauce
1 T. brown sugar
8-oz. can pineapple tidbits, drained and
    ¼ c. juice reserved

Heat oil in a skillet over medium heat. Add pork chops and cook until golden on both sides; drain. Stir in soup, vinegar, Worcestershire sauce, brown sugar, pineapple and reserved juice. Cover and simmer over low heat for 5 to 10 minutes until pork is cooked through. Serves 4.

Cheryl Brady
Canfield, OH

Sweet & Spicy Baby Back Ribs

2 slabs baby back ribs (about 5 lbs.), halved
3 green onions, chopped
1 T. fresh ginger, minced
1½ t. garlic, minced
1 T. oil
12-oz. bottle chili sauce
8-oz. bottle hoisin sauce
½ c. applesauce
½ c. regular or non-alcoholic beer
2 T. Worcestershire sauce
1 T. country-style Dijon mustard
1 to 3 t. hot pepper sauce

Preheat broiler with oven rack 5½ inches from heat. Coat the rack of a broiler pan and broiler pan with non-stick vegetable spray. Place ribs on rack in broiler pan. Broil 10 minutes.

Meanwhile, sauté green onions, ginger and garlic in hot oil in a small saucepan over medium heat for 3 to 5 minutes or until tender. Stir in remaining ingredients. Bring to a boil; reduce heat to medium-low and simmer 5 minutes.

Arrange half of ribs in a single layer in a lightly greased 7-quart oval slow cooker. Pour half of sauce mixture over ribs. Top with remaining ribs in a single layer. Pour remaining sauce mixture over ribs. Cover and cook on low setting 4 hours or until tender. Makes 8 servings.

Sweet & Spicy Baby Back Ribs

Pork Chops,
Cabbage & Apples

Pork Chops, Cabbage & Apples

This classic combination is always a hit.

3 t. paprika, divided
2 t. chopped fresh or 1 t. dried thyme, divided
2 t. kosher salt, divided
1½ t. pepper, divided
2 t. chopped fresh or 1 t. dried sage,
    divided
6 ½-inch thick bone-in pork loin chops
2 slices bacon
1 head cabbage, coarsely chopped
2 onions, thinly sliced
1 Granny Smith apple, peeled and sliced
1 T. tomato paste
12-oz. bottle lager beer or 1½ c. apple cider
Optional: fresh thyme sprigs

Combine 2 teaspoons paprika, one teaspoon fresh or ½ teaspoon dried thyme, one teaspoon salt, one teaspoon pepper and one teaspoon fresh or ½ teaspoon dried sage; rub over pork chops.

Cook bacon slices in a large, deep skillet over medium-high heat 6 to 8 minutes or until crisp; remove bacon and drain on paper towels, reserving drippings in skillet. Crumble bacon.

Cook pork in hot drippings 3 minutes on each side or until browned and cooked through; remove pork from skillet and keep warm.

Add cabbage, onion and apple to skillet. Cover and reduce heat to medium; cook, stirring occasionally, 15 minutes or until cabbage begins to wilt. Add tomato paste, beer or apple cider, bacon, remaining one teaspoon paprika, one teaspoon fresh or ½ teaspoon dried thyme, one teaspoon salt, ½ teaspoon pepper and one teaspoon fresh or ½ teaspoon dried sage, stirring to loosen browned bits from bottom of skillet. Cover and cook 15 minutes or until cabbage is tender and liquid is slightly thickened. Add pork and cook, uncovered, 5 minutes or until heated through. Garnish with fresh thyme sprigs, if desired. Serves 6.

Jo Ann
Gooseberry Patch

Red Beans & Rice

This recipe takes a shortcut by using canned beans in place of dried. Kick it up a notch by using andouille sausage and shaking a few drops of hot sauce on top! (Pictured on page 66)

1 lb. Kielbasa sausage, cut into ¼-inch slices
1 onion, chopped
1 green pepper, chopped
1 clove garlic, minced
2 16-oz. cans dark kidney beans, drained
14½-oz. can diced tomatoes
½ t. dried oregano
½ t. pepper
4 c. hot cooked rice

Cook Kielbasa sausage in a Dutch oven over low heat 6 minutes, stirring often. Add onion, green pepper and garlic; cook over medium-high heat 5 minutes or until tender.

Add beans, tomatoes, oregano and pepper; reduce heat and simmer, uncovered, 20 minutes, stirring occasionally. Serve over cooked rice. Serves 4 to 6.

Vickie
Gooseberry Patch

Ratatouille

This southern French dish is made with eggplant, zucchini, onions, peppers, tomato and garlic. There are many different variations, but this recipe is my favorite!

1 onion, chopped
3 to 4 cloves garlic, chopped
3 to 4 T. olive oil
2 zucchini, sliced
2 eggplants, peeled and cubed
2 green peppers, sliced
28-oz. can crushed tomatoes
1 t. dried parsley
1 t. dried oregano
1 t. dried basil
4 c. hot cooked rice

Sauté onion and garlic in oil in a large skillet over medium heat. Add remaining ingredients, except rice; simmer over medium heat for 30 minutes or until vegetables are tender. Serve over cooked rice. Serves 6 to 8.

Ginny Paccioretti
Oak Ridge, NJ

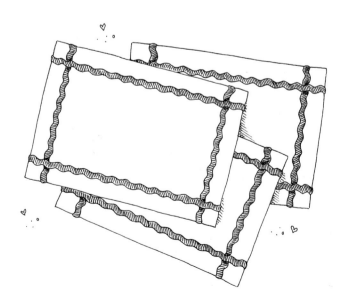

Creamy Penne with Swiss Chard

A lightly spiced pasta dish that's ready to serve in 30 minutes.

16-oz. pkg. penne pasta, uncooked
1 bunch Swiss chard, trimmed and sliced
1 T. butter
2 onions, sliced
3 cloves garlic, minced
¼ t. red pepper flakes
⅛ t. nutmeg
1 c. ricotta cheese
⅓ c. vegetable broth
¼ t. salt
½ c. oil-packed sun-dried tomatoes, sliced

Cook pasta according to package directions; add Swiss chard 2 minutes before end of cooking time. Drain; set aside.

Melt butter in a skillet over medium-high heat; add onion, garlic, pepper flakes and nutmeg. Heat until onion is translucent, about 10 minutes. In a blender, purée ricotta with broth and salt until smooth. In serving bowl, combine ricotta mixture with onion mixture, tomatoes and pasta mixture; toss to coat. Serves 6.

Jen Burnham
Delaware, OH

Risotto with Asparagus

Risotto should stand only briefly before being served to keep this pasta-like rice dish creamy and rich.

2 14½-oz. cans vegetable broth
2 T. olive oil
1 c. onion, chopped
1 c. celery, thinly sliced
2 cloves garlic, minced
1½ c. Arborio rice, uncooked
1 lb. asparagus, trimmed and cut into 1½-inch pieces
⅓ c. grated Parmesan cheese
1 T. butter, softened

Measure broth; add enough water to make 5¾ cups liquid. Bring to a simmer in a saucepan; reduce heat to low. Heat oil in a large skillet over medium heat; add onion, celery and garlic. Sauté for 4 to 5 minutes, until onion is translucent; add rice and stir for one minute. Add one cup hot broth; simmer, stirring often, until liquid is almost completely absorbed, about 4 minutes. Repeat with 2 additional cups hot broth, adding one cup at a time. Add asparagus and another cup hot broth; cook and stir until absorbed. Add another cup broth; cook and stir until rice and asparagus are tender-firm. Remove from heat; stir in cheese, butter and remaining hot broth. Let stand briefly before serving. Serves 3 to 5.

Suzie Raymond
South Bend, IN

Corn Dogs

Corn Dogs

1 c. all-purpose flour
2 T. sugar
1½ t. baking powder
1 t. salt
⅔ c. cornmeal
2 T. shortening
1 egg
¾ c. milk
8 to 10 hot dogs
8 to 10 wooden sticks
oil for deep frying

Combine flour, sugar, baking powder and salt; stir in cornmeal. Using a pastry cutter or 2 forks, cut in shortening until coarse crumbs form; set aside. Blend together egg and milk in a separate bowl. Stir into flour mixture. Thoroughly dry each hot dog with a paper towel to ensure batter will cling. Insert a stick into each; dip in mixture. Deep-fry in 350 to 375-degree oil 4 to 5 minutes or until golden. Makes 8 to 10.

Kay Marone
Des Moines, IA

Crunchy Pecan Fish

These flaky fillets get a double shot of toasty pecans.

1 lb. catfish or whitefish fillets
¼ c. bread crumbs
2 T. cornmeal
2 T. grated Parmesan cheese
2 T. ground pecans
¼ t. salt
¼ t. pepper
¼ c. all-purpose flour
¼ c. milk
oil for frying
⅓ c. chopped pecans

Divide fish into 4 portions; set aside. In a bowl, mix together bread crumbs, cornmeal, Parmesan cheese, ground pecans, salt and pepper. Coat each piece of fish with flour, then dip each in milk. Coat evenly with crumb mixture. Heat oil in a skillet; add fish and fry 4 to 6 minutes on each side. Add chopped pecans to skillet; cook and stir 2 more minutes. Serve fish topped with pecans. Serves 4.

Firecracker Grilled Salmon

4 6-oz. salmon fillets
¼ c. peanut oil
2 T. soy sauce
2 T. balsamic vinegar
2 T. green onions, chopped
1½ t. brown sugar, packed
1 clove garlic, minced
½ t. red pepper flakes
½ t. sesame oil
⅛ t. salt

Place salmon in a casserole dish. Whisk together remaining ingredients and pour over salmon. Cover with plastic wrap; refrigerate 4 to 6 hours. Remove salmon, discarding marinade. Place on an aluminum foil-lined grill; spray foil with non-stick vegetable spray. Grill 10 minutes per inch of thickness, measured at thickest part, until fish flakes easily with a fork. Turn halfway through cooking. Serves 4.

Sharon Demers
Dolores, CO

Firecracker Grilled Salmon

Cornmeal Fried Catfish & Fresh Tartar Sauce

Very easy to prepare!

3 catfish fillets
½ c. Dijon mustard
1 c. cornmeal
1 t. salt
½ t. pepper
2 T. oil

Rinse and dry fillets, then brush with mustard. Combine cornmeal, salt and pepper into a large plastic zipping bag; shake to mix well. Add fillets one at a time and shake to coat. Add oil to skillet and fry each fillet on both sides until golden. Place each fillet in a brown paper bag to keep crisp and repeat with remaining fillets, adding oil as needed. Serves 3.

Fresh Tartar Sauce:

½ c. sour cream
½ c. mayonnaise
1 t. lemon juice
2 T. onion, diced
1 T. fresh parsley, chopped

Blend all ingredients thoroughly in a small bowl. Cover and refrigerate until cold. Makes about one cup.

lemon love
Wrap halved lemons in cheesecloth and tie with twine for your dinner guests to squeeze over their fish. The cheesecloth will catch the seeds but allow the juice to run through.

Salmon Patties

A delicious standby...so quick to fix, and most of the ingredients are right in the pantry.

15½-oz. can salmon, drained and flaked
½ c. round buttery crackers, crushed
½ T. dried parsley
½ t. lemon zest
1 T. lemon juice
2 green onions, sliced
1 egg, beaten
2 T. oil
5 to 6 English muffins, split and toasted

Combine first 7 ingredients; form into 5 to 6 patties. Heat oil in a skillet over medium heat. Cook patties 4 to 5 minutes on each side, until golden. Serve on English muffins topped with Cucumber Sauce. Serves 5 to 6.

Cucumber Sauce:

⅓ c. cucumber, chopped
¼ c. plain yogurt
¼ c. mayonnaise
¼ t. dried tarragon

Combine all ingredients; chill until ready to serve.

Carol Hickman
Kingsport, TN

Chive & Dijon Crab Cakes

These have the perfect texture...moist inside, crunchy outside.

1 lb. fresh crabmeat, flaked
½ c. soft bread crumbs
2 T. fresh parsley
2 T. heavy cream
1 T. lemon juice
2 t. chives, chopped
1 t. Dijon mustard
⅛ t. cayenne pepper
1 egg
1 egg yolk
⅓ c. dry bread crumbs
¼ cup butter

Combine all ingredients except bread crumbs and butter in a large bowl; stir well to blend. Shape mixture into 8 patties; set aside. Place bread crumbs in a bowl and dip each patty in the bread crumbs; cover both sides well. Melt butter in a large skillet over medium-high heat. Add patties and cook 5 minutes or until golden, turning once. Repeat with remaining patties. Serves 4.

Garlicky Baked Shrimp

(Pictured on page 66)

2 lbs. uncooked large shrimp, rinsed and unpeeled
16-oz. bottle Italian salad dressing
1½ T. pepper
2 cloves garlic, pressed
2 lemons, halved
¼ c. fresh parsley, chopped
½ c. butter, cut into pieces

Place first 4 ingredients in a 13"x9" baking pan, tossing to coat. Squeeze juice from lemons over shrimp mixture and stir. Add lemon halves to pan. Sprinkle shrimp with parsley; dot with butter. Bake, uncovered, at 375 degrees for 25 minutes, stirring after 15 minutes. Serve in pan. Serves 6.

Shrimp & Mushroom Fettuccine

1 T. olive oil
1 portabella mushroom, sliced
1 c. onion, finely chopped
¼ c. flat-leaf parsley, chopped
¼ t. salt
1 clove garlic, minced
1 c. chicken broth
¼ c. sherry or chicken broth
1 lb. uncooked large shrimp, peeled and cleaned
8-oz. pkg. fettuccine pasta, cooked
½ c. grated Parmesan cheese
1 T. fresh chives, chopped

Heat oil in a large saucepan over medium-high heat. Add mushroom, onion, parsley, salt and garlic; sauté for 4 minutes, or until mushroom releases moisture, stirring frequently. Stir in broth, sherry or broth and shrimp; bring to a boil. Add fettuccine; cook for 3 minutes, or until shrimp turn pink, tossing to combine. Sprinkle with cheese and chives. Serves 4.

Diana Chaney
Olathe, KS

I like to keep frozen packages of peeled, uncooked shrimp on hand for quick, delicious meals...just thaw according to package directions. –Diana

Herbed Shrimp Tacos

juice of 1 lime
½ c. plus 1 T. fresh cilantro, chopped
    and divided
1 t. salt
½ t. pepper
⅛ t. dried thyme
⅛ t. dried oregano
1 lb. uncooked medium shrimp, peeled
    and cleaned
½ c. radishes, shredded
½ c. green cabbage, shredded
½ c. red onion, chopped
Optional: 2 T. oil
10 6-inch flour tortillas, warmed

Combine lime juice, one tablespoon cilantro, salt, pepper and herbs in a large plastic zipping bag; mix well. Add shrimp; seal bag and refrigerate up to 4 hours.

Mix together radishes, cabbage, onion and remaining cilantro; set aside.

Thread shrimp onto skewers. Grill over medium-high heat until pink and cooked through; or, heat oil in a skillet over medium heat and sauté shrimp until done, if desired. Spoon into warm tortillas; garnish with Guacamole and cabbage mixture. Serves 10.

Guacamole:

2 avocados, peeled, pitted and mashed
1 T. sour cream
1 T. hot pepper sauce
juice of 1 lime
1 t. garlic salt
¼ t. pepper

Combine all ingredients in a small bowl. Makes about 2 cups.

Laurie Vincent
Alpine, UT

Herbed
Shrimp Tacos

Laurie's Stuffed Peppers

Laurie's Stuffed Peppers

4 green, red or yellow peppers
2 T. olive oil
8-oz. pkg. mushrooms, finely chopped
1 onion, finely chopped
1 clove garlic, pressed
1 c. white rice, cooked
1 c. brown rice, cooked
3 to 4 dashes hot pepper sauce
salt and pepper to taste
2 15-oz. cans tomato sauce, divided
1 c. shredded mozzarella cheese
Optional: fresh thyme sprigs

Slice off tops of peppers; remove seeds. Fill a large soup pot with water; bring water to a boil over medium-high heat. Add peppers; boil 5 minutes. Remove peppers; set aside. Heat oil in a large skillet over medium heat; add mushrooms, onion and garlic. Sauté 5 minutes or until onion is tender. Add white rice, brown rice, hot pepper sauce, salt and pepper; cook 2 minutes. Add one can tomato sauce and simmer 5 minutes; spoon into peppers. Spread half can tomato sauce into an ungreased 13"x9" baking pan. Place filled peppers in pan; pour remaining sauce over top. Bake, uncovered, at 350 degrees for 25 minutes; sprinkle with cheese. Bake 10 more minutes or until cheese is melted. Garnish with thyme sprigs, if desired. Serves 4.

Laurie Patton
Pinckney, MI

Santa Fe Grilled Veggie Pizzas

Make sure to cut the vegetables into equal-size pieces so that they will grill evenly. (Pictured on page 66)

13.8-oz. tube refrigerated pizza dough
1 lb. portabella mushrooms, stems removed
1 red pepper, quartered
1 yellow pepper, quartered
1 zucchini, cut lengthwise into ½-inch thick slices
1 yellow squash, cut lengthwise into
    ½-inch thick slices
¾ t. salt
1 c. Alfredo sauce
1¼ c. smoked mozzarella cheese, shredded

Lightly dust 2 baking sheets with flour. On a lightly floured surface, press dough into a 15-inch by 11-inch rectangle. Cut into quarters; place 2 on each baking sheet. Lightly coat vegetables with non-stick vegetable spray; sprinkle with salt. Grill vegetables over medium-high heat until tender, about 10 minutes. Cut mushrooms and peppers into slices. Cut squash in half crosswise. Grill 2 pieces pizza dough at a time one minute or until golden. With tongs, turn dough over and grill 30 more seconds or until firm. Return to baking sheets. Spread sauce over crusts; top with vegetables and cheese. Grill pizzas, covered, 2 to 3 more minutes or until cheese melts. Serves 4.

April Jacobs
Loveland, CO

---

simple seasonings
Use herbs from your herb garden that you've dried to make a terrific seasoning blend. Combine one cup sea salt with 2 tablespoons each of rosemary, thyme, lemon balm, mint, tarragon, dill weed and paprika. Stir in 4 tablespoons parsley and basil. Blend, in batches, in a food processor, and store in a glass shaker.

Divine Chicken & Wild Rice
Casserole (page 107)

Tangy Corn Casserole
(page 120)

Beef & Broccoli Wellington
(page 102)

Shrimp & Feta Casserole
(page 115)

CASSEROLES GALORE

One-dish wonders for busy days

Shepherd's Pie

Shepherd's Pie

Traditionally an English dish made with lamb or mutton, this casserole has become a popular American dish typically made with ground beef.

4 to 5 potatoes, peeled and boiled
2 T. butter, softened
¼ to ½ c. milk
salt and pepper to taste
1 lb. ground beef
1 tomato, chopped
6 mushrooms, sliced
2 T. fresh parsley, chopped
1 T. tomato paste
¼ t. Worcestershire sauce
1 c. brown gravy
10-oz. pkg. frozen peas, thawed

Mash potatoes, butter, milk, salt and pepper together; set aside. Brown beef in a skillet over medium-high heat; drain. Add tomato, mushrooms, parsley, tomato paste, Worcestershire sauce and gravy; mix well. Add peas and simmer 5 minutes; pour into an ungreased 13"x9" baking pan. Spread mashed potatoes over top; bake, uncovered, at 400 degrees for 40 minutes. Serves 4 to 6.

Tami Davidson
Santa Clarita, CA

Easy Cheesy Enchiladas

Garnish with dollops of sour cream and a sprinkle of sliced green onions just before serving.

3 lbs. ground beef
2 1¼-oz. pkgs. taco seasoning mix
1 c. water
16-oz. can refried beans
2 pkgs. 10-inch flour tortillas
10¾-oz. can cream of mushroom soup
10¾-oz. can cream of chicken soup
2 10-oz. cans diced tomatoes with green chiles
1½ lbs. pasteurized process cheese spread, cubed

Brown ground beef in a large skillet over medium heat; drain. Add seasoning mix and water; simmer for 5 minutes. Add beans; cook 5 more minutes. Spread mixture down center of tortillas; roll up. Arrange seam-side down in 2 lightly greased 13"x9" baking pans; set aside. Combine remaining ingredients in a medium saucepan. Cook over medium heat until cheese is melted; spoon over enchiladas. Cover tightly with aluminum foil and freeze, or bake, covered, at 350 degrees for 15 minutes, until bubbly. Serves 12 to 16.

Julie Neathery
Oak Grove, LA

shopper's secret
Purchase prepared mashed potatoes at the grocery store. Heat up, blend in sour cream and cream cheese to taste, then reheat and stir until well blended...so yummy!

Pasta Bake Florentine

Pasta Bake Florentine

Not only is this baked pasta delicious, but the variety of vegetables makes it colorful and appealing as well.

2 T. olive oil
1 onion, finely chopped
¼ c. red pepper, chopped
½ c. mushrooms, sliced
1 lb. ground beef
½ t. salt
¼ t. garlic salt
¼ t. pepper
2 26-oz. jars pasta sauce
1 c. marinated artichokes, drained and chopped
10-oz. pkg. frozen spinach, thawed and drained
16-oz. pkg. rotini pasta, cooked
8-oz. pkg. shredded mozzarella cheese

Heat olive oil in a Dutch oven over medium heat. Sauté onion, red pepper and mushrooms until tender, about 5 minutes. Stir in ground beef, salt, garlic salt and pepper. Cook until beef is browned, about 5 to 7 minutes; drain. Stir in pasta sauce, artichokes and spinach until well combined. Stir in cooked pasta. Transfer to a lightly greased 13"x9" baking pan; sprinkle with cheese. Bake, uncovered, at 350 degrees for 15 to 20 minutes or until heated through and cheese is melted. Serves 8.

Jenny Flake
Gilbert, AZ

Pastitsio

Think of this as a Greek lasagna...filled with wonderful ingredients and absolutely delicious!

1 lb. ground beef, browned
1 onion, chopped
1 clove garlic, minced
8-oz. can tomato sauce
1 t. dried oregano
1 t. salt
½ t. cinnamon
2 c. elbow macaroni, uncooked and divided
¼ c. butter
3 T. all-purpose flour
¼ t. pepper
¼ t. nutmeg
2 c. milk
2 eggs, beaten
¼ c. grated Parmesan cheese

Combine beef, onion and garlic in a skillet; cook over medium heat until onion and garlic are tender. Stir in tomato sauce, oregano, salt and cinnamon; simmer for 5 minutes. Set aside. Spread one cup uncooked macaroni in a greased 8"x8" baking pan; cover with uncooked beef mixture. Top with remaining macaroni; set aside. Melt butter in a saucepan; whisk in flour, pepper and nutmeg until smooth. Gradually pour in milk; heat until thickened. Remove from heat; whisk in eggs and Parmesan cheese. Pour over uncooked macaroni; bake uncovered at 350 degrees for 45 minutes or until top is golden. Serves 4.

Lindsey Hignite
Morrisville, NC

try this table setting
Small pears, apples and Jack-be-Little pumpkins make the cutest placecards. Simply hole-punch tags, slip a ribbon through each and tie to the stems.

Gourmet Beef-Noodle Casserole

Cream cheese and Cheddar cheese make this casserole extra rich and creamy.

1 lb. ground beef
14½-oz. can diced tomatoes
8-oz. can tomato sauce
½ c. green pepper, chopped
4-oz. can sliced mushrooms, drained
1 clove garlic, chopped
2 t. salt
2 t. sugar
½ c. Burgundy wine or beef broth
8-oz. pkg. cream cheese, softened
1 c. sour cream
⅓ c. onion, chopped
2 c. shredded Cheddar cheese, divided
8-oz. pkg. wide egg noodles, cooked and divided

Brown ground beef in a skillet over medium-high heat; drain. Add tomatoes with juice, sauce, green pepper, mushrooms, garlic, salt, sugar and wine or broth; cover and simmer over low heat 10 minutes. In a medium bowl, blend cream cheese, sour cream, onion and one cup Cheddar cheese; set aside. In an ungreased 13"x9" baking pan, layer half the beef mixture, half the noodles and half the cream cheese mixture; repeat layers. Top with remaining Cheddar cheese. Bake, uncovered, at 350 degrees for 40 minutes. Serves 6 to 8.

Michelle Greeley
Hayes, VA

Gourmet
Beef-Noodle
Casserole

Tamale Pot Pie

Tamale Pot Pie

Not your "usual" pot pie filling...this will be a hit!

1 lb. ground beef
2 c. frozen corn, thawed
14½-oz. can diced tomatoes
2¼-oz. can sliced ripe olives, drained
1 c. plus 2 T. biscuit baking mix, divided
1 T. chili powder
2 t. ground cumin
½ t. salt
½ c. cornmeal
½ c. milk
2 T. chopped green chiles
1 egg, beaten

Cook ground beef in a large skillet over medium heat until browned; drain. Stir in corn, tomatoes with juice, olives, 2 tablespoons baking mix, chili powder, cumin and salt. Bring to a boil; boil, stirring frequently, one minute. Keep warm over low heat. Stir together remaining baking mix and remaining ingredients until blended. Pour beef mixture into an ungreased 9"x9" baking pan. Spread cornmeal mixture over beef mixture. Bake, uncovered, at 400 degrees for 20 to 30 minutes or until golden. Serves 6.

Marian Buckley
Fontana, CA

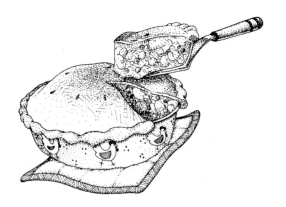

Johnny Marzetti

This hearty dish brings back childhood memories of family potlucks at Grandma's house.

1½ lbs. ground beef
1.31-oz. pkg. Sloppy Joe seasoning mix
6-oz. can tomato paste
1¼ c. water
4 c. elbow macaroni, cooked
15¼-oz. can corn, drained
8-oz. pkg. shredded Cheddar cheese, divided
Optional: 4-oz. can sliced mushrooms, drained

Cook ground beef in a skillet over medium-high heat until browned; drain. Stir in seasoning mix, tomato paste and water; heat and stir until blended. Spoon into a lightly greased 13"x9" baking pan; stir in macaroni, corn, one cup cheese and mushrooms, if desired. Bake, uncovered, at 350 degrees for 45 minutes. Sprinkle with remaining cheese; return to oven and bake until cheese melts. Serves 4 to 6.

Heather Neibar
South Bend, IN

Johnny Marzetti

Beef & Broccoli
Wellington

Steak & Onion Pie

*Try substituting tiny pearl onions…they are just as
tasty and will save with prep time.*

1 c. onion, diced
½ c. shortening
1 lb. round steak, cubed
⅛ t. ground ginger
2 t. salt
½ c. all-purpose flour
½ t. paprika
⅛ t. allspice
⅛ t. pepper
1½ c. boiling water
2 c. potatoes, diced

Sauté onion in shortening until tender; set
onion aside and reserve drippings. Toss steak with
ginger, salt, flour, paprika, allspice and pepper;
brown steak in reserved drippings. Add boiling
water; cover and simmer 45 minutes. Add
potatoes; simmer 10 minutes. Pour into a greased
8"x8" baking pan; place cooked onion on top.
Cover with Egg Crust; bake at 450 degrees for
30 minutes. Serves 6.

Egg Crust:
1 c. all-purpose flour
⅓ c. shortening
½ t. salt
1 egg, beaten

Combine flour, shortening and salt; add egg.
Mix thoroughly. Roll out slightly larger than top
of baking pan.

Tracey Clevenger
Clymer, PA

Beef & Broccoli Wellington

*Ground beef makes this a quick take on an old
classic…yummy!*

1½ lbs. ground beef
1 onion, chopped
6½-oz. can mushroom stems and pieces, drained
20-oz. pkg. frozen chopped broccoli, thawed
2 8-oz. pkgs. shredded mozzarella cheese
8-oz. container sour cream
2 8-oz. tubes refrigerated crescent rolls

Brown ground beef with onion and mushrooms in a skillet over medium heat; drain. Stir in
broccoli and cheese. When cheese is melted, stir
in sour cream. Line a lightly greased 13"x9" baking
pan with one tube crescent rolls. Spoon ground
beef mixture over rolls; arrange remaining tube
of rolls on top. Bake, uncovered, at 350 degrees
for 15 minutes or until golden. Cut into squares
to serve. Serves 6.

Cindy Kerekes
Wharton, NJ

Mexican Lasagna

1 lb. ground beef
16-oz. can refried beans
2 t. dried oregano
1 t. ground cumin
¾ t. garlic powder
2 c. picante sauce
1½ c. water
9 lasagna noodles, uncooked and divided
16-oz. container sour cream
¾ c. green onions, thinly sliced
2¼-oz. can sliced black olives, drained
1 c. shredded Monterey Jack cheese

"Use a colorful tablecloth or runner and napkins in vivid hues to give the table a Mexican flair." —Jo Ann

Cook ground beef in a large non-stick skillet until browned; drain. Wipe skillet clean. Return beef to skillet; stir in refried beans and seasonings.

Combine picante sauce and water. Pour 1⅓ cups picante mixture into a lightly greased 13"x9" baking pan. Arrange 3 uncooked noodles over picante mixture. Spread half of beef mixture evenly over noodles. Pour one cup picante mixture over beef mixture and top with 3 more noodles. Spread remaining beef mixture over noodles. Top with 3 remaining noodles. Pour remaining picante mixture evenly over noodles. Cover and bake at 350 degrees for 1½ hours.

Combine sour cream, onions and olives in a small bowl. Remove lasagna from oven; spread sour cream mixture over lasagna and sprinkle with cheese. Return to oven and bake, uncovered, 10 more minutes. Let stand 10 minutes before serving. Serves 6.

Jo Ann
Gooseberry Patch

Mexican Lasagna

Crunchy Biscuit
Chicken

Crunchy Biscuit Chicken

Refrigerated canned biscuits make this hearty casserole come together in a snap.

2 c. cooked chicken, diced
10¾-oz. can cream of chicken soup
14½-oz. can green beans
1 c. shredded Cheddar cheese
4-oz. can sliced mushrooms
½ c. mayonnaise-type salad dressing
1 t. lemon juice
10-oz. tube refrigerated flaky biscuits
1 to 2 T. butter, melted
¼ c. Cheddar cheese croutons, crushed

Combine first 7 ingredients in a medium saucepan over medium heat; cook until hot and bubbly. Pour hot chicken mixture into an ungreased 13"x9" baking pan. Separate biscuit dough into 10 biscuits. Arrange biscuits over chicken mixture. Brush each biscuit with butter; sprinkle with croutons. Bake, uncovered, at 375 degrees for 25 to 30 minutes or until deep golden brown. Serves 4 to 6.

Mary Makulec
Rockford, IL

Amy's Chicken Tetrazzini

I make this casserole to take to new moms… they always ask for the recipe!

½ c. butter
½ c. all-purpose flour
½ t. salt
¼ t. pepper
2 c. chicken broth
2 T. sherry or chicken broth
2 c. milk or whipping cream
8-oz. pkg. spaghetti, cooked
2 c. cooked chicken, cubed
¾ c. grated Parmesan cheese, divided
Optional: 4-oz. can sliced mushrooms, drained

Melt butter in a large saucepan over medium heat. Add flour, salt and pepper; cook until bubbly. Add broth, sherry or broth and milk or cream; bring to a boil for one minute. Stir in spaghetti, chicken, ¼ cup Parmesan cheese and mushrooms, if desired; mix well. Spread into a lightly greased 13"x9" baking pan; sprinkle with remaining Parmesan cheese. Bake, uncovered, at 350 degrees for 30 minutes. Serves 6 to 8.

Amy Tague
Lebanon, IN

Chicken, beans, cheese and biscuits... what more could you want? –Mary

Chicken-Artichoke Bake

An impressive dinner in no time. Try it!

2 to 3 lbs. boneless, skinless chicken breasts
14½-oz. can chicken broth
14-oz. can artichoke hearts, drained
    and quartered
¼ c. sliced mushrooms
2 T. butter
¼ t. salt
¼ t. pepper
¾ c. half-and-half
½ c. grated Parmesan cheese
½ t. dried rosemary
¼ c. all-purpose flour

In a large skillet over medium-high heat, simmer chicken in broth until juices run clear; discard broth. Place chicken in a greased 13"x9" baking pan. Top with artichokes and mushrooms; set aside. Combine butter, salt, pepper, half-and-half, cheese and rosemary in a saucepan; bring to a boil. Blend in flour; pour over chicken. Bake, uncovered, at 350 degrees for 30 minutes. Serves 6 to 8.

Kristine Kundrick
Fenton, MI

King Ranch Chicken Casserole

Make a double batch and freeze one...you'll be ready for the next school potluck!

1 c. onion, diced
1 c. green pepper, diced
8-oz. pkg. sliced mushrooms
¼ c. butter
10¾-oz. can cream of mushroom soup
10¾-oz. can cream of chicken soup
10-oz. can diced tomatoes with green chiles
1 clove garlic, minced
2 T. chili powder
1 T. chicken broth
12 6-inch corn tortillas, torn into quarters
    and divided
2 c. cooked chicken, diced and divided
16-oz. pkg. shredded Cheddar cheese, divided

In a large skillet over medium heat, sauté onion, pepper and mushrooms in butter. Add soups, tomatoes with juice, garlic, chili powder and broth; heat until bubbly and set aside. Arrange half the tortillas in a lightly greased 13"x9" baking pan; top with half the chicken, half the sauce and half the cheese. Repeat layers. Cover tightly with aluminum foil and freeze or bake at 350 degrees for about 30 minutes, until hot and bubbly. Serves 6.

Linda Behling
Cecil, PA

heat & eat instructions
Thaw overnight in refrigerator. Follow baking instructions above.

Divine Chicken & Wild Rice Casserole

2 6.2-oz. pkgs. fast-cooking long-grain and wild rice mix
¼ c. butter
4 stalks celery, chopped
2 onions, chopped
2 8-oz. cans sliced water chestnuts, drained
5 c. cooked chicken, chopped
4 c. shredded Cheddar cheese, divided
2 10¾-oz. cans cream of mushroom soup
2 8-oz. containers sour cream
1 c. milk
½ t. salt
½ t. pepper
2 c. soft bread crumbs
2¼-oz. pkg. sliced almonds, toasted

Prepare rice mixes according to package directions. Melt butter in a large skillet over medium heat; add celery and onions. Sauté 10 minutes or until tender. Stir in cooked rice, water chestnuts, chicken, 3 cups cheese and next 5 ingredients. Spoon mixture into a lightly greased 4-quart casserole dish. Top with bread crumbs.

Bake, uncovered, at 350 degrees for 35 minutes. Sprinkle with remaining cheese and almonds; bake 5 more minutes. Serves 10 to 12.

NOTE: *You can divide this casserole evenly between 2 greased 13"x9" baking pans. They'll just be slightly shallow as opposed to brimming over. Bake as directed above or freeze casseroles up to one month. Remove from freezer and let stand at room temperature one hour. Bake, covered, at 350 degrees for 30 minutes. Uncover and bake 55 more minutes. Sprinkle with remaining one cup cheese and almonds; bake 5 more minutes.*

Divine Chicken &
Wild Rice Casserole

Golden Chicken Divan

*This weeknight winner is quick and easy to make…
it bakes in just 15 minutes!*

1 lb. broccoli, chopped
1½ c. cooked chicken, cubed
10¾-oz. can cream of broccoli soup
⅓ c. sour cream
½ t. garlic powder
½ t. onion powder
¼ t. seasoned salt
½ c. shredded Cheddar cheese
1 T. butter, melted
2 T. dry bread crumbs

Cover broccoli with water in a saucepan; bring to a boil over medium heat. Cook 5 minutes or until tender; drain. In a large bowl, combine broccoli, chicken, soup, sour cream, garlic powder, onion powder and salt. Spread in a greased 8"x8" baking pan; sprinkle with cheese. Mix together melted butter and bread crumbs; sprinkle over cheese. Bake uncovered at 450 degrees for 15 minutes or until bubbly and golden. Serves 6.

*Amy Kim
Ann Arbor, MI*

Golden
Chicken Divan

Cheesy Turkey Rellenos

Try tossing in some jalapeños for a spicier version!

4 4-oz. cans whole green chiles, drained
    and rinsed
¼ lb. Pepper Jack cheese, sliced into
    ½-inch strips
2 c. cooked turkey, sliced into ½-inch strips
½ c. all-purpose flour
½ t. baking powder
¼ t. salt
½ c. milk
3 eggs, beaten
⅔ c. shredded Cheddar cheese

    Slice chiles up one side; remove seeds and spread open flat. Arrange in a greased 11"x7" baking pan. Fill each chile half with Pepper Jack cheese and turkey strips. Fold chiles closed and place seam-side down in dish. In a medium bowl, combine flour, baking powder and salt. Whisk together milk and eggs; slowly add to flour mixture, beating until smooth. Pour over chiles. Bake, uncovered, at 450 degrees for 15 minutes. Remove from oven and turn off heat. Sprinkle Cheddar cheese over top and return to oven until cheese is melted. Serves 6.

Vickie
Gooseberry Patch

Chicken & Dressing Casserole

Great for any gathering!

½ c. butter
1 c. celery, chopped
1 c. onion, chopped
2 c. cornbread crumbs
2 c. bread crumbs
dried sage to taste
10¾-oz. can cream of chicken soup
Optional: ¼ to ½ c. water
5 boneless, skinless chicken breasts,
    cooked and diced
10½-oz. jar chicken gravy

    Heat butter in a large skillet over medium heat. Add celery and onion; cook until tender. Combine celery mixture, cornbread crumbs, bread crumbs, sage and soup. If desired, add water to reach desired consistency. Transfer to a lightly greased 13"x9" baking pan. Arrange chicken over top; spread gravy over chicken. Bake, covered, at 375 degrees for one hour. Serves 12.

Tracie Loyd
Powell, TN

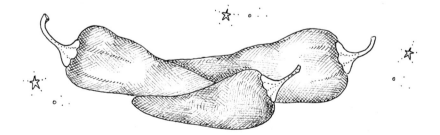

Hot Chicken Salad

Add a crunchy topping of crushed potato chips, buttery crackers or bread crumbs if you'd like.

4 c. cooked chicken, diced
½ c. green onions, chopped
1 c. celery, chopped
⅔ c. slivered almonds
¼ c. black olives, sliced
10¾-oz. can cream of chicken soup
1 c. mayonnaise
1 t. lemon juice
2 c. shredded Cheddar cheese

Combine all ingredients except cheese; mix well. Spread into an ungreased 13"x9" baking pan; sprinkle cheese over top. Bake, uncovered, at 325 degrees for 25 minutes until cheese is melted and bubbly. Serves 10 to 12.

Karen Hoag
Jackson, NE

Potluck Poppy Seed Chicken

4 boneless, skinless chicken breasts, cooked
    and cubed
10¾-oz. can cream of chicken soup
8-oz. container sour cream
½ c. butter, melted
1 sleeve round buttery crackers, crushed
2 T. poppy seed

Stir together chicken, soup and sour cream in a lightly greased 8"x8" baking pan. Mix butter, crackers and poppy seed; spread mixture over chicken. Bake, uncovered, at 350 degrees for 30 minutes or until bubbly. Serves 4.

Jennifer Langley
Kannapolis, NC

Mexican Chicken Casserole

This has been an evolving dish for about the past five years. It can be adapted for those who love a little bit of zing and for those who like a tamer side.

4 boneless, skinless chicken breasts, cooked
    and shredded
2 10¾-oz. cans cream of chicken soup
10½-oz. can tomatoes with chiles
1 t. pepper
1 T. fresh cilantro, chopped
2 cloves garlic, pressed
1 t. onion powder
1 t. cayenne pepper
8-oz. pkg. pasteurized process cheese spread,
    cubed
2 c. spicy nacho-flavored tortilla chips, crushed
Garnish: sour cream, sliced jalapeños, shredded
    lettuce, diced tomatoes

Combine all ingredients except tortilla chips and garnish. Mix well and pour into a lightly greased 13"x9" baking pan. Bake, uncovered, at 425 degrees for 20 minutes, or until bubbly. Stir well and top with crushed chips to cover. Bake uncovered for an additional 10 minutes. Let stand for 5 minutes before serving. Garnish with desired toppings. Serves 6.

Michelle Townsend
Billings, MO

Hashbrown-Pork Chop Casserole

Serve a quick vegetable like steamed corn or broccoli along with these chops for a flavorful weeknight meal.

5 bone-in pork chops
1 T. oil
1 c. sour cream
10¾-oz. can cream of celery soup
½ c. milk
32-oz. pkg. frozen shredded hashbrowns, thawed
1 c. onion, chopped
1 c. shredded Cheddar cheese

In a large skillet over medium heat, brown pork chops on both sides in hot oil. Set aside. Combine sour cream, soup and milk in a large bowl; stir in hashbrowns and onion. Spread sour cream mixture in an ungreased 13"x9" baking pan and sprinkle with cheese. Top with pork chops. Bake, uncovered, at 375 degrees for 45 to 50 minutes or until heated through and pork chops are fully cooked. Serves 5.

Shirley Flanagan
Wooster, OH

Hashbrown-Pork Chop Casserole

Blue-Ribbon Ham Casserole

A tried & true county fair blue-ribbon winner!

1½ lbs. yams, boiled, peeled and sliced
 ¾-inch thick and divided
2 c. cooked ham, chopped
1½ c. Golden Delicious apples, peeled, cored,
 sliced and divided
¼ t. salt
¼ t. paprika
½ c. brown sugar, packed
2 T. bourbon or apple juice
2 T. butter

Arrange half the yams in a greased 2-quart round casserole dish; set aside. Layer ham evenly over yams, then layer apples evenly over ham. Arrange remaining yams over apples; sprinkle with salt and paprika. Set aside. Combine brown sugar and bourbon or apple juice; sprinkle evenly over ingredients in casserole dish. Dot with butter. Bake, covered, for 20 minutes. Baste with pan juices; bake, uncovered, for 25 more minutes. Baste and serve. Serves 6.

Laura Jones
Louisville, KY

---

an apple a day
Golden Delicious apples have the perfect amount of tartness to complement the sweet yams and salty ham. Experiment with your favorite varieties if you'd like.

Party Paella Casserole

Here's a great use for rotisserie chicken, shrimp and yellow rice.

2 8-oz. pkgs. yellow rice
1 lb. uncooked medium shrimp, peeled
 and cleaned
1 T. fresh lemon juice
½ t. salt
¼ t. pepper
2 cloves garlic, minced
1½ T. olive oil
2½-lb. lemon-and-garlic deli roast whole
 chicken, boned and coarsely shredded
5 green onions, chopped
8-oz. container sour cream
1 c. frozen English peas, thawed
1 c. green olives with pimentos,
 coarsely chopped
1½ c. shredded Monterey Jack cheese
½ t. smoked Spanish paprika

Prepare rice according to package directions. Remove from heat and let cool 30 minutes; fluff with a fork.

Meanwhile, toss shrimp with lemon juice, salt and pepper in a bowl. Sauté shrimp and garlic in hot oil in a large non-stick skillet 2 minutes or just until done. Remove from heat.

Combine shredded chicken, cooked rice, onions, sour cream and peas in a large bowl; toss well. Add shrimp and olives, tossing gently. Spoon rice mixture into a greased 13"x9" baking pan.

Combine cheese and paprika, tossing well; sprinkle over casserole. Bake, uncovered, at 400 degrees for 15 minutes, or just until cheese is melted and casserole is thoroughly heated. Serves 8.

Party Paella Casserole

Shrimp & Feta Casserole

Shrimp & Feta Casserole

Chunky salsa is the secret ingredient in this savory dinner.

2 eggs, beaten
1 c. evaporated milk
1 c. plain yogurt
3-oz. pkg. crumbled feta cheese
2 c. shredded Swiss cheese
¼ c. fresh parsley, chopped
1 t. dried basil
1 t. dried oregano
4 cloves garlic, minced
8-oz. pkg. angel hair pasta, cooked and divided
16-oz. jar chunky salsa
1 lb. medium shrimp, peeled, cleaned and divided
8-oz. pkg. shredded mozzarella cheese

In a medium bowl, combine first 9 ingredients; set aside. Spread half the pasta in a greased 13"x9" baking pan. Cover with salsa; add half the shrimp. Spread remaining pasta over shrimp; top with egg mixture. Add remaining shrimp and top with mozzarella cheese. Bake, uncovered, at 350 degrees for 30 minutes. Let stand 5 minutes before serving. Serves 6 to 8.

Jill Valentine
Jackson, TN

make it easier

To bake this when you're on vacation, purchase a large disposable roasting pan for easy clean-up. French bread is perfect for sopping up the savory sauce.

Down-Home Tuna Casserole

My family loves this creamy casserole! As the parents of two young children, my husband and I believe in the importance of sharing meals together. When I serve this casserole, everyone races to the table where we can sit as a family and share our blessings.

8-oz. pkg. egg noodles, uncooked
2 T. butter
1 c. celery, chopped
¼ c. onion, chopped
10¾-oz. can cream of mushroom soup
2 T. flour
¾ c. milk
¼ t. pepper
¼ t. dried thyme
9¼-oz. can tuna, drained and flaked
1 sleeve round buttery crackers, crushed
¼ c. Parmesan cheese, grated

Cook noodles according to package directions and place in a greased 1½-quart casserole dish. Melt butter in a saucepan and cook celery and onions until tender. Add to noodles. In a separate bowl, blend soup, flour, milk, pepper and thyme; add tuna. Add to noodle mixture and mix well. Combine cracker crumbs and Parmesan cheese and sprinkle over top. Bake, uncovered, at 350 degrees for 25 minutes. Serves 4 to 6.

Karen Urfer
New Philadelphia, OH

Quick Pizza Mac

1½ c. elbow macaroni, cooked
8-oz. jar pizza sauce
8-oz. container cottage cheese
4-oz. pkg. sliced pepperoni, halved
½ c. onion, chopped
½ t. dried basil
1 T. grated Parmesan cheese

In a lightly greased 2-quart casserole dish, combine all ingredients except Parmesan cheese; blend well. Sprinkle Parmesan over top. Cover; bake at 350 degrees for 30 to 35 minutes, or until heated through. Serves 6.

Sheila Murray
Lancaster, CA

Mom's Macaroni & Cheese

A warm, tasty dinner that'll please the kids as well as Mom and Dad.

1½ c. elbow macaroni, uncooked
4 T. all-purpose flour
4 T. butter
1½ t. salt
¼ t. pepper
½ t. dry mustard
½ t. paprika
2½ c. milk
1 T. Worcestershire sauce
10-oz. pkg. sharp Cheddar cheese, cubed

Prepare macaroni according to package directions; spread in an ungreased 13"x9" baking pan. Set aside. Combine remaining ingredients in a heavy saucepan; heat until cheese is melted and smooth, stirring often. Pour over macaroni; bake, uncovered, at 400 degrees for 30 minutes. Serves 4.

April Farley
Lowell, MA

Eggplant Parmesan

This is a down-home dish that's great to enjoy with family and friends no matter what the occasion. Serve it atop spaghetti.

2 eggs, beaten
1 T. water
2 eggplants, peeled and sliced ¼-inch thick
2 c. Italian-flavored dry bread crumbs
1½ c. grated Parmesan cheese, divided
27¾-oz. jar garden-style pasta sauce, divided
1½ c. shredded mozzarella cheese

Combine eggs and water in a shallow bowl. Dip eggplant slices into egg mixture. Arrange slices in a single layer on a greased baking sheet; bake at 350 degrees for 25 minutes or until golden. Set aside. Mix bread crumbs and ½ cup Parmesan cheese; set aside. Spread a small amount of sauce in an ungreased 13"x9" baking pan; layer half the eggplant, one cup sauce and one cup crumb mixture. Repeat layers. Cover and bake for 45 minutes. Uncover; sprinkle with mozzarella cheese and remaining Parmesan cheese. Bake, uncovered, 10 more minutes. Cut into squares. Serves 6 to 8.

Tammy Dillow
Raceland, KY

crumbs in an instant
Homemade bread crumbs are a snap! Just place Italian bread cubes in a food processor and pulse until the texture becomes fine.

Eggplant Parmesan

Mom's Squash Casserole

Tomato-Zucchini Casserole

1 c. shredded Cheddar cheese
⅓ c. grated Parmesan cheese
½ t. dried oregano
½ t. dried basil
1 clove garlic, minced
3 zucchini, thinly sliced and divided
2 tomatoes, sliced and divided
¼ c. butter
2 T. onion, minced
½ c. Italian-flavored dry bread crumbs

Combine cheeses, oregano, basil and garlic; set aside. Spread half the zucchini and half the tomatoes in a greased 8"x 8" baking pan; sprinkle with half the cheese mixture. Repeat layers; set aside. Melt butter in a small skillet; add onion and sauté until tender. Remove from heat; stir in bread crumbs. Sprinkle over cheese layer; cover with aluminum foil. Bake at 350 degrees for 30 minutes; uncover and bake 25 more minutes. Serves 8.

Jeanne Hodack
Norwich, NY

Mom's Squash Casserole

Loosely cover the casserole with aluminum foil halfway through the baking time so that the crackers don't over-brown.

1½ lbs. zucchini, sliced
1½ lbs. yellow squash, sliced
1 onion, chopped
1 egg, beaten
½ t. salt
¼ t. pepper
½ c. butter, melted and divided
2 c. round buttery crackers, crushed

Cook zucchini and squash in boiling salted water until tender, about 12 to 15 minutes; drain and mash. Add onion, egg, salt, pepper and half the melted butter. Pour mixture into a greased 13"x9" baking pan. Sprinkle with cracker crumbs; drizzle with remaining butter. Bake, uncovered, at 350 degrees for one hour. Serves 10 to 12.

Cheryl Donnelly
Arvada, CO

freezer friendly
What's one of the many advantages of making casseroles? They can be made ahead and frozen for busy weeknights. Just be sure to wrap them carefully in plastic wrap and aluminum foil.

Buttery Cauliflower Casserole

1 head cauliflower, broken into flowerets
1 c. sour cream
1 c. shredded Cheddar cheese
½ c. round buttery crackers, crushed
¼ c. green peppers, chopped
¼ c. red peppers, chopped
1 t. salt
¼ c. grated Parmesan cheese

Place cauliflower in a saucepan filled with one inch water; cook until crisp-tender. Drain. Stir in sour cream, cheese, crushed crackers, peppers and salt; spoon into a greased 2-quart casserole dish. Sprinkle with Parmesan cheese; bake, uncovered, at 325 degrees for 30 minutes. Serves 6 to 8.

Holly Sutton
Middleburgh, NY

Cheesy Broccoli-Rice Casserole

I'm always asked to bring this yummy casserole along to family gatherings. Once you taste it, you'll see why!

10-oz. pkg. frozen chopped broccoli, thawed
1 c. instant rice, uncooked
1 c. water
10¾-oz. can cream of celery soup
8-oz. jar pasteurized process cheese sauce
¼ c. butter, melted
½ c. celery, diced
½ c. onion, chopped

Mix together all ingredients; spoon into a lightly greased 2-quart casserole dish. Bake, uncovered, at 350 degrees for one hour and 15 minutes, stirring every 20 minutes. Serves 4 to 6.

Darla Manninen
South Range, MI

Creamed Spinach Casserole

Only four ingredients...a breeze to make!

2 10-oz. pkgs. frozen chopped spinach,
    thawed and drained
8-oz. pkg. cream cheese, softened
¼ c. milk
salt and pepper to taste
⅓ c. seasoned croutons, crushed

Mix together all ingredients except croutons. Spoon mixture into an ungreased one-quart casserole dish. Sprinkle with croutons. Bake uncovered at 350 degrees for 25 to 30 minutes or until heated through. Serves 6.

Leah Finks
Gooseberry Patch

Sweet Potato Crunch

½ c. sugar
1 c. butter, melted and divided
2 eggs, beaten
1 t. vanilla extract
½ c. milk
3 c. sweet potatoes, peeled, boiled and mashed
1 c. brown sugar, packed
½ c. all-purpose flour

Whisk together sugar, ½ cup butter, eggs, vanilla and milk in a large bowl; blend in sweet potatoes. Spoon into a buttered 13"x9" baking pan; set aside. Combine brown sugar, flour and remaining butter; sprinkle over potato mixture. Bake, uncovered, at 350 degrees for 25 minutes. Serves 4.

Theresa Fussell
Thibodaux, LA

Onion-Potato Gratin

Serve these with a tender pork roast for a very special "meat and potatoes" dinner.

5 potatoes, peeled, sliced and divided
2 T. olive oil, divided
1 onion, chopped
1 c. whipping cream
1 t. fresh rosemary, minced
salt and pepper to taste
¾ c. shredded fontina cheese, divided

Place sliced potatoes in a bowl, cover with water and set aside. Heat one tablespoon olive oil in a small skillet until smoking hot; add onion. Cook until onion has caramelized to a dark brown color, about 5 minutes, stirring frequently; set aside to cool. Mix together cream, rosemary, salt and pepper; set aside. Heat remaining olive oil in a 2-quart oven-safe casserole dish. Drain potatoes; add enough potatoes to cover bottom. Cook until browned; remove from heat. Sprinkle with half the onion and half the cheese; drizzle with half the cream mixture. Add a layer of uncooked potatoes, remaining onion and cheese; drizzle with remaining cream mixture. Top with any remaining uncooked potatoes. Bake, uncovered, at 425 degrees for 25 to 35 minutes; cool 5 minutes. Invert onto a plate. Serves 6.

Kathy Unruh
Fresno, CA

Tangy Corn Casserole

10-oz. pkg. frozen corn, thawed and drained
½ c. onion, chopped
½ c. green pepper, sliced into strips
½ c. water
1 c. yellow squash, chopped
1 tomato, chopped
1 c. shredded Cheddar cheese, divided
⅔ c. cornmeal
½ c. milk
2 eggs, beaten
¾ t. salt
¼ t. pepper
¼ t. hot pepper sauce
Garnish: tomato slices and green pepper,
   sliced into rings

In a medium saucepan, combine corn, onion, green pepper and water. Bring to a boil; reduce heat to medium-low. Cover and simmer 5 minutes or until vegetables are crisp-tender. Do not drain. In a large bowl, combine squash, tomato, ¾ cup cheese, cornmeal, milk, eggs, salt, pepper and hot pepper sauce. Add corn mixture to squash mixture; stir to blend. Pour into a greased 1½-quart casserole dish. Bake, uncovered, at 350 degrees for 45 to 50 minutes, or until golden brown and bubbly. Top with remaining cheese, tomato slices and green pepper rings. Serves 8.

Dave Slyh
Galloway, OH

Tangy Corn Casserole

Baked Four-Cheese
Spaghetti with Italian
Sausage (page 140)

Loaded Potato
Soup (page 126)

Slow-Cooker
Roast for Tacos
(page 142)

Hot Fudge
Spoon Cake
(page 146)

SLOW COOKER SENSATIONS

Soul-satisfying dishes using an old favorite

Spicy White Cheese Dip

Spicy White Cheese Dip

This crowd-pleaser gets its kick from canned diced tomatoes with green chiles.

2 lb. white American deli cheese slices, torn
½ c. onion, finely chopped
1 t. jarred minced garlic
2 10-oz. cans diced tomatoes with green chiles
¾ c. milk
½ t. ground cumin
½ t. coarsely ground pepper
assorted chips

   Place all ingredients, except chips, in a 6-quart slow cooker. Cover and cook on low setting 3 hours, stirring gently every hour. Adjust slow cooker setting to warm. Stir before serving. Serve with assorted chips. Makes about 8 cups.

---

kitchen secret: chopping an onion
Trim the stem and root ends; discard. Remove the papery outer skins. Then stand the onion upright on a cutting board and cut a thin slice off one side. Make vertical slices through the onion to within ¼ inch of the bottom. Rotate the onion 90 degrees and repeat. Finally, turn the onion so that the cut side is flat on the board. Cut vertically through the onion.

Easy Slow-Cooker Bean Dip

This dip is perfect to tote to potlucks and family gatherings.

4 16-oz. cans refried beans
1-lb. pkg. Colby Jack cheese, cubed
1¼-oz. pkg. taco seasoning mix
1 bunch green onions, chopped
1 c. sour cream
8-oz. pkg. cream cheese, cubed

   Place all ingredients in a 3½-quart slow cooker; stir to mix. Cover and cook on low setting 2½ hours. Stir often. Makes 11 cups.

Marni Senner
Long Beach, CA

Barbecue Chicken Wings

My family loves it when I make these wings for dinner along with potato salad and baked beans.

3 lbs. chicken wings
1½ c. barbecue sauce
¼ c. honey
2 t. mustard
1½ t. Worcestershire sauce

   Arrange chicken wings on broiler pan. Broil 4 to 5 inches from heat, turning once, about 10 minutes until chicken is golden. Place chicken in a 4-quart slow cooker. Combine barbecue sauce, honey, mustard and Worcestershire sauce in a bowl; mix well and pour over chicken. Cover and heat on low setting for 2 to 2½ hours. Makes about 2½ dozen.

Sharon Crider
Lebanon, MO

Russian Beef Borscht

*Serve in big soup bowls, dolloped with sour cream…
there's nothing better on a cold day!*

4 c. cabbage, thinly sliced
1½ lbs. beets, peeled and grated
5 carrots, peeled and sliced
1 parsnip, peeled and sliced
1 c. onion, chopped
1 lb. stew beef, cubed
4 cloves garlic, minced
14½-oz. can diced tomatoes
3 14½-oz. cans beef broth
¼ c. lemon juice
1 T. sugar
1 t. pepper

In a 6-quart slow cooker, layer ingredients in
order given. Cover and cook on low setting for
7 to 9 hours, just until vegetables are tender. Stir
well before serving. Serves 8 to 10.

Rita Morgan
Pueblo, CO

Loaded Potato Soup

*Since this recipe takes eight hours to cook, it's best
to put it on first thing in the morning so it'll be ready
when you walk in the door from work.*

4 lbs. redskin potatoes, peeled and cut into
    ¼-inch thick slices
½ c. onion, chopped
2 14-oz. cans chicken broth
2 t. salt
½ t. pepper
2 c. half-and-half
Garnish: shredded Cheddar cheese, cooked
    and crumbled bacon, sliced green onions

Layer sliced potatoes in a lightly greased 5-quart
slow cooker; top with chopped onion.
Stir together chicken broth, salt and pepper;
pour over potatoes and onion. Broth will not completely cover potatoes and onion. Cover and cook
on low setting 8 hours or until potatoes are tender.
Mash mixture with a potato masher; stir in half-
and-half. Cover and cook on high setting 20 more
minutes, or until mixture is thoroughly heated.
Ladle into bowls and garnish. Serves 8.

easy does it!
Scrub the crockery liner
gently…a nylon scrubbie
is just right for removing
cooked-on food
particles.

Loaded Potato Soup

Down-on-the-Bayou Gumbo

Down-on-the-Bayou Gumbo

You can't help but smile with a bowl of gumbo in front of you!

3 T. all-purpose flour
3 T. oil
½ lb. smoked sausage, sliced ½-inch thick
2 c. frozen okra
14½-oz. can diced tomatoes
1 onion, chopped
1 green pepper, chopped
3 cloves garlic, minced
¼ t. cayenne pepper
¾ lb. cooked medium shrimp, peeled
1½ c. long-cooking rice, cooked

Stir together flour and oil in a small saucepan over medium heat. Cook, stirring constantly, for 5 minutes. Reduce heat and cook, stirring constantly, for about 10 minutes or until mixture turns reddish brown. Spoon mixture into a 4 to 5-quart slow cooker; stir in remaining ingredients except shrimp and rice. Cover and cook on high setting for one hour; then 5 hours on low setting. Twenty minutes before serving, add shrimp to slow cooker; mix well. Cover and cook on low setting. Ladle gumbo over cooked rice in soup bowls. Serves 6.

Sue Neely
Greenville, IL

Rio Grande Green Pork Chili

Makes a wonderful buffet dish served with warm flour tortillas, or spoon over potato-filled burritos…yum!

3 lbs. boneless pork loin, cubed
1 clove garlic, minced
3 T. olive oil
½ c. all-purpose flour
2 14½-oz. cans beef broth
32-oz. can tomato juice
14½-oz. can crushed tomatoes
7-oz. can diced green chiles
4-oz. can chopped jalapeño peppers
⅓ c. dried parsley
¼ c. lemon juice
2 t. ground cumin
1 t. sugar
¼ t. ground cloves

In a heavy skillet over medium heat, sauté pork and garlic in oil. Add flour, stirring until thoroughly mixed. Place browned pork in a 6-quart slow cooker. Add remaining ingredients; cover and cook on low setting for 6 to 8 hours, until pork is tender. Serves 12 to 14.

Debby Heatwole
Canadian, TX

terrific topper!
There's no such thing as too much chili! Top hot dogs and baked potatoes with extra chili, or spoon into flour tortillas and sprinkle with shredded cheese for quick burritos.

Mom's Firehouse Chili

This tastes even better if it's refrigerated overnight, then reheated.

1½ lbs. boneless beef chuck roast, cubed
3 onions, sliced
2 c. water
28-oz. can crushed tomatoes
6-oz. can tomato paste
2 stalks celery, sliced
1 green pepper, cut into strips
16-oz. can kidney beans, drained and rinsed
16-oz. can white beans, drained and rinsed
pepper, garlic powder, parsley, chili powder
    and hot pepper sauce to taste
14¾-oz. can corn, drained

Place beef, onions and water in a 5-quart slow cooker. Add tomatoes and tomato paste; stir well. Add celery, green pepper and beans. Stir in seasonings to taste; top with corn. Cover and cook on low setting for 8 to 10 hours or on high setting for 5 to 6 hours, stirring occasionally. Serves 6.

Wendy Lee Paffenroth
Pine Island, NY

Slow-Cooker Mac & Cheese

A handy dish that's simple to make.

2 c. cooked elbow macaroni
2 T. oil
12-oz. can evaporated milk
1½ c. milk
3 c. pasteurized process cheese spread,
    shredded
¼ c. butter, melted
2 T. dried, minced onion

Combine macaroni and oil; toss to coat. Pour into a lightly greased 3 to 4-quart slow cooker; stir in remaining ingredients. Cover and cook on low setting for 3 to 4 hours; stir occasionally. Serves 4 to 6.

Paula Schwenk
Pennsdale, PA

quick cleanup!
Slow-cooker disposable liners are readily available and make cleanup a snap.

Beef Burgundy Stew

This classic recipe works well in a slow cooker.

6 slices bacon, chopped
2 lbs. stew beef
16-oz. pkg. frozen pearl onions, thawed
8-oz. pkg. mushrooms, quartered
6 redskin potatoes, quartered
2 carrots, peeled and cut into ½-inch pieces
14-oz. can beef broth
1 c. Burgundy, dry red wine or beef broth
2 T. tomato paste
1 T. fresh thyme leaves
1 t. salt
¼ t. pepper
3 cloves garlic, minced
2 T. cornstarch
2 t. cold water

Cook bacon in a large skillet over medium-high heat until crisp. Remove bacon, reserving drippings in pan. Set bacon aside.

Brown beef, in batches, in drippings until browned on all sides. Combine reserved bacon, beef, onions and remaining ingredients except cornstarch and water in a 5-quart slow cooker. Cover and cook on low setting 7 hours or until beef and vegetables are tender. Whisk together cornstarch and water. Stir into stew. Cover and cook on high setting one hour or until slightly thickened. Serves 6 to 8.

Beef Burgundy Stew

Jen's Pulled Pork

*There's no right or wrong amount of sauce to use…
simply stir in as much as you'd like. You can also
add sliced jalapeños, minced garlic or sautéed onions
and green peppers.*

3 to 4-lb. boneless pork loin roast, halved
2-ltr. bottle cola
2 28-oz. bottles honey barbecue sauce
8 to 10 hamburger buns, split

Place roast in a 5-quart slow cooker; add cola.
Cover and cook on high setting one hour; reduce
heat to low setting and cook, fat-side up, 10 to
12 more hours. Remove from slow cooker; remove
and discard any fat. Discard cooking liquids; clean
and wipe slow cooker with a paper towel. Shred
pork and return to slow cooker; add barbecue
sauce to taste. Cover and cook on low setting
one more hour, or until heated through. Add more
sauce, if desired. Serve on buns. Serves 8 to 10.

*Jennifer Inacio
Hummelstown, PA*

Jen's Pulled Pork

Sweet &
Sauerkraut Brats

Greek Chicken Pitas

Top with crumbled feta cheese and sliced black olives.

1 onion, diced
3 cloves garlic, minced
1 lb. boneless, skinless chicken breasts,
　　cut into strips
1 t. lemon-pepper seasoning
½ t. dried oregano
¼ t. allspice
¼ c. plain yogurt
¼ c. sour cream
½ c. cucumber, peeled and diced
4 rounds pita bread, halved and split

　　Place onion and garlic in a 3 to 4-quart slow cooker; set aside. Sprinkle chicken with seasonings; place in slow cooker. Cover and cook on high setting for 4 to 5 hours or until chicken is no longer pink. Stir together yogurt, sour cream and cucumber in a small bowl; chill. Fill pita halves with chicken and drizzle with yogurt sauce. Serves 4.

Peggy Pelfrey
Fort Riley, KS

Sweet & Sauerkraut Brats

Perfect for tailgating or a fall supper, these sandwiches go nicely with chips, fries or potato salad.

1½ to 2 lbs. bratwurst, cut into bite-size pieces
27-oz. can sauerkraut
4 tart apples, cored, peeled and chopped
¼ c. onion, chopped
¼ c. brown sugar, packed
1 t. caraway seed
4 to 6 hard rolls, split
Optional: spicy mustard

　　Place bratwurst in a 5 to 6-quart slow cooker. Toss together sauerkraut, apple, onion, brown sugar and caraway seed; spoon over bratwurst. Cover and cook on high setting one hour; reduce heat to low setting and cook 2 to 3 more hours, stirring occasionally. Fill rolls, using a slotted spoon. Serve with mustard, if desired. Serves 4 to 6.

Jo Ann
Gooseberry Patch

I like to pop this into the slow cooker on Saturday mornings. Later, when I get home from a day of barn sale-ing with friends, I know a hearty meal will be ready to serve my family! —Jo Ann

Country Captain

We discovered this curry-flavored dish with the unusual name on a trip to southern Georgia.

2 T. olive oil
3-lb. chicken, quartered and skin removed
2 cloves garlic, minced
1 onion, chopped
1 green pepper, chopped
½ c. celery, chopped
2 t. curry powder
⅓ c. currants or raisins
14½-oz. can whole tomatoes, chopped
1 t. sugar
salt and pepper to taste
hot cooked rice
Garnish: ¼ c. slivered almonds

Heat oil in a skillet over medium heat. Sauté chicken just until golden; place in a 4 to 5-quart slow cooker and set aside. Add garlic, onion, green pepper, celery and curry powder to skillet; sauté briefly. Remove from heat; stir in remaining ingredients except rice and almonds. Pour over chicken. Cover and cook on low setting for 6 hours, until chicken is no longer pink. Serve over cooked rice; garnish with almonds. Serves 4.

Marlene Darnell
Newport Beach, CA

French Country Chicken

This recipe is completely my own and we really love it! It has a very fancy taste, yet takes only minutes to prepare. The white wine really makes this dish, but you can use chicken broth instead.

1 onion, chopped
6 carrots, peeled and sliced diagonally
6 stalks celery, sliced diagonally
6 boneless, skinless chicken breasts
1 t. dried tarragon
1 t. dried thyme
pepper to taste
10¾-oz. can cream of chicken soup
1½-oz. pkg. onion soup mix
⅓ c. dry white wine or chicken broth
2 T. cornstarch
hot cooked rice or mashed potatoes

Combine onion, carrots and celery in a 5 to 6-quart slow cooker. Arrange chicken on top; sprinkle with seasonings. Mix together chicken soup and onion soup mix; spoon over chicken. Cover and cook on high setting for 4 hours, stirring after one hour. At serving time, stir together wine or broth and cornstarch; pour over chicken and mix well. Cook uncovered for 10 more minutes, until thickened. Stir again; serve over cooked rice or mashed potatoes. Serves 6.

Teri Lindquist
Gurnee, IL

timeless table setting
A single big blossom floating in a water-filled juice tumbler is a charming touch on the dinner table. Set one at each guest's place...sweet!

Lemony "Baked" Chicken

A perfectly golden chicken is the result of slow cooking this main dish. Stir a little lemon zest and chopped parsley into steamed rice for a perfect side dish.

3½ to 4-lb. roasting chicken
2 T. olive oil
1 lemon, halved
2 cloves garlic, minced
1 t. dried parsley
1 t. salt
½ t. pepper
Garnish: additional lemon wedges, parsley

Pat chicken dry with a paper towel; rub with oil. Place lemon halves inside chicken cavity; tie ends of legs together with string and tuck wing tips under. Place chicken in a 5-quart oval slow cooker. Sprinkle with seasonings. Cover and cook on high setting one hour; reduce heat to low setting and cook 4½ hours, or until a thermometer inserted into thigh registers 170 degrees. Garnish with lemon and parsley. Serves 4.

Sharon Lundberg
Longwood, FL

Lemony "Baked" Chicken

Sesame Chicken

All the flavor of traditional sesame chicken is in this recipe, but without the work of breading and frying the chicken pieces.

1¼ c. chicken broth
½ c. brown sugar, packed
¼ c. cornstarch
2 T. rice vinegar
2 T. soy sauce
2 T. sweet chili sauce
2 T. honey
2 t. sesame oil
1½ lb. skinned and boned chicken breasts,
    cut into 1-inch pieces
2 c. sugar snap peas
2 c. carrots, peeled and crinkle-cut
1½ T. sesame seeds, toasted
hot cooked rice
Garnish: chopped green onions

Whisk together first 8 ingredients in a 4-quart slow cooker. Stir in chicken. Cover and cook on high setting 2½ hours, or until chicken is no longer pink, stirring after 1½ hours.

Steam sugar snap peas and carrots until crisp-tender. Stir vegetables and sesame seeds into the slow cooker. Serve over cooked rice. Garnish with green onions. Serves 4 to 6.

Sesame
Chicken

Arroz con Pollo

Chicken and rice with a Spanish accent!

¼ t. saffron
2 T. boiling water
3 lbs. boneless, skinless chicken breasts
1 T. oil
2 onions, finely chopped
4 cloves garlic, minced
1 t. salt
¼ t. pepper
1½ c. long-cooking rice, uncooked
28-oz. can whole tomatoes, chopped
1 c. chicken broth
½ c. dry white wine or chicken broth
1 green pepper, finely chopped
1 c. frozen green peas, thawed
Garnish: sliced green olives with pimentos
Optional: hot pepper sauce

Combine saffron and boiling water in a cup; set aside. In a skillet over medium-high heat, cook chicken in oil just until golden. Place chicken in a 5-quart slow cooker and set aside. Add onion to skillet. Reduce heat to medium; stir and cook until softened. Add garlic, salt and pepper; cook one minute, stirring constantly. Add uncooked rice; cook and stir until coated. Add saffron mixture, tomatoes, broth and wine or broth; pour over chicken. Cover and cook on low setting for 6 to 8 hours, until chicken juices run clear and rice is tender. Increase heat to high setting; add green pepper and peas. Cover and cook 20 more minutes. Garnish with olives; serve with hot pepper sauce, if desired. Serves 6.

Michelle Sheridan
Upper Arlington, OH

Maple Praline Chicken

Any day is Mardi Gras when you serve this delicious chicken!

6 boneless, skinless chicken breasts
2 T. Cajun seasoning
¼ c. butter, melted
½ c. maple syrup
2 T. brown sugar, packed
1 c. chopped pecans
6-oz. pkg. cooked long-grain and wild rice

Sprinkle chicken with Cajun seasoning. In a skillet over medium-high heat, cook chicken in butter until golden. Arrange chicken in a 4 to 5-quart slow cooker. Mix together syrup, brown sugar and pecans; pour over chicken. Cover and cook on low setting for 6 to 8 hours. Serve with cooked rice. Serves 6.

Jill Valentine
Jackson, TN

Slow-Cooker Cassoulet

½ lb. cooked ham, cubed
½ lb. Italian sausage, cooked and sliced
1 onion, diced
3 16-oz. cans navy beans, drained and rinsed
8-oz. can tomato sauce
¼ c. water
¼ c. catsup
2 T. brown sugar, packed
½ t. salt
½ t. dry mustard
¼ t. pepper

Combine all ingredients in a 4 to 5-quart slow cooker; mix well. Cover and cook on low setting for 2 to 3 hours, until hot and bubbly. Serves 4 to 6.

Jennifer Denny
Delaware, OH

Irish Corned Beef Dinner

Serve with rye bread and spicy mustard for a tasty meal.

3-lb. corned beef brisket
4 to 6 potatoes, peeled and quartered
1 lb. carrots, peeled, halved and cut into sticks
1 head cabbage, cut into wedges
2 onions, quartered
12-oz. can beer or non-alcoholic beer
1 bay leaf
2 to 3 c. water

Place corned beef in a 6-quart slow cooker. Arrange vegetables around beef; add beer, bay leaf and enough water to cover. Cover and cook on high setting for 3½ to 4 hours. Discard bay leaf. To serve, arrange vegetables on a large serving platter. Slice corned beef and arrange on platter. Serves 6.

Lisanne Miller
York, ME

"Potatoes can be peeled and quartered the night before...just cover them with water before popping them in the fridge." —Lisanne

Beef Chow Mein

Delicious made with pork, too...serve over steamed rice or crunchy chow mein noodles.

1½ lbs. beef round steak, cubed
4-oz. can sliced mushrooms, drained
4 stalks celery, sliced
2 onions, sliced
3 cubes beef bouillon
1 c. boiling water
3 T. soy sauce
2 t. Worcestershire sauce
2 T. cornstarch
2 T. cold water
16-oz. can Chinese vegetables, drained

Place beef, mushrooms, celery and onions in a 4-quart slow cooker. Dissolve bouillon cubes in boiling water; add to slow cooker along with sauces. Cover and cook on low setting for 8 to 10 hours. One hour before serving, dissolve cornstarch in cold water; add to slow cooker along with Chinese vegetables. Serves 4.

Patsy Roberts
Center, TX

homemade take-out dinner
Purchase Chinese take-out boxes and chopsticks at your local party supply store to use as serving dishes. Fun!

Pot Roast & Sweet Potatoes

The sweet potatoes have such a good flavor in this recipe.

2 T. oil
1½ to 2-lb. boneless beef chuck roast
1 onion, thinly sliced
3 sweet potatoes, peeled and quartered
⅔ c. beef broth
¾ t. celery salt
¼ t. salt
¼ t. pepper
¼ t. cinnamon
1 T. cornstarch
2 T. cold water

Heat oil in a skillet over medium heat. Add roast and cook until brown on all sides; drain. Place onion and sweet potatoes in a 4-quart slow cooker; top with roast. Combine broth and seasonings; pour over roast. Cover and cook on low setting 7 to 8 hours or on high setting 4 to 5 hours.

Place roast on a serving platter, surrounded with vegetables; keep warm. Combine cornstarch and water in a small saucepan; add one cup of juices from slow cooker. Cook and stir over medium heat until thickened and bubbly; continue cooking and stirring 2 more minutes. Serve gravy with roast. Serves 4 to 6.

Barbara Scmeckpeper
Minoka, IL

Pot Roast & Sweet
Potatoes

Baked Four-Cheese Spaghetti with Italian Sausage

Open sausage casings using kitchen shears; then just squeeze the sausage into the pan for browning.

8 oz. spaghetti, uncooked
1 lb. Italian sausage (about 4 links)
8-oz. container pre-chopped green
    pepper-and-onion mix
2 t. minced garlic
1 T. oil
24-oz. jar fire-roasted tomato and garlic
    pasta sauce
16-oz. package shredded sharp Cheddar cheese
8-oz. package shredded mozzarella cheese, divided
4 oz. fontina cheese, shredded
½ c. shredded Parmesan cheese

Cook pasta according to package directions in a Dutch oven. Drain and return to pan.

Meanwhile, brown sausage, pepper mix and garlic in oil in a large nonstick skillet over medium-high heat, stirring often, 8 to 10 minutes or until sausage crumbles and is no longer pink. Drain. Stir sausage mixture, pasta sauce and Cheddar cheese into pasta. Spoon half of pasta mixture into a lightly greased 5-quart slow cooker.

Combine mozzarella cheese and fontina cheese. Sprinkle half of mozzarella mixture over pasta mixture in slow cooker. Top with remaining pasta mixture, remaining mozzarella mixture and Parmesan cheese. Cover and cook on low setting 3 hours. Let stand, covered, 10 minutes before serving. Serves 8 to 10.

Baked Four-Cheese
Spaghetti with Italian
Sausage

Sweet & Spicy Country Ham

This ham brings back memories of Christmas at Grandma's house.

6-lb. bone-in country ham
30 whole cloves
3 c. apple cider, divided
1 c. brown sugar, packed
1 c. maple syrup
2 T. cinnamon
2 T. ground cloves
1 T. nutmeg
2 t. ground ginger
zest of 1 orange
Optional: 1 T. vanilla extract

Make shallow cuts in fat on outside of ham one inch apart in a diamond pattern. Insert cloves in centers of diamonds; place in a 6 to 7-quart slow cooker. Pour in enough cider to cover all but top 2 inches of ham. Pack brown sugar over top of ham, pressing firmly; drizzle with syrup. Sprinkle with spices, zest and vanilla, if desired. Add remaining cider without going over fill line. Cover and cook on low setting for 8 to 10 hours. Serves 12.

Claire Bertram
Lexington, KY

Chinese-Style BBQ Pork

We ate this pork roast when we lived in China. Serve it with steamed rice and stir-fried veggies like broccoli, carrots and peppers.

2-lb. boneless pork roast
¼ c. soy sauce
¼ c. hoisin sauce
3 T. catsup
3 T. honey
2 t. garlic, minced
2 t. fresh ginger, peeled and grated
1 t. sesame oil
½ t. Chinese 5-spice powder
½ c. chicken broth

Place roast in a large plastic zipping bag and set aside. In a small bowl, whisk together remaining ingredients except broth; pour over roast. Seal bag; refrigerate at least 2 hours, turning occasionally. Remove roast from bag, reserving marinade. Place roast in a 4-quart slow cooker; pour marinade over roast. Cover and cook on low setting for 8 hours. Remove pork from slow cooker; keep warm. Add broth to liquid in slow cooker; cover and cook on low setting for 30 minutes, or until thickened. Shred pork with 2 forks and stir into sauce in slow cooker. Serves 6.

Ruth Leonard
Columbus, OH

Honey-Mustard Short Ribs

If your grocer carries boneless short ribs, cooking time can be reduced by about an hour.

3 to 4 lbs. bone-in beef short ribs
salt and pepper to taste
1 c. hickory smoke-flavored barbecue sauce
3 T. honey
1 T. Dijon mustard
3 cloves garlic, minced
2 T. cornstarch
2 T. cold water

  Sprinkle ribs with salt and pepper; place in a 4-quart slow cooker and set aside. Combine barbecue sauce, honey, mustard, garlic and additional salt and pepper, if desired; pour over ribs. Cover and cook on low setting for 6 to 7 hours. During the last 30 minutes of cooking, whisk cornstarch into water; add to slow cooker, stirring until thickened. Serves 4.

David Wink
Marion, OH

Slow-Cooker Roast for Tacos

Don't forget to offer all the tasty taco toppers… shredded cheese, sour cream, lettuce, tomatoes, onions and salsa. Olé!

4 to 5-lb. beef chuck roast
1 T. chili powder
1 t. ground cumin
1 t. onion powder
1 t. garlic powder
2 14 ½-oz. cans Mexican-style stewed tomatoes
taco shells

  Place roast in a 5 to 6-quart slow cooker; sprinkle with seasonings. Pour tomatoes with juice over roast. Cover and cook on low setting for 8 to 10 hours. Using 2 forks, shred roast and spoon into taco shells. Makes 10 cups.

Dana Thompson
Prospect, OH

Slow-Cooker
Roast for Tacos

Spoon Bread Florentine

This side dish is deliciously different and so simple to make.

10-oz. pkg. frozen chopped spinach, thawed
   and drained
6 green onions, sliced
1 red pepper, chopped
6-oz. pkg. cornbread mix
4 eggs, beaten
½ c. butter, melted
1 c. cottage cheese
1¼ t. seasoned salt

   Combine all ingredients in a large bowl; mix well. Spoon into a lightly greased 3-quart slow cooker. Cover with lid slightly ajar to allow moisture to escape. Cook on low setting for 3 to 4 hours or on high setting for one hour and 45 minutes to 2 hours, until edges are golden and a knife tip inserted in center tests clean. Serves 8.

Jo Ann
Gooseberry Patch

Mexicali Rice

Serve this with chicken or turkey breasts to make it even heartier!

15¼-oz. can corn, drained
15-oz. can black beans, drained and rinsed
4-oz. can diced green chiles
1 onion, chopped
1 red pepper, chopped
2 c. long-cooking rice, uncooked
3½ c. boiling water
½ c. frozen orange juice concentrate, thawed
4½ T. lime juice, divided
1½ T. ground cumin
1 T. chili powder
⅓ c. fresh cilantro, chopped
½ t. salt

   Combine corn, black beans, chiles, onion, pepper, rice, water, orange juice, ¼ cup lime juice, cumin and chili powder in a 3-quart slow cooker. Cover and cook on low setting for 2½ to 3 hours. Stir in remaining lime juice, cilantro and salt; mix well. Serves 4 to 6.

Marian Buckley
Fontana, CA

Slow-Simmered Green Beans

1½ lbs. green beans, trimmed and sliced
1 stalk celery, diced
¼ c. onion, chopped
¼ c. butter, sliced
4 cubes beef bouillon
1 T. sugar
1 t. garlic salt
¼ t. dill seed

   Combine all ingredients in a 3-quart slow cooker. Cover and cook on low setting for 3 to 4 hours. Serves 6 to 8.

Cathy Lipchak
Mechanicsville, VA

picnic perferct
Keep picnics festive and comfy...
bring along colorful, soft quilts and
blankets for lunch in the shade.
Once lunch is over, those soft
and cozy quilts also create a
perfect spot for napping!

Double-Berry Cobbler

Who would guess that this homestyle cobbler is made in a slow cooker?

1 c. all-purpose flour
1½ c. sugar, divided
1 t. baking powder
¼ t. salt
¼ t. cinnamon
¼ t. nutmeg
2 eggs, beaten
2 T. milk
2 T. oil
2 c. blackberries
2 c. blueberries
¾ c. water
1 t. orange zest
Optional: ice cream or whipped topping

Combine flour, ¾ cup sugar, baking powder, salt and spices in a medium bowl; set aside. In a small bowl, combine eggs, milk and oil; stir into flour mixture until moistened. Spread batter evenly in a 3 to 4-quart slow cooker; set aside. Combine berries, water, zest and remaining sugar in a large saucepan. Bring to a boil; remove from heat and pour over batter without stirring. Cover and cook on high setting for 2 to 2½ hours, or until a toothpick inserted in center comes out clean. Uncover and let stand 30 minutes. Spoon into bowls, topped with ice cream or whipped topping, if desired. Serves 6.

Becky Weatherman
Mocksville, NC

Roll up plastic cutlery in paper napkins and stack in a child's vintage sand pail...oh-so easy for party guests to grab and go! —Becky

Favorite Caramel Apples

For a special treat, press warm caramel apples into chopped peanuts, candy-coated chocolates, candy corn or red cinnamon candies.

2 14-oz. pkgs. caramels, unwrapped
¼ c. water
½ t. cinnamon
8 wooden craft sticks
8 apples

Combine caramels, water and cinnamon in a 3-quart oval slow cooker. Cover and cook on high setting one hour to 1½ hours, stirring every 20 minutes.

Insert sticks into apples. Reduce heat to low setting; dip apples into hot caramel and turn to coat, scraping excess caramel from bottom of apples with a knife. Place on greased wax paper to cool. Makes 8.

Graceann Frederico
Irondequoit, NY

chocolate-drizzled caramel apples
Make caramel apples extra special! Microwave mini chocolate chips for 30 seconds, stir and then drizzle over apples.

Favorite Caramel Apples

Slow-Cooked
Brown Sugar Apples

Hot Fudge Spoon Cake

This gooey chocolate cake is heavenly.

1 c. all-purpose flour
1¾ c. brown sugar, packed and divided
¼ c. plus 3 T. baking cocoa, divided
2 t. baking powder
¼ t. salt
½ c. milk
2 T. butter, melted
½ t. vanilla extract
1¾ c. hot water
Optional: vanilla ice cream

Combine flour, one cup brown sugar, 3 tablespoons cocoa, baking powder and salt in a medium bowl. Whisk in milk, butter and vanilla. Spread evenly in a 3½-quart slow cooker. Mix together remaining ¾ cup brown sugar and ¼ cup cocoa; sprinkle evenly over top of batter. Pour in hot water; do not stir. Cover and cook on high setting for 2 hours, or until a toothpick inserted one-inch deep comes out clean. Spoon warm cake into bowls; top with vanilla ice cream, if desired. Serves 6.

Sara Plott
Monument, CO

Slow-Cooked Brown Sugar Apples

Nothing says comfort like the aroma of these apples cooking…unless, of course, it's sitting down to enjoy them.

6 apples, cored
¾ c. orange juice
½ c. apple cider
½ c. brown sugar, packed
¼ t. cinnamon
Optional: frozen whipped topping, thawed

Peel a strip around the top of each apple to help prevent cracking. Arrange apples in a 4 to 5-quart slow cooker. In a large bowl, combine remaining ingredients except whipped topping. Spoon over apples. Cover and cook on low setting for 3 to 4 hours, or until apples are tender. Cool slightly and serve warm with whipped topping, if desired. Serves 6.

Lynn Williams
Muncie, IN

we all scream for ice cream
While vanilla is the natural choice to serve alongside warm cobblers and pies, set up an ice cream bar with a variety of flavors to make dessert even more fun.

Hot Fudge
Spoon Cake

Triple Chocolate-Nut
Clusters

Triple Chocolate-Nut Clusters

Candy making has never been so easy! The slow cooker is the perfect tool to keep this candy mixture warm while you're spooning it out.

16-oz. jar dry-roasted peanuts
9¾-oz. can salted whole cashews
2 c. pecan pieces
18 2-oz. chocolate bark coating squares,
    cut in half
12-oz. package semi-sweet chocolate morsels
4 1-oz. bittersweet chocolate baking squares,
    broken into pieces
1 T. shortening
1 t. vanilla extract

    Combine all ingredients except vanilla in a 5-quart slow cooker; cover and cook on low setting 2 hours or until chocolate is melted. Stir in vanilla. Drop candy by heaping teaspoonfuls onto wax paper. Let stand at least 2 hours, or until firm. Store in an airtight container. Makes about 6 dozen.

candy for a crowd
Wrap up bagfuls of homemade chocolates and give them as gifts to family and friends.

Bananas Foster

Be sure your bananas are ripe but not too soft; otherwise they'll turn into mush in the slow cooker.

½ c. butter, melted
¼ c. brown sugar, packed
6 bananas, cut into one-inch slices
¼ c. rum or ¼ t. rum extract
vanilla ice cream

    Stir together butter, brown sugar, bananas and rum or extract in a 3-quart slow cooker. Cover and cook on low setting for one hour. To serve, spoon over scoops of vanilla ice cream. Serves 4.

Jo Ann
Gooseberry Patch

Guests will flip over this decadent dessert!
—Jo Ann

Turkey Panini
(page 170)

Cheeseburger
Soup (page 169)

Cheesy Wild Rice Soup
(page 157)

Grilled Cuban Sandwiches
(page 174)

SCRUMPTIOUS SOUPS
& SANDWICHES

Simple solutions for easy lunches & dinners

Black Beans &
Vegetable Chili

Black Beans & Vegetable Chili

This vegetarian chili, filled with black beans, peppers, squash and tomatoes and served over rice, is hearty and filling.

1 onion, coarsely chopped
1 T. oil
28-oz. can diced tomatoes
⅔ c. picante sauce
1½ t. ground cumin
1 t. salt
½ t. dried basil
15-oz. can black beans, drained and rinsed
1 green pepper, cut into ¾-inch pieces
1 red pepper, cut into ¾-inch pieces
1 yellow squash or zucchini, cut into
    ½-inch pieces
hot cooked rice
Garnish: shredded Cheddar cheese,
    sour cream, chopped fresh cilantro
Optional: additional picante sauce

Sauté onion in oil in a Dutch oven over medium-high heat, stirring constantly, until tender. Add tomatoes with juice, picante sauce and seasonings; stir well. Bring to a boil; cover, reduce heat and simmer 5 minutes. Stir in beans, peppers and squash. Cover and cook over medium-low heat 25 minutes or until vegetables are tender, stirring occasionally.

To serve, ladle chili over hot cooked rice in individual bowls. Top each serving with cheese, sour cream and cilantro. Serve with additional picante sauce, if desired. Serves 4 to 6.

perfect pairing
Nothing goes better with hearty chili than warm cornbread! If you like your cornbread crisp, prepare it in a vintage sectioned cast-iron skillet...each wedge of cornbread will bake up with its own golden crust.

Farmstead Split Pea Soup

Fill a thermos with this hearty soup...it's terrific for an autumn picnic.

8 c. water
16-oz. pkg. bag split peas, rinsed and drained
1½ lb. ham bone with meat
2 onions, chopped
3 leeks, white part only, chopped
2 stalks celery, chopped
1 carrot, peeled and chopped
1 c. dry white wine or vegetable broth
1 clove garlic, finely chopped
½ t. dried marjoram
¼ t. dried thyme
salt and pepper to taste

Combine all ingredients except salt and pepper in a Dutch oven. Bring to a boil. Cover, reduce heat and simmer for 2 to 2½ hours or until peas are soft. Remove ham bone and cool to warm. Remove meat from bone and add to Dutch oven. Add salt and pepper to taste. Serves 6.

Jo Ann
Gooseberry Patch

Cool Gazpacho Soup

So refreshing on a steamy day. Garnish with thin slices of lemon.

3 tomatoes, chopped
2 cucumbers, peeled and chopped
½ red onion, chopped
I green pepper, chopped
I yellow pepper, chopped
I clove garlic, minced
32-oz. bottle cocktail vegetable juice
I T. olive oil
I T. lemon juice

Combine all ingredients in a deep bowl; mix gently. Cover and refrigerate for at least 4 hours; serve chilled. Serves 6.

Sharon Tillman
Hampton, VA

simple supper
Take it easy and have a leftovers night once a week. Set out leftovers so everyone can choose their favorite. End with ice cream for dessert… what could be simpler?

Rainy-Day Tomato Soup

Topped with buttery fresh-baked croutons, here is a modern take on a classic comfort food.

2 T. olive oil
I onion, thinly sliced
3 to 4 T. garlic, chopped
I c. celery, chopped
½ c. carrot, peeled and cut into 2-inch sticks
28-oz. can crushed tomatoes
2½ c. vegetable broth
2 t. dried basil
I t. dried thyme

Heat oil in a Dutch oven over medium heat; add onion and garlic and sauté until onion is translucent. Add celery and carrot; cook 5 more minutes. Add remaining ingredients and bring to a boil. Cover, reduce heat and simmer 1½ hours or until thickened. Ladle soup into 4 bowls; top with Italian Croutons. Serves 4.

Italian Croutons:
I loaf day-old bread, crusts removed
½ c. butter, melted
I T. Italian seasoning

Cube bread and place in a large plastic zipping bag; set aside. Combine butter and seasoning; pour over bread. Mix well; arrange bread cubes on an ungreased baking sheet. Bake at 425 degrees for 10 minutes; turn bread cubes and bake 5 more minutes.

Rosie Sabo
Toledo, OH

Rainy-Day
Tomato Soup

Cheesy Wild Rice Soup

Cheesy Wild Rice Soup

Garnish each bowl of this soup with a little extra crispy bacon...yummy!

9 to 10 slices bacon, diced
1 onion, chopped
2 10¾-oz. cans cream of potato soup
1½ c. wild rice, cooked
2 pts. half-and-half
2 c. American cheese, shredded
Optional: Biscuit Bowls

In a skillet over medium heat, sauté bacon and onion together until bacon is crisp and onion is tender. Drain and set aside. Combine soup and rice in a medium saucepan; stir in bacon mixture, half-and-half and cheese. Cook over low heat until cheese melts, stirring occasionally. Serve in Biscuit Bowls, if desired. Serves 6 to 8.

Tanya Graham
Lawrenceville, GA

Biscuit Bowls:

16.3-oz. tube refrigerated jumbo flaky biscuits
non-stick vegetable spray

Flatten each biscuit into a 5-inch round. Invert eight 6-ounce custard cups, several inches apart, on a lightly greased baking sheet. Spray bottoms of cups with non-stick vegetable spray; form flattened biscuits around cups. Bake at 350 degrees for 14 minutes. Cool slightly and remove biscuit bowls from cups. Return to oven and bake 7 to 10 more minutes, or until golden. Makes 8.

Anna McMaster
Portland, OR

Pumpkin Chowder

This blend of everyday ingredients is anything but ordinary.

8-oz. pkg. bacon, diced
2 c. onions, chopped
2 t. curry powder
2 T. all-purpose flour
1-lb. pie pumpkin, peeled, seeded and chopped
2 potatoes, peeled and cubed
4 c. chicken broth
1 c. half-and-half
salt and pepper to taste
Garnish: toasted pumpkin seeds, sliced
   green onions

Cook bacon in a stockpot over medium heat for 5 minutes; add onion. Sauté for 10 minutes; add curry and flour, stirring until smooth and creamy, about 5 minutes. Add pumpkin, potatoes and broth; simmer until potatoes are tender, about 15 minutes. Pour in half-and-half; season with salt and pepper. Simmer for 5 minutes; do not boil. Spoon into serving bowls; garnish with toasted pumpkin seeds and sliced green onions. Serves 6.

Sandy Westendorp
Grand Rapids, MI

creative candle

Guests will love the smell of spicy pumpkin, and it's so easy to create. Cut off the top of a pumpkin, scrape out the insides and punch several holes in the pumpkin shell with an apple corer. Rub cinnamon into the "walls" of the pumpkin and place a tealight inside.

Bean & Ham Soup

This soup is sure to become a comfort food favorite.

16-oz. pkg. dried Great Northern beans,
    rinsed
8 c. water
1½ lb. ham bone
2 potatoes, peeled and cubed
2 carrots, peeled and chopped
2 stalks celery, chopped
1 onion, chopped
¾ t. dried thyme
½ t. salt
¼ t. pepper
hot pepper sauce to taste

Combine beans and water in a large Dutch oven; bring to a boil. Reduce heat; simmer for 2 minutes. Remove from heat; cover and let stand for one hour. Bring beans to a boil; add ham bone. Reduce heat; simmer for one hour. Remove ham bone and cool. Remove meat from bone, discarding bone; add meat to soup. Stir in remaining ingredients. Cover; simmer until vegetables are tender, about 30 minutes. Serves 4 to 6.

Shannon Cronin
Hinton, IA

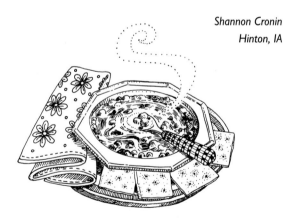

Parmesan-Onion Soup

A rich and flavorful soup that'll warm you to your toes!

3 T. butter, melted
4 c. onions, thinly sliced
½ t. sugar
1 T. all-purpose flour
4 c. water
salt and pepper to taste
4 French bread slices, toasted
½ c. freshly grated Parmesan cheese

Combine butter, onions and sugar in a large saucepan; sauté 20 to 25 minutes or until onions are golden. Stir in flour; cook for 3 to 5 minutes. Add water and simmer, partially covered, for 30 minutes. Add salt and pepper, blending well. Fill 4 oven-proof bowls, arranged on a rimmed baking sheet, with soup; top each with a bread slice and sprinkle generously with Parmesan cheese. Bake at 400 degrees until cheese melts.

Texas Ranch Soup

So good, this may make only two Texas-size servings!

1½ lbs. ground beef, browned
2 15-oz. cans ranch-style beans
2 15-oz. cans corn
2 14½-oz. cans diced tomatoes
1¼ oz. pkg. taco seasoning mix
Garnish: crushed tortilla chips,
    shredded Cheddar cheese

Combine all ingredients except garnish in a large stockpot; bring to a boil. Reduce heat and simmer 15 minutes. Spoon into serving bowls; garnish with tortilla chips and cheese. Serves 6.

Deborah Neuman
San Felipe, TX

Parmesan-Onion Soup

Curried
Harvest Bisque

Curried Harvest Bisque

Top with ham for an elegant beginning to a holiday meal.

1 lb. butternut squash, peeled and cut into
   1-inch cubes
5 c. chicken broth
¼ c. butter
¼ c. all-purpose flour
1 t. curry powder
¾ c. half-and-half
1 T. lime juice
½ t. salt
¼ t. white pepper
Garnish: diced ham

Combine squash and broth in a 4-quart Dutch oven. Cook over medium heat until squash is tender, about 15 minutes. Using a slotted spoon, transfer squash to a blender; process until smooth. Add broth to squash; set aside. Melt butter in Dutch oven; stir in flour and curry powder. Cook over medium heat, stirring until smooth. Add squash mixture; increase heat to medium-high and stir until soup thickens slightly. Reduce heat to low; add remaining ingredients except ham and heat through without boiling. Garnish with ham. Serves 4.

Kathy Grashoff
Fort Wayne, IN

Tailgate Seafood Chowder

This is so easy to make…but, your guests will think you worked for hours!

½ c. butter
1 lb. shrimp, peeled, cleaned and chopped
3 8-oz. cans chopped clams, drained
2 10½-oz. cans she-crab soup
2 19-oz. cans chunky clam chowder
½ c. vermouth or chicken broth
pepper to taste
Garnish: fresh parsley, chopped

Melt butter in a large saucepan over medium heat; add shrimp to pan. Cook 2 to 3 minutes or until shrimp turn pink. Add remaining ingredients except parsley; cook until heated through. Garnish with fresh parsley. Serves 8 to 10.

Kathleen Brillinger
Norwich, NY

recycled radiance

Give old candles new glow! Grate partially burned candles with a kitchen grater, then layer clear glass jars with wax shavings in different colors. Push a wick down into the center and enjoy the candles a second time.

Hearty Minestrone

This soup is worth the extra time it takes to prepare...you may even want to double the recipe!

2 slices bacon, diced
¼ lb. ham, diced
½ lb. Italian sausage, casings removed
1 onion, chopped
3 cloves garlic, chopped
3 stalks celery, chopped
1 leek, chopped
2 zucchini, chopped
2 qts. beef broth
16-oz. can kidney beans, drained and rinsed
½ head cabbage, shredded
1 c. dry red wine or beef broth
14.5-oz. can diced tomatoes
½ c. uncooked elbow macaroni
pepper to taste
2 t. dried basil
Garnish: Parmesan cheese, grated

Cook bacon, ham and sausage in a large skillet over medium heat until bacon is crisp and sausage crumbles and is no longer pink. Add onion, garlic, celery, leek and zucchini. Cook 10 minutes. Heat broth in a large Dutch oven. Add bacon mixture, kidney beans, cabbage and wine or broth. Simmer, partially covered, for 1½ hours. Add tomatoes with juice, macaroni, pepper and basil. Cook 15 minutes. Serve with cheese. Serves 6 to 8.

Teresa Sullivan
Westerville, OH

Traditional Wedding Soup

Prepare the meatballs ahead and freeze them until you're ready to make the soup.

2 qts. chicken broth
4 ripe tomatoes, peeled, seeded, chopped
  and juice reserved
1 head escarole, washed and chopped
1 T. dried basil
1 T. dried parsley
pepper to taste
Garnish: fresh parsley, Parmesan cheese

In soup pot, bring broth to a boil; add all ingredients except Meatballs and garnish. Bring to a boil. Add Meatballs, a few at a time. Bring to a boil again, reduce heat and simmer until Meatballs are thoroughly cooked, about one hour. Garnish with fresh parsley and Parmesan cheese. Serves 6 to 8.

Meatballs:
1 lb. ground beef
1 egg
1 clove garlic, minced
1 T. dried parsley
¼ c. bread crumbs
¼ c. grated Parmesan cheese

Combine all ingredients. Shape into 2-inch balls.

Marisa Adams
Manchester, CT

Chili with Corn Dumplings

Dumplings created with cornmeal and fresh cilantro make this chili extra special and so satisfying.

4½ lbs. ground beef
2¼ c. onion, chopped
3 15-oz. cans corn, undrained and divided
3 14½-oz. cans stewed tomatoes
3 15-oz. cans tomato sauce
1 T. hot pepper sauce
6 T. chili powder
1 T. garlic, minced
1⅓ c. biscuit baking mix
⅔ c. cornmeal
⅔ c. milk
3 T. fresh cilantro, chopped

Brown beef and onion in a Dutch oven over medium heat; drain. Set aside 1½ cups of drained corn; stir remaining corn with liquid, tomatoes with juice, sauces, chili powder and garlic into beef mixture. Bring to a boil. Cover, reduce heat and simmer 15 minutes. Combine baking mix and cornmeal in a medium bowl; stir in milk, cilantro and reserved corn just until moistened. Drop dough by rounded tablespoonfuls onto simmering chili. Cook over low heat, uncovered, 15 minutes. Cover and cook 15 to 18 more minutes or until dumplings are dry on top. Serves 10.

Tanya Graham
Lawrenceville, GA

Chili with Corn Dumplings

Country Comfort
Chicken Soup

Country Comfort Chicken Soup

This warm and cozy soup is perfect on a chilly wintry day.

9 c. water
2 c. baby carrots, sliced
1 c. celery, chopped
2 T. garlic, minced
1½ t. seasoned salt
1 t. dried parsley
1 t. poultry seasoning
½ t. salt
¼ t. pepper
6 boneless, skinless chicken thighs
4 cubes chicken bouillon
5 c. fine egg noodles, uncooked

Place all ingredients except noodles in a large Dutch oven. Bring to a boil; cover, reduce heat and simmer until chicken and vegetables are tender, about one hour. Remove chicken from simmering broth; let chicken cool slightly. Stir noodles into broth; simmer, uncovered, until done, about 5 minutes. While noodles are cooking, dice chicken and return to soup. Serves 8.

Chicken Tortilla Soup

This is a great make-ahead soup, but don't ladle it over the tortilla chips until just before serving.

1 c. red onion, chopped
1 red pepper, chopped
2 cloves garlic, minced
2 boneless, skinless chicken breasts
1 T. oil
7 c. chicken broth
9-oz. pkg. frozen corn, thawed
1 t. ground cumin
2 c. tortilla chips, lightly crushed
1 c. shredded Cheddar cheese
Optional: sour cream, chopped fresh
    cilantro

Sauté onion, pepper, garlic and chicken in oil in a Dutch oven 7 to 8 minutes; remove chicken. Pour in broth; bring to a simmer. Add corn and cumin; cook 10 minutes. Shred chicken; stir into soup. Place some chips in each bowl; ladle soup over chips. Sprinkle with cheese; stir. Top with sour cream and cilantro, if desired. Serves 6 to 8.

Lynnette Zeigler
South Lake Tahoe, CA

garnishes galore

It's the unexpected touches that make the biggest impression. When serving soup or chili, offer guests a variety of fun toppings…fill bowls with shredded cheese, oyster crackers, chopped onions, sour cream and crunchy croutons. Then invite everyone to dig in!

Homestyle Kale Soup

Warm and filling for a family on the go.

4 10½-oz. cans chicken broth
4 10½-oz. cans beef broth
8 c. kale, shredded
3 potatoes, peeled and cubed
1 T. oil
1 onion, chopped
3 carrots, peeled and sliced
2 stalks celery, chopped
14½-oz. can diced tomatoes
1½ lbs. Kielbasa sausage, sliced
16-oz. can pinto beans
hot pepper sauce to taste

Combine first 4 ingredients in a large Dutch oven; cook over medium heat until potatoes are tender. Heat oil in a large skillet; add onions, carrots and celery. Sauté until tender; add to broth mixture. Stir in tomatoes with juice and Kielbasa sausage; simmer for 30 minutes. Add beans; season with hot pepper sauce. Simmer until thoroughly heated. Serves 10.

Tracy Melancon
APO, AE

Callie Coe's Chicken & Dumplings

This Southern favorite is the ultimate comfort food. Like biscuit dough, the less the dumpling dough is handled, the lighter and more tender it will be.

3 to 4 lbs. bone-in chicken, cut up
3 qts. water
salt and pepper to taste
4 eggs, hard-boiled, peeled and chopped

Place chicken pieces in a large pan; add water, salt and pepper. Bring to a boil; reduce heat and simmer until tender and juices run clear when chicken is pierced with a fork, about one hour. Remove chicken, reserving broth in pan. Let chicken cool; remove meat, discarding bones, and return meat to chicken broth. Add chopped eggs. Bring broth to a boil and add Dumplings one batch at a time; stir well before adding each new batch. After adding last batch, cover and simmer until tender, about 20 minutes. Remove from heat; let stand a few minutes before serving. Serves 4 to 6.

Dumplings:

4 c. self-rising flour
1 to 1¼ c. warm water

Mix flour with enough water to make a dough that can be rolled out. Divide dough into 4 batches. Roll out each batch of dough ½-inch thick on a lightly floured surface; cut into strips.

Marilyn Meyers
Orange City, FL

"My grandma always made her chicken and dumplings for family reunions. She would roll out the dough with a jelly glass." –Marilyn

Callie Coe's
Chicken & Dumplings

Red Barn Chowder

Red Barn Chowder

Enjoy the spicy taste of this delicious, hearty chowder filled with sausage and vegetables.

1 lb. ground hot Italian sausage, crumbled
1 onion, chopped
3 stalks celery, chopped
1 green pepper, chopped
1 red pepper, chopped
2 zucchini, quartered and sliced
3 to 4 cloves garlic, chopped
28-oz. can stewed tomatoes
10-oz. can diced tomatoes with green chiles
6-oz. can tomato paste
1 c. water
2 t. dried basil
salt and pepper to taste
1 c. canned garbanzo beans, drained
    and rinsed

Combine sausage, onion, celery, peppers, zucchini and garlic in a large saucepan. Sauté until sausage is browned and vegetables are tender; drain. Stir in tomatoes with juice, tomato paste, water, basil, salt and pepper; cook until heated through. Add garbanzo beans; heat through. Serves 8 to 10.

Suzanne Pottker
Elgin, IL

soup secret
Warmed soup bowls are a thoughtful touch. Set oven-safe crocks on a baking sheet and place in a warm oven for a few minutes. Remove from oven and ladle in hot, hearty soup…mmm, pass the bread!

My son's favorite! When his first-grade class made recipe holders for Mothers' Day, he insisted that I put this recipe in the holder. Kids really do like this soup…the jalapeño doesn't taste hot when it's done. –Lacy

Cheeseburger Soup

All the ingredients of your favorite cheeseburger are included in this chunky soup. (Pictured on page 150)

2 c. potatoes, peeled and cubed
2 carrots, peeled and grated
1 onion, chopped
1 jalapeño pepper, seeded and chopped
1 clove garlic, minced
1½ c. water
1 T. beef bouillon granules
½ t. salt
1 lb. ground beef, browned and drained
2½ c. milk, divided
3 T. all-purpose flour
8-oz. pkg. pasteurized process cheese spread,
    cubed
Optional: ¼ to 1 t. cayenne pepper
Garnish: ½ lb. bacon, crisply cooked and crumbled

Combine first 8 ingredients in a large saucepan; bring to a boil over medium heat. Reduce heat and simmer until potatoes are tender. Stir in beef and 2 cups milk.

Whisk together flour and remaining milk in a small bowl until smooth; gradually whisk into soup. Bring to a boil; cook 2 minutes or until thick and bubbly, stirring constantly. Reduce heat; add cheese and stir until melted. Add cayenne pepper, if desired. Garnish with bacon. Serves 6 to 8.

Lacy Mayfield
Earth, TX

Stuffed Pockets

3 whole pita rounds, cut in half
lettuce leaves
6 slices deli ham, thinly sliced
6 slices Cheddar cheese
1 red onion, sliced into rings
1 tomato, sliced
ranch-style salad dressing to taste
4 slices bacon, crisply cooked and crumbled

Slightly open pita halves and stuff with lettuce, ham, cheese, onion and tomato. Top with salad dressing and crumbled bacon. Makes 6.

Chicken Salad Sandwiches

Served with slices of fresh melon or strawberries, these sandwiches are great for a quick and tasty lunch.

1¼ lbs. chicken breast, cooked and diced
1 c. celery, thinly sliced
1 c. seedless red grapes, halved
½ c. raisins
½ c. plain yogurt
¼ c. mayonnaise
2 T. shallots, chopped
2 T. fresh tarragon, chopped
½ t. salt
⅛ t. white pepper
6 whole-wheat buns, split
lettuce leaves

Combine chicken, celery, grapes and raisins in a large bowl. Blend together yogurt, mayonnaise, shallots, tarragon, salt and pepper in a small bowl. Add yogurt mixture to chicken mixture; stir gently to coat. Divide mixture evenly among buns. Place lettuce leaves over chicken mixture and place tops on buns. Makes 6.

Susan Smith
London, OH

Turkey Panini

Use leftover turkey after a big holiday feast for these delicious sandwiches. Pile on the turkey and use your homemade cranberry sauce, if desired. Shaved deli turkey makes a fine substitute.

¼ c. whole-berry cranberry sauce
2 to 3 t. prepared horseradish
2 T. mayonnaise
4 ½-inch thick large slices ciabatta bread
4 ⅜-inch thick slices cooked turkey breast or
  deli turkey
salt and pepper to taste
4 slices provolone cheese
4 slices bacon, crisply cooked
1½ T. olive oil
Optional: mixed salad greens

Combine cranberry sauce and horseradish, stirring well. Spread mayonnaise on one side of each slice of bread. Spread cranberry-horseradish sauce on 2 slices of bread; top each sandwich with 2 turkey slices and sprinkle with salt and pepper. Arrange 2 cheese slices on each sandwich; top with 2 bacon slices. Cover with tops of bread, mayonnaise side down. Brush tops and bottoms of sandwiches with olive oil. Cook on a panini press 3 minutes or until cheese begins to melt and bread is toasted. Serve hot. Garnish with mixed salad greens, if desired. Makes 2.

panini press alternative
If you don't have a panini press, cook your sandwiches in a skillet and place another heavy skillet topped with cans over the sandwich to press it. It'll work just as well.

Turkey Panini

Mark's Egg Salad Sandwiches

6 eggs, hard-boiled, peeled and chopped
1/3 c. celery, finely chopped
1/3 c. onion, finely chopped
3 to 4 T. mayonnaise-type salad dressing
1 to 2 t. mustard
1 t. Worcestershire sauce
1/2 t. salt
1/4 t. pepper
1/2 t. dry mustard
1 T. dill weed
1 loaf sliced bread

Mix all ingredients except bread in a small bowl; refrigerate about one hour. Spread on half of bread slices; top with remaining bread slices. Makes 6 to 8.

Connie Herek
Bay City, MI

mix-and-match
Whip up several different kinds of sandwiches (or stop at the local deli for a few!) and cut each one into four sections. Arrange them on a large platter with chips and pickles…everyone will love the variety, and the preparation couldn't be easier.

Mark's Egg Salad Sandwiches

Tomato Sandwiches

Use garden tomatoes warm from the summer sun to make these sandwiches extra special.

3 tomatoes, thickly sliced
10 sprigs watercress
1 red onion, sliced
1 green pepper, sliced
10 slices pumpernickel bread
salt and pepper to taste
mayonnaise to taste

Place 2 tomato slices, 2 sprigs of watercress, a slice of onion and 2 slices of green pepper on half of the bread slices. Sprinkle with salt and pepper. Spread mayonnaise over remaining bread slices and top sandwiches. Makes 5.

Diane Long
Delaware, OH

The Ultimate Shrimp Sandwich

¾ lb. cooked shrimp, chopped
¼ c. green pepper, chopped
¼ c. celery, chopped
¼ c. cucumber, chopped
¼ c. tomato, diced
¼ c. green onion, chopped
¼ c. mayonnaise
Optional: hot pepper sauce to taste
6 split-top rolls, split and lightly toasted
2 T. butter, softened
1 c. shredded lettuce

Combine shrimp and next 6 ingredients; add hot pepper sauce, if desired, and toss well. Set aside. Spread rolls evenly with butter; divide lettuce among rolls. Top with shrimp mixture. Makes 6.

Karen Pilcher
Burleson, TX

Grilled Veggie Sandwich

Use any of your favorite freshly picked vegetables for this sandwich!

¼ c. balsamic vinegar
2 T. olive oil
1 T. fresh basil, chopped
2 t. molasses
1½ t. fresh thyme, chopped
¼ t. salt
¼ t. pepper
3 zucchini, sliced
1 yellow pepper, coarsely chopped
2 red peppers, coarsely chopped
1 onion, sliced
16-oz. loaf French bread
¾ c. crumbled feta cheese
2 T. mayonnaise
¼ c. freshly grated Parmesan cheese

Whisk together vinegar, olive oil, basil, molasses, thyme, salt and pepper. Place zucchini, peppers and onion in a large plastic zipping bag. Add vinegar mixture; seal and refrigerate 2 hours, turning bag occasionally. Remove vegetables from bag and set aside; reserve marinade. Slice bread loaf in half horizontally and brush 3 or 4 tablespoons reserved marinade over inside of bread. Lightly coat grill with non-stick vegetable spray; add vegetables and grill 5 minutes, basting occasionally with remaining marinade. Turn vegetables, baste and grill 2 more minutes. Place bread, cut sides down on grill and grill 3 minutes or until vegetables are tender and bread is toasted.

Combine feta cheese and mayonnaise; spread evenly over cut sides of bread. Layer grilled vegetables on bottom half of bread; add Parmesan cheese and top with remaining bread. Slice into 8 sections. Makes 8.

Wendy Jacobs
Idaho Falls, ID

Santa Fe Sandwiches

Add a fresh fruit salad for a quick and tasty meal with friends.

6 hoagie buns, split in half horizontally
½ c. mayonnaise
½ c. sour cream
½ t. chili powder
½ t. cumin
¼ t. salt
6 tomatoes, sliced
8-oz. pkg. sliced cooked turkey
½ c. sliced black olives
⅓ c. green onion, sliced
3 avocados, peeled, pitted and sliced
8-oz. pkg. shredded Cheddar cheese
Garnish: shredded lettuce, salsa

Arrange hoagie buns cut sides up on an ungreased baking sheet; set aside. Combine mayonnaise and next 4 ingredients; spread over hoagie buns. Layer remaining ingredients except garnish in the order listed equally on top of each bun; bake at 350 degrees for 15 minutes. Slice each sandwich in half to serve; garnish with shredded lettuce and salsa. Makes 12.

Deanne Birkestrand
Minden, NE

delightful decoration
Wrap Santa Fe Sandwiches in parchment paper to keep them fresh before serving. Tie a gingham ribbon around each and tuck white daisies in the knots...guests will feel so special.

Grilled Cuban Sandwiches

A great combination of flavors...some Cuban sandwiches have layers of thinly sliced cooked pork, too. You can also grill sandwiches on a countertop grill or cook in a panini press. (Pictured on page 150)

1 loaf French bread, halved lengthwise
2 T. Dijon mustard
6 oz. thinly sliced Swiss cheese
6 oz. sliced deli ham
8 dill pickle sandwich slices

Spread cut sides of bread with mustard. Arrange half of cheese and ham on bottom half of bread; top with pickle slices. Repeat with remaining cheese and ham; cover with top half of bread. Slice into quarters. Arrange sandwiches in a lightly greased skillet; place a heavy skillet on top of sandwiches. Cook over medium-high heat 2 minutes on each side or until golden and cheese is melted. Makes 4.

Gladys Kielar
Perrysburg, OH

Reuben Sandwich

2 slices corned beef
1 slice Swiss cheese
2 slices dark rye or pumpernickel bread
4 T. sauerkraut
1½ T. Thousand Island dressing
3 T. butter

Place one slice corned beef and cheese on a slice of bread. Top with sauerkraut and dressing. Add a second slice of corned beef and remaining bread. Melt butter in a skillet over medium heat; add sandwich to pan. Grill each side until cheese melts and bread is toasted. Makes one.

Linda Webb
Delaware, OH

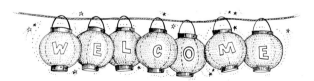

Turkey-Veggie Bagels

Instead of bagels, you can also slice a loaf of round bread in half and layer on all the goodies. Replace the top of the loaf, cut into wedges and secure the sandwich in plastic wrap…an easy take-along lunch.

4 onion bagels, sliced in half
4 leaves romaine lettuce
8 slices deli smoked turkey
1 cucumber, thinly sliced
2 to 4 radishes, thinly sliced
1 to 2 carrots, peeled and shredded
¼ c. cream cheese with chives and onions

Arrange 4 bagel halves on a serving tray. Place a lettuce leaf on each; top with turkey, cucumber, radish and carrot. Spread cream cheese on top halves of bagels; place on bottom halves. Makes 4.

April Jacobs
Loveland, CO

sandwich smorgasbord

Easiest-ever sandwiches for a get-together... provide a big platter of cold cuts, a basket of fresh breads and a choice of condiments so guests can make their own.

Turkey-Veggie Bagels

Italian Meatball Subs

Look for packages of frozen, cooked meatballs in your grocer's freezer if you don't have time to make your own.

1 onion, sliced
½ c. green pepper, sliced
2 T. water
8-oz. can pizza sauce
24 meatballs, cooked
4 Italian hard rolls, sliced and hollowed out
½ c. shredded provolone cheese

Cook onion, pepper and water, covered, in a large saucepan over medium heat just until tender; drain. Stir in pizza sauce and meatballs; cook until hot and bubbly. Fill each roll with 6 meatballs; top with sauce. Sprinkle with cheese and add roll tops. Place sandwiches in a lightly greased 13"x9" baking pan. Bake at 400 degrees for 10 to 15 minutes or until bread is crusty and cheese is melted. Makes 4.

Dana Thompson
Prospect, OH

"Pass any leftover sauce for dipping." –Dana

Italian Meatball Subs

Roast Beef & Pepper Panini

Your favorite sandwich shop couldn't make them any tastier.

8 thick slices Italian bread
8 slices deli roast beef
4 slices mozzarella cheese
8-oz. jar roasted red peppers, drained and chopped
2 T. green olives with pimentos, diced
1 T. olive oil

Top 4 slices of bread with roast beef, cheese, peppers and olives; add remaining bread slices. Brush oil on both sides of sandwiches. Heat a large skillet over medium heat; add sandwiches and cook 2 to 3 minutes on each side or until golden and cheese is melted. Slice sandwiches in half to serve. Makes 4.

Jennie Gist
Gooseberry Patch

Hula Ham Wraps

¾ lb. deli ham, sliced into strips
20-oz. can pineapple tidbits, drained
2 carrots, peeled and shredded
1 head napa cabbage, shredded
1 c. sour cream
¼ c. white wine vinegar
1 t. salt
¼ t. pepper
Optional: 1 t. caraway seed
12 10-inch flour tortillas

Combine ham, pineapple, carrots and cabbage in a large bowl; set aside. In a separate bowl, whisk together sour cream, vinegar, salt, pepper and caraway seed, if desired. Pour over ham mixture; toss. Divide among tortillas and roll into wraps. Makes 12.

Nancy Wise
Little Rock, AR

Yummy Blue Cheese Burgers

These mouthwatering burgers will be a hit at your next cookout.

2 lbs. ground beef
Cajun seasoning to taste
1 c. half-and-half
1 clove garlic, finely minced
1 t. dried rosemary
1 t. dried basil
4-oz. container crumbled blue cheese
6 kaiser rolls, split, toasted and buttered
Optional: sliced mushrooms, sliced onion, butter

Shape beef into 6 patties; sprinkle with Cajun seasoning. Grill patties over medium-high heat, 350 to 400 degrees, to desired doneness, turning to cook on both sides. Combine half-and-half, garlic and herbs in a saucepan. Bring to a boil; reduce heat and simmer until mixture is thickened and reduced by half. Add blue cheese; stir just until melted. Place burgers on bottom halves of rolls; spoon sauce over burgers. If desired, sauté mushrooms and onion in butter until tender; spoon onto burgers. Top with remaining roll halves. Makes 6.

Lynn Daniel
Portage, MI

Kentucky Hot Brown

Tender turkey is hidden under lots of bubbly cheese and bacon.

2 T. butter
2 T. all-purpose flour
salt and cayenne pepper to taste
¼ t. curry powder
1 c. milk
¾ c. shredded American cheese, divided
¾ c. shredded sharp Cheddar cheese, divided
4 slices bread, toasted
4 slices turkey
8 slices bacon, slightly cooked

Melt butter in a saucepan; whisk in flour, salt, cayenne pepper and curry powder. Stir until bubbly; remove from heat. Pour in milk; return to heat and cook until thickened. Stir in ¼ cup American cheese and ¼ cup Cheddar cheese. Cook until cheese melts; set aside. Place one piece of toast each on 4 oven-safe plates; place one slice of turkey on top of each. Cover each with butter mixture; top with remaining cheeses and bacon. Place plates under broiler; broil until bacon is fully cooked. Makes 4.

Renee Brooks
Utica, KY

Philly Cheesesteak Sandwiches

Onion, garlic, mushrooms and green pepper spooned over layers of beef and topped with melted cheese make a hearty meal-on-a-bun.

2 T. butter
1 lb. beef top or rib-eye steak, thinly sliced
seasoned salt and pepper to taste
1 onion, sliced
1 clove garlic, minced
Optional: 1 c. sliced mushrooms
1 green pepper, thinly sliced
1 lb. provolone, Gouda or Swiss cheese, sliced
6 hoagie buns or baguettes, split

Melt butter in a skillet over medium heat until slightly browned. Add steak; sprinkle with seasoned salt and pepper and sauté just until browned. Add onion, garlic, mushrooms (optional), and green pepper; stir. Cover and simmer 5 to 7 minutes or until onion and pepper are tender. Add additional salt and pepper to taste. Remove from heat; set aside. Place 2 to 3 cheese slices in each bun; top each with 2 to 3 table-spoonfuls of steak mixture. Top with additional cheese, if desired. Wrap each sandwich in aluminum foil; bake at 350 degrees for 10 to 15 minutes, or until cheese is melted. Makes 6.

Amy Michalik
Norwalk, IA

festive fries

For zesty French fries that are anything but boring, spray frozen fries with non-stick olive oil spray and sprinkle with your favorite spice blend like Italian, Cajun or steakhouse seasoning. Spread on a baking sheet and bake as directed...wow!

Mexican Burgers

Chili powder, cumin and Pepper Jack cheese add a little zip to these tasty burgers.

1 avocado, peeled, pitted and diced
1 plum tomato, diced
2 green onions, chopped
1 to 2 t. lime juice
1¼ lbs. ground beef
1 egg, beaten
¾ c. to 1 c. nacho-flavored tortilla chips,
    crushed
¼ c. fresh cilantro, chopped
½ t. chili powder
½ t. ground cumin
salt and pepper to taste
1¼ c. shredded Pepper Jack cheese
5 hamburger buns, split

Combine avocado, tomato, onions and lime juice; mash slightly and set aside. Combine ground beef, egg, chips and seasonings in a large bowl. Form into 5 patties; grill over medium-high heat to desired doneness, turning to cook on both sides. Sprinkle cheese over burgers; grill until melted. Place burgers on bottoms of buns; top with avocado mixture and bun tops. Makes 5.

Stacie Avner
Delaware, OH

Lettuce Wedge Salad
(page 200)

Country Butterscotch
Yams (page 183)

Three-Cheese
Pasta Bake
(page 188)

Orange-Wild Rice
Chicken Salad
(page 204)

SAVORY SIDES & SALADS

The perfect accompaniment to round out your meal

Creamy Potatoes au Gratin

Creamy Potatoes au Gratin

4 potatoes, peeled, sliced and divided
1 onion, thinly sliced
salt and pepper to taste
3 T. butter
3 T. all-purpose flour
½ t. salt
2 c. milk
2 c. shredded Cheddar cheese, divided

Arrange half the potatoes in a greased 1½-quart casserole dish. Top with onion and remaining potatoes; add salt and pepper to taste. In a saucepan, melt butter over medium heat. Add flour and salt; stir constantly with a whisk one minute. Stir in milk; cook until thickened. Stir in 1½ cups cheese; stir until melted. Pour over potatoes; cover with aluminum foil. Bake at 400 degrees for one hour. Uncover; sprinkle with remaining cheese. Bake 12 more minutes or until golden. Serves 4.

Tami Bowman
Marysville, OH

Garlic Smashed Potatoes

5 lbs. potatoes, peeled and cubed
1 head garlic
1 T. oil
½ c. butter
8-oz. pkg. cream cheese, softened
1 c. sour cream
salt to taste

Place potatoes in a Dutch oven, cover with water and bring to a boil. Cook until potatoes are tender. Drain and set aside. Cut garlic horizontally and place in a baking pan. Drizzle with oil and bake at 350 degrees for 30 minutes or until tender. Using a fork, remove skin and mash garlic. Mash potatoes. Add garlic and remaining ingredients; blend well. Spoon potatoes into a greased 13"x9" baking pan. Cover and refrigerate overnight. When ready to serve, heat oven to 350 degrees and bake for 50 to 60 minutes. Serves 8.

Vickie
Gooseberry Patch

Country Butterscotch Yams

(Pictured on page 180)

8 yams, peeled, sliced and boiled
½ c. corn syrup
½ c. brown sugar, packed
¼ c. half-and-half
2 T. butter
½ t. salt
½ t. cinnamon

Arrange yams in an ungreased 13"x9" baking pan; bake at 325 degrees for 15 minutes. Combine remaining ingredients in a 2-quart saucepan; boil 5 minutes, stirring constantly. Pour over yams; bake 15 more minutes, basting often. Serves 6.

Charlotte Weaver
Purcell, OK

Butternut Squash & Apples

2-lb. butternut squash, peeled
2 Rome apples, cored
¼ c. brown sugar, packed
1 T. all-purpose flour
1 T. butter, melted
¼ t. salt

Cut squash in half lengthwise and discard seeds; cut each half into ½-inch thick slices and place in a greased 13"x9" baking pan. Slice apples into 8 wedges and layer over squash. Combine brown sugar, flour, butter and salt in a small bowl; sprinkle over apples. Cover and bake at 350 degrees for 30 minutes; uncover and bake 20 more minutes or until squash is tender. Serves 6.

Janice McCatty
Royal Oak, MI

Roasted Root Vegetables

Roasting brings out the natural sweetness of vegetables.

4 redskin potatoes, peeled and quartered
4 turnips, peeled and quartered
2 parsnips, peeled and cut into one-inch slices
2 carrots, peeled and thickly sliced
1 yam, peeled and cut into one-inch slices
16 pearl onions, peeled
4 beets, peeled and quartered
8 cloves garlic
½ c. olive oil
2 T. fresh rosemary, chopped
salt and pepper to taste

Place all of the ingredients in a large plastic zipping bag. Close bag; turn several times to coat vegetables evenly. Spread mixture in a roasting pan; bake at 450 degrees for one hour. Serves 8.

Jennifer Wickes
Pine Beach, NJ

flavor booster

Be sure to place warm melted butter on the table for guests to brush over vegetables or rolls. Make a natural butter brush by bundling sprigs of fresh herbs such as thyme, oregano, parsley or rosemary, then bind them together with jute... adds extra flavor too!

Kickin' Chili Fries

Hearty chili and melted cheese over French fries... yum!

32-oz. pkg. frozen French fries
15-oz. can chili without beans
8-oz. jar pasteurized process cheese sauce

Fry or bake French fries according to package directions; place on a serving platter and keep warm. Heat chili and cheese sauce separately, according to package directions. Spoon hot chili over fries; top with hot cheese sauce and serve immediately. Serves 8.

Colleen Lambert
Casco, WI

Quick Rice & Black Beans

This simple, foolproof recipe goes very well with grilled chicken.

1 T. olive oil
1 green pepper, chopped
1 onion, chopped
2 cloves garlic, minced
1 c. long-cooking rice, uncooked
16-oz. can black beans, drained and rinsed
16-oz. jar salsa
1 c. water

Heat oil in a large skillet over medium heat. Sauté pepper, onion and garlic for about 5 minutes or until onion is tender. Add rice, stirring to coat with oil. Add beans, salsa and water, stirring to mix. Cover and simmer over medium-low heat for 20 minutes, stirring once or twice, until rice is tender. Serves 4 to 6.

Erin Tingle
Ephrata, PA

Kickin' Chili Fries

Hoppin' John

Hoppin' John

This dish is popular in the South. It's traditionally eaten on New Year's Day and promises good luck.

1 c. dried black-eyed peas
10 c. water, divided
6 slices bacon, coarsely chopped
¾ c. onion, chopped
1 stalk celery, chopped
¾ t. cayenne pepper
1½ t. salt
1 c. long-cooking rice, uncooked

Rinse peas and place in a large saucepan with 6 cups water. Bring to a boil; reduce heat and simmer 2 minutes. Remove from heat, cover and let stand one hour. Drain and rinse.

In same pan, cook bacon until crisp, reserving 3 tablespoons drippings in pan. Add peas, remaining water, onion, celery, cayenne pepper and salt. Bring to a boil, cover and reduce heat. Simmer 30 minutes. Add rice; cover and simmer 20 more minutes or until peas and rice are tender. Serves 4 to 6.

Gnocchi with Mushroom Sauce

Gnocchi are little Italian dumplings made from potatoes. They're used much like pasta, either in soups or with sauces...give them a try!

12-oz. pkg. gnocchi, uncooked
2 cloves garlic, minced
1 T. oil
3 c. sliced mushrooms
1 c. vegetable broth
1 t. dried rosemary
½ t. salt
½ t. pepper
2 T. grated Parmesan cheese

Prepare gnocchi according to package directions. Sauté garlic in oil in a skillet for 2 minutes. Add mushrooms; cook until tender. Stir in broth, rosemary, salt and pepper; reduce heat and simmer until liquid is almost absorbed. Spoon over gnocchi. Sprinkle with Parmesan cheese. Serves 4.

Kristy Rangel
Racine, WI

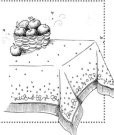

bountiful baskets
Centerpieces don't need to be fussy...fresh fruit tucked into a basket, bowl or vintage colander always looks (and tastes) terrific!

Three-Cheese Pasta Bake

This yummy mac and cheese dish gets a great update with penne pasta and a trio of cheeses. (Pictured on page 180)

8-oz. pkg. penne pasta, uncooked
2 T. butter
2 T. all-purpose flour
1½ c. milk
½ c. half-and-half
1 c. shredded white Cheddar cheese
¼ c. grated Parmesan cheese
2 c. shredded Gruyère cheese, divided
1 t. salt
¼ t. pepper
pinch of nutmeg

Prepare pasta according to package directions. Meanwhile, melt butter in a saucepan over medium heat. Whisk in flour until smooth; cook, whisking constantly, one minute. Gradually whisk in milk and half-and-half; cook, whisking constantly, 3 to 5 minutes or until thickened. Stir in Cheddar cheese, Parmesan cheese, one cup Gruyère cheese and next 3 ingredients until smooth. Stir together pasta and cheese mixture; pour into a lightly greased 11"x7" baking pan. Top with remaining one cup Gruyère cheese. Bake, uncovered, at 350 degrees for 15 minutes, or until golden and bubbly. Serves 4.

Corn Fritters

These can be made in a deep fryer if you prefer.

1 egg
½ c. milk
12-oz. can corn
1 T. shortening, melted
1 c. all-purpose flour
1 T. sugar
½ t. salt
1 t. baking powder
oil for frying

In a large mixing bowl, combine egg and milk. Add corn and shortening, stirring to combine. In a separate bowl, sift together flour, sugar, salt and baking powder. Slowly add to egg mixture, stirring just until dry ingredients are moistened. Pour oil into a skillet and drop batter by tablespoonfuls into skillet. Fry until thoroughly cooked, about 5 minutes. Drain on paper towels and repeat procedure. Makes about 20.

outdoor supper settings
Use a fisherman's stool to hold desserts or baskets of apples. Create an easy tablecloth by covering your picnic table with newspaper and keep sodas cool by icing them down in a clean minnow bucket.

Corn Pudding

9 ears corn
4 eggs, beaten
½ c. half-and-half
1½ t. baking powder
⅓ c. butter
2 T. sugar
2 T. all-purpose flour
1 T. butter, melted
⅛ t. pepper

Remove and discard husks and silks from corn. Cut off tips of corn kernels into a bowl; scrape milk and remaining pulp from cob with a paring knife to measure 3 to 4 cups total. Set corn aside.

Combine eggs, half-and-half and baking powder, stirring well with a wire whisk. Melt ⅓ cup butter in a large saucepan over low heat; add sugar and flour, stirring until smooth. Remove from heat; gradually add egg mixture, whisking constantly until smooth. Stir in corn. Pour corn mixture into a greased 1 to 1½-quart casserole dish. Bake, uncovered, at 350 degrees for 40 to 45 minutes or until pudding is set. Drizzle with melted butter; sprinkle with pepper.

Broil 5½ inches from heat 2 minutes or until golden. Let stand 5 minutes before serving. Serves 6 to 8.

Corn Pudding

Easy Fancy
Broccoli

Easy Fancy Broccoli

⅓ c. pine nuts
¼ c. butter
1 T. olive oil
6 cloves garlic, thinly sliced
1 lb. broccoli flowerets
½ t. salt
⅛ t. red pepper flakes

Toast pine nuts in a large skillet over medium heat 6 minutes or until golden. Remove from skillet and set aside.

Heat butter and oil in same skillet over medium heat until butter melts. Add garlic; sauté one to 2 minutes or until golden. Add broccoli, salt and red pepper flakes. Sauté 8 minutes or until broccoli is tender. Stir in pine nuts before serving. Serves 6.

Jo Ann
Gooseberry Patch

Bagged broccoli flowerets make this side dish a cinch to prepare! –Jo Ann

veggie love
Get kids to eat their vegetables! Serve fresh cut-up vegetables with small cups of creamy salad dressing or even peanut butter for dipping.

Crispy Fried Zucchini

Sometimes I like to use a mixture of grated Parmesan, Romano and Asiago cheeses in this recipe.

1 c. Italian-flavored dry bread crumbs
½ c. grated Parmesan cheese
salt and pepper to taste
2 to 4 zucchini, cut into slices or strips
2 eggs, beaten
oil for frying
Garnish: marinara sauce, horseradish sauce

Combine crumbs, cheese, salt and pepper in a bowl; set aside. Dip zucchini into beaten eggs, then into crumb mixture to coat evenly. Heat oil in a skillet; fry zucchini a few at a time, until tender and golden. Serve with sauces for dipping. Serves 6 to 8.

Staci Meyers
Cocoa, FL

crispy coating
Batter-fried veggies will be crispier if they're patted dry before being dipped into batter. Drying ensures the coating will cling.

Caramelized Brussels Sprouts

4 lbs. Brussels sprouts, trimmed
½ c. butter
4 onions, cut into strips
¼ c. red wine vinegar, divided
2 T. sugar
salt and pepper to taste
Optional: ½ c. pistachio nuts, chopped

Steam Brussels sprouts for 8 to 10 minutes or until just crisp-tender. Melt butter in a deep skillet. Add onions and 3 tablespoons vinegar; cook until golden. Add Brussels sprouts, sugar and remaining vinegar. Sauté over medium heat until sprouts are lightly caramelized. Sprinkle with salt, pepper and nuts, if desired. Serves 8.

Beth Schlieper
Lakewood, CO

Orange-Glazed Carrots

Add a spoonful of orange marmalade or apricot jam...the kids will be happy to eat their veggies tonight!

16-oz. pkg. peeled baby carrots
½ c. orange juice
5 T. brown sugar, packed
2 T. butter
⅛ t. salt

Place carrots in a medium saucepan. Cover with water and boil until tender; drain and return to saucepan. Add orange juice to saucepan; simmer until juice is nearly evaporated. Stir in remaining ingredients; heat until butter is melted and mixture is well blended. Serves 4 to 6.

Staci Meyers
Cocoa, FL

Green Bean Bundles

Easy and delicious! The most obvious time-saver in this recipe is to not make the bundles, but it's definitely worth the effort.

3 14½-oz. cans whole green beans, drained
8 slices bacon, cut in half crosswise
6 T. butter, melted
½ c. brown sugar, packed
2 to 3 cloves garlic, minced

Gather beans in bundles of 10; wrap each bundle with a half-slice of bacon. Arrange bundles in a lightly greased 13"x9" baking pan. Mix melted butter, sugar and garlic in a small bowl; spoon over bundles. Cover and bake at 375 degrees for 30 minutes. Uncover and bake 15 more minutes. Serves 8.

Wendy Sensing
Brentwood, TN

This is one of our favorite side dishes to bring to church get-togethers. The pan always comes home empty and someone always wants the recipe, especially the garlic lovers. —Wendy

> ### twice as nice
> Turn leftover mashed potatoes into twice-baked potatoes. Stir in minced onion, crumbled bacon and shredded cheese to taste; pat into individual ramekins. Bake at 350 degrees until hot and golden... delicious!

Green Bean Bundles

Fried Okra Salad

Fried Okra Salad

The okra soaks up all the yummy sweet vinaigrette in this salad...a nice contrast to the crunchy bacon.

2-lb. pkg. frozen breaded okra
10 slices bacon, crisply cooked and crumbled
6 plum tomatoes, chopped
1 bunch green onions, chopped
½ c. olive oil
¼ c. sugar
2 T. vinegar

Fry okra according to package directions; drain. Combine okra, bacon, tomatoes and green onions; set aside. Mix together remaining ingredients; pour dressing over okra mixture. Serve immediately. Serves 8.

Lisa Martin
Tulsa, OK

Company Creamed Spinach

Just like what you order at a fancy steakhouse!

10-oz. pkg. frozen chopped spinach
1 T. dried, minced onion
1½ T. bacon bits
½ to ¾ c. sour cream

Prepare spinach according to package directions; add onion and bacon bits to cooking water half-way through cooking time. Drain well; stir in sour cream to desired consistency. Serves 4.

Zana Shults
Marlton, NJ

Roasted Asparagus with Feta

Sometimes I add freshly chopped basil, garlic and bowtie pasta...delicious any way you make it!

1 bunch asparagus, trimmed
1 to 2 t. olive oil
coarse salt to taste
2 tomatoes, chopped
8-oz. pkg. crumbled feta cheese

Arrange asparagus spears in a lightly greased 2-quart casserole dish; sprinkle with olive oil and add salt to taste. Bake at 400 degrees for 15 to 20 minutes or until tender; let cool. Chop into 2-inch pieces and toss with tomatoes and feta cheese. Serves 4.

Denise Neal
Yorba Linda, CA

Melon Salad with Honey Dressing

1 cantaloupe melon, peeled and seeded
1 honeydew melon, peeled and seeded
3 T. lime juice
2 T. balsamic vinegar
3 T. honey
2 c. baby Bibb lettuce, torn
2 c. arugula

Cut melons into chunks. In a small bowl, combine lime juice, vinegar and honey. Pour over melon and toss. Place lettuce and arugula on salad plates. Using a slotted spoon, spoon fruit mixture onto lettuce; drizzle dressing over top. Serves 4.

evening shade
If you have a heat wave this summer, enjoy an evening supper under the shade of old trees, on the porch or in a gazebo.

Apple-Broccoli Salad

Waldorf Slaw

Apple-Broccoli Salad

Loaded with raisins, pecans and bacon, this yummy salad gets coated in a creamy dressing.

4 c. broccoli flowerets
½ c. raisins
½ c. chopped pecans, toasted
6 slices bacon, crisply cooked and crumbled
2 Red Delicious apples, cored and diced
1 red onion, chopped
1 c. mayonnaise
½ c. sugar
2 T. cider vinegar

Combine first 6 ingredients in a large bowl. Combine mayonnaise, sugar and vinegar; add to broccoli mixture, stirring to coat. Cover and chill. Serves 6.

Waldorf Slaw

Everyone will love this tangy salad that's easily made ahead.

16-oz. pkg. coleslaw mix
2 c. Braeburn apples, cored, peeled and chopped
1 c. Bartlett pears, cored, peeled and chopped
½ c. raisins
3 T. chopped walnuts
½ c. mayonnaise
½ c. buttermilk
1 t. lemon zest
2 T. lemon juice
¼ t. salt
⅛ t. pepper

Combine coleslaw, apples, pears, raisins and walnuts in a large bowl; set aside. Combine remaining ingredients, stirring well with a whisk. Drizzle mayonnaise mixture over coleslaw mixture and toss to coat. Cover and refrigerate 30 minutes. Serves 10.

Lori Rosenberg
University Heights, OH

Mandarin Orange Salad

Quick and easy to prepare, this salad is best topped with a sweet dressing like Raspberry Vinaigrette.

4 c. green or red leaf lettuce, torn into
    bite-size pieces
2 15-oz. cans mandarin oranges, drained
½ c. walnut pieces, toasted
½ red onion, sliced

    Combine all ingredients. Toss with desired amount of Raspberry Vinaigrette. Serves 4.

Raspberry Vinaigrette:

⅓ c. raspberry vinegar
⅓ c. seedless raspberry jam
1 t. coriander or ground cumin
½ t. salt
¼ t. pepper
¾ c. olive oil

    Combine first 5 ingredients in blender. Turn blender on high; gradually add oil. Chill.

easiest-ever side salad
Whip up a marinated salad to keep in the fridge...cut up crunchy veggies and toss with Italian salad dressing.

Mandarin Orange Salad

Fresh Corn Salad

Fresh Corn Salad

Use Silver Queen or another sweet corn variety for this sugary-sweet salad with an oil and vinegar dressing. Using corn freshly cut from the cob yields the sweetest kernels.

6 ears white or yellow corn, husks removed
¼ c. sugar
¼ c. cider vinegar
¼ c. olive oil
½ t. salt
½ t. pepper
I red onion, diced
I red pepper, diced
¼ c. fresh parsley, coarsely chopped

Cook corn in boiling salted water in a large stockpot 3 to 4 minutes; drain. Plunge corn into ice water to stop the cooking process; drain. Cut kernels from cobs.

Whisk together sugar and next 4 ingredients in a large bowl; add corn, onion, pepper and parsley, tossing to coat. Cover and chill at least 2 hours. Serves 8 to 10.

a new twist
Use old serving dishes in a new way for a fresh look. Handed-down cream-and-sugar sets can hold sauces, bread sticks can be arranged in gravy boats and a trifle dish can make a great salad bowl.

Three-Bean Basil Salad

Fresh vegetables and basil from your garden will make this wonderful side dish even better!

2 c. canned kidney beans, drained and rinsed
2 c. garbanzo beans, drained and rinsed
2 c. green beans
I red onion, sliced into rings
I carrot, peeled and shredded
½ c. white vinegar
½ c. oil
6 T. sugar
I T. fresh basil, minced
¾ t. dry mustard
salt and pepper to taste

Combine beans in a large bowl with onion and carrot. In a separate bowl, combine remaining ingredients; add to bean mixture and toss. Chill overnight before serving. Serves 10.

Cucumber Salad

This garden-fresh salad comes together superfast!

I T. oil
I t. dried parsley
2 to 3 T. sour cream
2 to 3 T. vinegar
½ t. dill weed
I onion, sliced
2 to 3 cucumbers, peeled and sliced
salt and pepper to taste

Combine first 5 ingredients; stir. Add onion, cucumbers and salt and pepper to taste. Chill at least one hour. Serves 4 to 6.

Patricia Jarman
Valrico, FL

Lettuce Wedge Salad

(Pictured on page 180)

4 to 6 slices bacon
1 onion, sliced
1 c. buttermilk
½ c. sour cream
1-oz. pkg. ranch salad dressing mix
¼ c. fresh basil, chopped
2 cloves garlic
1 head iceberg lettuce, cut into 4 wedges
Optional: shredded fresh basil

Cook bacon in a large skillet over medium heat until crisp. Remove bacon and drain on paper towels, reserving one tablespoon drippings in skillet. Crumble bacon and set aside.

Sauté onion in hot drippings in skillet over medium heat 10 minutes or until tender and golden. Remove from heat; cool.

Process onion, and next 5 ingredients in a blender or food processor until smooth, stopping to scrape down sides. Top each lettuce wedge with dressing; sprinkle with bacon and top with shredded fresh basil, if desired. Serves 4.

Jo Ann
Gooseberry Patch

Vegetable Pasta Salad

So easy to make and even better when you use fresh, crunchy vegetables from your garden!

¼ c. fresh parsley, loosely packed
2 T. oil
2 T. wine vinegar
2 T. water
1 or 2 cloves garlic
½ t. dry mustard
¼ t. salt
¼ t. pepper
2 oz. uncooked linguine noodles, broken
1 carrot, peeled and cut into julienne strips
1 turnip, peeled and cut into julienne strips
1 zucchini, cut into julienne strips
½ c. frozen or fresh peas
2-oz. pkg. mozzarella cheese, shredded

To prepare dressing, combine parsley, oil, vinegar, water, garlic, mustard, salt and pepper in a blender; blend until combined. Set aside.

Cook linguine according to package directions. Drain and rinse with cold water. In a large bowl, combine linguine and remaining ingredients. Add dressing; toss to coat. Serves 4.

Susan Kennedy
Delaware, OH

"Who can resist a simple iceberg wedge, especially when it's icy cold?" —Jo Ann

pretty pantry
Homemade preserves are beautiful displayed in an old-fashioned corner cupboard. Bright red tomatoes, green pickles and golden corn are particularly nice.

Summer Tortellini Salad

8-oz. pkg. cheese-filled tortellini, cooked and
 cooled
1 tomato, chopped
3 to 4 slices hard salami, sliced into strips
3 to 4 mushrooms, sliced
4 to 5 Kalamata olives, chopped
½ c. mild Cheddar cheese, cubed
½ c. mozzarella cheese, cubed
½ c. provolone cheese, cubed
¼ c. olive oil
1 clove garlic, finely minced
¼ t. garlic salt
⅛ t. pepper
2 to 3 T. cider vinegar
Optional: 1 t. red pepper flakes
Garnish: fresh basil leaves

In a large bowl, combine tortellini, tomato, salami, mushrooms, olives and cheeses; set aside. Whisk together remaining ingredients until thoroughly mixed. Pour dressing over salad; toss well. Refrigerate for 2 hours. Toss just before serving. Garnish with fresh basil leaves. Serves 4 to 6.

Jen Eveland-Kupp
Blandon, PA

makeover in minutes
Include any of your favorite veggies in this pasta salad...a garnish of basil leaves makes a nice presentation.

Summer
Tortellini Salad

Spinach Salad &
Hot Bacon Dressing

Spinach Salad & Hot Bacon Dressing

The hot and savory dressing is the key ingredient to this salad's fantastic taste.

10-oz. bag spinach, torn into bite-size pieces
4 eggs, hard-boiled, peeled and sliced
1 tomato, chopped
1 red onion, sliced
8 to 10 large mushrooms, sliced

Toss together all ingredients; serve with Hot Bacon Dressing. Serves 4.

Hot Bacon Dressing:
1 lb. bacon, cut into 1-inch pieces
1 onion, chopped
1 clove garlic, minced
½ c. brown sugar, packed
½ c. red wine vinegar
2 c. water, divided
¼ t. salt
½ t. pepper
1 T. cornstarch

In a large skillet, sauté bacon, onion and garlic until bacon is crisp. Add brown sugar, vinegar, 1½ cups water, salt and pepper; simmer until mixture is reduced by half. In a bowl, mix together cornstarch and remaining water; add to pan and simmer until thick and bubbly. Makes 2 cups.

Kristie Rigo
Friedens, PA

German Potato Salad

This recipe was one of my first cooking successes as a new bride. My husband and his family raved over it!

6 redskin potatoes
10 slices bacon, chopped
1 red onion, finely chopped
4 t. flour
1 T. sugar
salt and pepper to taste
½ c. cider vinegar
½ c. water
¼ c. fresh parsley, minced
1 t. celery seed

Steam potatoes until tender; cool and peel. Thinly slice potatoes and transfer to a large bowl. Cook bacon in a heavy skillet over medium heat until crisp. Add onion; cook one minute. Stir in flour and sugar. Season with salt and pepper; stir. Mix together vinegar and water; pour over bacon mixture. Stir until thickened. Pour over potatoes. Stir in parsley and celery seed. Serves 6 to 8.

Calla Andrews
Long Beach, CA

Carrot-Raisin Salad

Grandma made this salad often. It's always very good!

2 c. carrots, peeled and shredded
1 c. raisins
½ c. walnuts, chopped
½ c. mayonnaise
lettuce leaves

Mix together all ingredients except lettuce leaves in a large bowl. Cover and refrigerate overnight. Serve on lettuce leaves. Serves 4.

Jackie Crough
Salina, KS

Orange-Wild Rice Chicken Salad

Heads up! This isn't your ordinary chicken salad... it's better! This salad boasts wild rice, sugar snap peas and mandarin oranges. (Pictured on page 180)

6-oz. pkg. cooked long-grain and wild rice
2 c. cooked chicken breast, shredded
1 c. sugar snap peas, trimmed
15-oz. can mandarin oranges, drained
½ c. honey-Dijon salad dressing

Combine all ingredients in a large bowl; mix well. Cover and chill until serving time. Serves 4.

Rhonda Reeder
Ellicott City, MD

---

no waste
When draining canned fruit, reserve the juice and freeze it in ice cube trays... oh-so handy for adding a little sweetness to marinades and dressings.

Mom's Yummy Cornbread Salad

This salad disappears from the table so quickly...you might want to double the recipe!

1 to 2 c. cornbread, cubed
8¾-oz. can corn, drained
½ c. green onions, chopped
½ c. cucumber, chopped
½ c. broccoli, chopped
½ c. red pepper, chopped
½ c. tomato, chopped
½ c. canned pinto or garbanzo beans,
   drained and rinsed
½ c. shredded Cheddar cheese
½ c. buttermilk ranch salad dressing
½ t. salt
½ t. pepper

Combine all ingredients in a large bowl. Cover and refrigerate at least 4 hours before serving. Serves 6.

Denise Neal
Castle Rock, CO

Mom was a great cook, and it makes me feel close to her when I prepare her recipes. When I compiled a family cookbook recently, this recipe was a must-have. –Denise

Mom's Yummy
Cornbread Salad

Mom's Antipasto Salad

Mom's Antipasto Salad

Antipasto is the Italian word meaning "before the pasta" and is usually served as an appetizer course. But with all the hearty ingredients this salad offers, it can easily stand alone as a main-dish salad.

1 head iceberg lettuce, chopped
½ c. Kalamata olives, quartered
½ lb. thick-sliced salami, quartered
2 6-oz. jars marinated artichokes, drained and coarsely chopped
1 zucchini, diced
10-oz. pkg. grape tomatoes, halved
1 green pepper, chopped
1 red onion, sliced vertically
6 to 8 pepperoncini, coarsely chopped
1½ c. grated Parmesan cheese
½ c. Italian salad dressing
5-oz. pkg. garlic-flavored croutons

Combine first 10 ingredients; toss gently. Cover and chill until serving time. Just before serving, add dressing to taste; top with croutons. Serves 10.

Yvonne Van Brimmer
Apple Valley, CA

Every time I take this to a church potluck my bowl comes back empty! I love to make people happy with my cooking. –Yvonne

Twelve-Layer Salad

Layer this salad in a glass bowl so the variety of colors can be seen!

12-oz. pkg. frozen peas
1 head iceberg lettuce, shredded
¾ c. fresh parsley, chopped
4 eggs, hard-boiled, peeled and chopped
1 red pepper, thinly sliced
4 carrots, peeled and shredded
1 c. black olives, sliced
2 T. fresh dill, chopped
1 c. radishes, sliced
¾ lb. Swiss or Cheddar cheese, shredded
½ lb. bacon, crisply cooked and crumbled
1 red onion, thinly sliced
Garnish: 2 T. fresh parsley, chopped

Cook peas in water until crisp-tender; set aside. Line bottom of a 3-quart straight-sided bowl with lettuce. Layer all ingredients except garnish in the order listed, adding peas after olives. Spread half of Dressing over salad; reserve remaining Dressing to serve on the side. Garnish salad with parsley. Cover tightly with plastic wrap and refrigerate for 6 to 12 hours. Serves 10 to 12.

Dressing:

2 c. mayonnaise
½ c. sour cream
¼ c. fresh chives, chopped
2 T. sugar
1 T. tarragon vinegar
salt and pepper to taste
½ c. fresh parsley, chopped

Combine all ingredients; mix well.

Kristi Warzocha
Lakewood, OH

Mocha Pecan Mud Pie
(page 236)

Mom's Blackberry Crisp
(page 237)

Crustless Coconut Pie
(page 235)

Grandma's Chocolate
Cake (page 217)

BLUE-RIBBON CAKES & PIES

Showstopping sweet endings everyone will love

Old-Fashioned Fruitcake

Old-Fashioned Fruitcake

What would Christmas be without a fruitcake?
You'll like this one.

1 c. butter, softened
2½ c. sugar
6 eggs
2 t. brandy flavoring
4 c. all-purpose flour
1½ t. cinnamon
1 t. nutmeg
1 t. salt
1½ lbs. candied mixed fruit
1 lb. raisins
¾ lb. candied pineapple
¾ lb. whole candied cherries
2 c. pecan halves
Garnish: light corn syrup,
   pecan halves
Optional: cloth soaked in wine

In a large bowl, beat butter and sugar with
an electric mixer until fluffy. Add eggs, one at a
time, beating just until yellow disappears. Stir in
flavoring. Sift together next 4 ingredients and mix
thoroughly with butter mixture. Work the fruit
and nuts into batter with hands. Grease and flour
a 10" tube pan. Fill pan ⅔ full with batter. Bake
at 275 degrees for 3 hours. One-half hour before
cake is done, brush top with corn syrup, decorate
with pecan halves and finish baking; cool.
If desired, place cake, wrapped in a wine-soaked
cloth, in an airtight container. Store in a cool place
for several weeks to blend and mellow the cake.
Serves 16.

Carrot Cake

I remember my mother baking this for my father's
birthday...it was his favorite cake!

4 eggs, beaten
1½ c. oil
2½ c. sugar
3 c. all-purpose flour
2 t. baking powder
2 t. baking soda
1 t. salt
2 t. cinnamon
3 c. carrots, peeled and grated
2 8-oz. cans crushed pineapple, drained
1½ to 2 c. nuts, chopped
1 t. vanilla extract

In a large mixing bowl, combine eggs, oil
and sugar, blending well. Add next 5 ingredients
and stir until smooth. Stir in carrots, pineapple,
nuts and vanilla. Pour into 3 greased and floured
9" cake pans. Bake at 350 degrees for 25 to
30 minutes or until a wooden pick inserted in
center comes out clean. Cool in pans for 10 minutes. Remove from pans and cool completely.
Spread Frosting between layers and on top and
sides of cake. Serves 12.

Frosting:
2 8-oz. pkgs. cream cheese, softened
½ c. butter, softened
2 16-oz. pkgs. powdered sugar, sifted
2 t. vanilla extract
1 c. nuts, chopped

Beat together first 4 ingredients; stir in nuts.

Karen Moran
Navasota, TX

Caramel Cake

I'm always asked to bring this cake to family gatherings.

8-oz. container sour cream
¼ c. milk
1 c. butter, softened
2 c. sugar
4 eggs
2¾ c. all-purpose flour
2 t. baking powder
½ t. salt
1 t. vanilla extract

Combine sour cream and milk; set aside. Beat butter at medium speed with an electric mixer until creamy. Gradually add sugar, beating well. Add eggs, one at a time, beating until blended after each addition.

Combine flour, baking powder and salt; add to butter mixture alternately with sour cream mixture, beginning and ending with flour mixture. Beat at medium-low speed until blended after each addition. Stir in vanilla. Pour batter into 2 greased and floured 9" round cake pans. Bake at 350 degrees for 30 to 35 minutes or until a wooden pick inserted in center comes out clean. Cool in pans on wire racks 10 minutes. Remove from pans to wire racks and let cool one hour or until completely cool. Spread Whipped Cream Caramel Frosting between layers and on top and sides of cake. Serves 8.

Caramel Cake

Whipped Cream Caramel Frosting:

1 c. butter
2 c. dark brown sugar, packed
¼ c. plus 2 T. whipping cream
2 t. vanilla extract
3¾ c. powdered sugar

Melt butter in a 3-quart saucepan over medium heat. Add brown sugar; bring to a boil, stirring constantly. Stir in whipping cream and vanilla; bring to a boil. Remove from heat; let cool one hour. Transfer to a mixing bowl. Sift powdered sugar into sugar mixture. Beat at high speed with an electric mixer until creamy and spreading consistency. Makes 3¾ cups.

Million-Dollar Pound Cake

2 c. butter, softened
3 c. sugar
6 eggs
4 c. all-purpose flour
¾ c. milk
1 t. almond extract
1 t. vanilla extract
Optional: sweetened whipped cream,
    blueberries, sliced peaches

Beat butter at medium speed with an electric mixer about 2 minutes or until creamy. Gradually add sugar, beating 5 to 7 minutes.

Add eggs, one at a time, beating just until yellow disappears after each addition.

Add flour to butter mixture alternately with milk, beginning and ending with flour. Beat at low speed just until blended after each addition. (Batter should be smooth.) Stir in extracts. Pour batter into a greased and floured 10" tube pan. Bake at 300 degrees for one hour and 40 minutes or until a long wooden pick inserted in center comes out clean. Cool in pan on a wire rack 10 to 15 minutes. Remove from pan and cool completely on wire rack. Top each serving with whipped cream, blueberries and sliced peaches, if desired. Serves 10 to 12.

Million-Dollar Pound Cake

Fresh Strawberry Shortcake

When time is short, use split biscuits, cubed angel food cake or waffles for a speedy version of strawberry shortcake.

1 qt. strawberries, hulled and sliced
1 c. sugar, divided
2 c. all-purpose flour
4 t. baking powder
¼ t. salt
⅛ t. nutmeg
½ c. butter
½ c. milk
2 eggs, separated
2 c. sweetened whipped cream
Optional: fresh mint sprigs

Gently toss together strawberries and ½ cup sugar; chill. In a large bowl, combine flour, ¼ cup sugar, baking powder, salt and nutmeg; cut in butter with a pastry blender or 2 forks until mixture is crumbly. Combine milk and egg yolks; mix well. Add to flour mixture, stirring just until moistened. Divide dough in half; pat into 2 greased 9" round cake pans. In a small bowl, beat egg whites at medium speed with an electric mixer until stiff peaks form; spread over dough. Sprinkle with remaining sugar. Bake at 300 degrees for 40 to 45 minutes or until golden. Cool 10 minutes before removing from pan to a wire rack. Cool completely. Place one cake layer on a large serving plate; spread with half the whipped cream. Spoon half the strawberries over cream. Repeat layers. Garnish with mint, if desired. Serves 8.

Nancy Ramsey
Delaware, OH

Italian Cream Cake

A tried & true recipe handed down from Grandma.

2 c. sugar
½ c. butter, softened
½ c. shortening
5 eggs, separated
2 c. all-purpose flour
1 t. baking soda
½ t. salt
½ c. buttermilk
1 c. chopped pecans
2 c. sweetened flaked coconut
Garnish: sweetened flaked coconut,
   chopped pecans

Beat sugar, butter and shortening at medium speed with an electric mixer until creamy. Add egg yolks, one at a time, beating until blended after each addition. Combine flour, baking soda and salt in a separate mixing bowl. Add to sugar mixture, alternately with buttermilk, beginning and ending with flour mixture. Beat at medium-low speed until blended after each addition. Stir in pecans and coconut; set aside.

In a small bowl, beat egg whites at high speed with an electric mixer until stiff. Fold into batter and pour into 2 greased and floured 8" round cake pans. Bake at 350 degrees for 20 to 30 minutes. Cool in pans on wire racks 10 minutes. Remove from pans to wire racks to cool completely. Spread with Frosting and garnish with sweetened flaked coconut and chopped pecans. Serves 8.

Frosting:

8-oz. pkg. cream cheese, softened
½ c. butter
1 t. vanilla extract
16-oz. pkg. powdered sugar
¾ t. butter flavoring

Beat together all ingredients until smooth.

Kim Schooler
Norman, OK

Boston Cream Cake

Drizzled with rich hot fudge…perfect for chocolate lovers!

6 egg whites
½ c. applesauce
18¼-oz. pkg. yellow cake mix
1-oz. pkg. instant sugar-free
   vanilla pudding mix
1½ c. milk
⅔ c. hot fudge topping, divided

Beat egg whites at high speed with an electric mixer for 30 seconds. Add applesauce and beat 10 more seconds. Gradually add cake mix. Beat at high speed for 2 minutes. Divide and spread batter equally among 4 greased and floured 8" round cake pans. Bake at 350 degrees for 15 minutes or until a wooden pick inserted in center comes out clean. Cool in pans on wire racks 10 minutes. Remove from pans; cool completely on wire racks.

Beat pudding mix and milk at low speed with an electric mixer for 2 minutes; refrigerate until cakes are completely cooled.

To assemble cakes, place one cake layer on a cake plate. Spread half of pudding mixture on cake. Place second cake layer on top of pudding mixture. Spread ⅓ cup hot fudge topping on top of cake. Repeat for second cake. Keep refrigerated until ready to serve. Serves 16.

Sheri Vanderzee
Midland Park, NJ

Old-Fashioned
Jam Cake

Old-Fashioned Jam Cake

For neat slices, cut with an electric knife.

1 c. plus 6 T. shortening, divided
5¾ c. sugar, divided
½ c. water
½ c. applesauce
1 c. seedless blackberry jam
2 eggs
3 c. all-purpose flour
½ c. baking cocoa
1 t. baking powder
1 t. baking soda
½ t. salt
1 t. each cinnamon, allspice and nutmeg
1 c. buttermilk
1 c. raisins
1 c. chopped pecans
6 T. butter
1½ c. milk
1½ t. vanilla extract

Beat one cup shortening until creamy; gradually beat in 2 cups sugar. Add water; beat until fluffy. Beat in applesauce and jam; add eggs, one at a time, beating until blended after each addition. Combine flour, cocoa, baking powder, baking soda, salt and spices; add to shortening mixture alternately with buttermilk. Stir in raisins and pecans. Pour into 3 lightly greased 9" round cake pans. Bake at 350 degrees for 24 minutes or until a wooden pick inserted in center comes out clean. Cool in pans 10 minutes; remove from pans and cool completely on wire racks.

Combine 3 cups sugar, remaining shortening, butter and milk in a heavy saucepan. Bring to a boil; remove from heat. Heat remaining sugar in a separate saucepan over medium heat until sugar melts and is golden. Stirring rapidly, pour into sugar mixture in saucepan; bring to a boil over medium heat. Cook, stirring for about 15 minutes, until icing reaches soft-ball stage, or 234 to 243 degrees on a candy thermometer. Remove from heat; stir in vanilla. Let stand 10 minutes, then beat icing with a wooden spoon until thick and creamy but still hot. Spread frosting between layers and on sides and top of cake; smooth with spatula dipped in hot water, if necessary. Serves 12.

Pineapple Upside-Down Cake

I received this recipe from a coworker. It's so simple to make…perfect for the working person!

18¼-oz. pkg. yellow cake mix
1 c. brown sugar, packed
20-oz. can sliced pineapple, drained and
  juice reserved
10-oz. jar maraschino cherries, drained

Prepare cake batter according to package directions. Spread brown sugar in the bottom of a greased 13"x9" baking pan. Pour pineapple juice over sugar; arrange pineapple slices in one layer over brown sugar mixture. Place a cherry in the center of each pineapple slice. Pour cake batter evenly over the top. Bake at 350 degrees for 40 minutes or until a wooden pick inserted in center comes out clean. Serves 12 to 16.

Phyllis Peters
Three Rivers, MI

Dreamy Orange Chiffon Cake

A light-textured cake with a delicate orange flavor.

1 orange
2 c. all-purpose flour
1½ c. sugar
1 T. baking powder
1 t. salt
½ c. oil
5 eggs, separated
¾ c. water
1 t. vanilla extract
½ t. cream of tartar

Grate zest from orange; set aside. Combine flour, sugar, baking powder and salt in a large mixing bowl. Gradually pour in oil, beating with a mixer. Add egg yolks, water, vanilla and orange zest. In another mixing bowl, beat egg whites until soft peaks form. Add cream of tartar; beat until stiff peaks form. Fold into flour mixture, combine thoroughly and pour into a lightly greased 10" tube pan. Bake at 325 degrees for one hour, or until a wooden pick inserted in center comes out clean. Cool and remove from pan. Serves 10 to 12.

Grandma's Chocolate Cake

A creamy cocoa frosting tops this rich and decadent cake...the ultimate chocolate indulgence! (Pictured on page 208)

3 c. all-purpose flour
2 c. sugar
⅓ c. baking cocoa
2 t. baking soda
½ t. salt
2 eggs
2 t. vanilla extract
¾ c. oil
2 T. vinegar
2 c. cold water

In a large bowl, combine flour and next 4 ingredients; mix well. Combine eggs and remaining ingredients in a separate bowl. Add egg mixture to flour mixture; mix well. Spread in a greased 13"x9" baking pan. Bake at 350 degrees for 30 to 35 minutes or until a wooden pick inserted in center comes out clean. Cool completely before spreading with Chocolate Frosting. Serves 12.

Chocolate Frosting:
⅔ c. butter-flavored shortening
⅔ c. baking cocoa
4 c. powdered sugar
3 t. vanilla extract
¼ c. milk

Mix together all ingredients; blend until smooth.

Regina Wood
Ava, MO

Grandma always made this when we went to visit at her house. —Regina

White Christmas
Coconut Sheet Cake

White Christmas Coconut Sheet Cake

This is so easy and delicious…no one will guess it started with a cake mix!

18¼-oz. pkg. white cake mix
¾ c. cream of coconut
¼ c. butter, melted
3 eggs
½ c. water
¾ c. lemon curd
4 1-oz. sqs. white baking chocolate, chopped
½ c. sour cream
1 c. whipping cream
¼ c. powdered sugar
6-oz. pkg. frozen shredded coconut, thawed
Optional: maraschino cherries with stems,
   lemon zest

Combine first 5 ingredients in a large bowl; beat at low speed with an electric mixer one minute. Increase speed to medium and beat 1½ minutes. Spread batter into a greased and floured 13"x9" baking pan. Bake at 350 degrees for 35 minutes or until a wooden pick inserted in center comes out clean. Remove pan to a wire rack; spread lemon curd over hot cake. Let cool completely in pan on wire rack. (Cake will sink slightly in center.)

Microwave white chocolate in a small microwave-safe bowl at high one minute or until melted, stirring after 30 seconds. Stir in sour cream. Cover and chill 30 minutes.

Beat whipping cream and powdered sugar in a large bowl at medium speed until stiff peaks form. Add white chocolate mixture and beat at low speed just until combined. Spread whipped cream topping over cake; sprinkle with coconut. Cover and chill 8 hours. Garnish with maraschino cherries and lemon zest, if desired. Store in refrigerator. Serves 15.

Jo Ann
Gooseberry Patch

Cherry-Chocolate Marble Cake

Mmmm, think chocolate-covered cherries in a cake.

1 c. butter, softened
2 c. sugar
3 eggs
6 T. maraschino cherry juice
6 T. water
2 t. almond extract
3¾ c. all-purpose flour
2¼ t. baking soda
¾ t. salt
1½ c. sour cream
¾ c. maraschino cherries, drained and
   chopped
¾ c. chopped walnuts
3 1-oz. sqs. unsweetened baking chocolate,
   melted
Garnish: powdered sugar

Beat butter and sugar in a large mixing bowl at medium speed with an electric mixer; add eggs, one at a time, beating well after each addition. Mix in cherry juice, water and almond extract; set aside. Combine flour, baking soda and salt; blend into butter mixture alternately with sour cream. Place half the batter in another mixing bowl; stir in cherries and walnuts. Set aside. Blend chocolate into remaining batter; set aside. Spoon half the cherry batter into a greased 10" angel food baking pan; spoon half the chocolate batter on top. Repeat layers. Bake at 350 degrees for one hour and 15 minutes or until a wooden pick inserted in the center comes out clean. Cool in pan for 30 minutes; remove to a serving platter to cool completely. Sprinkle with powdered sugar before slicing. Serves 15 to 18.

Sharon Webb
Clinton, IL

Texas Sheet Cake

This chocolatey delight is a crowd pleaser and perfect topped with colorful sprinkles for a child's birthday cake!

1 c. butter
1 c. water
¼ c. baking cocoa
2 c. all-purpose flour
2 c. sugar
½ t. salt
2 eggs, beaten
½ c. sour cream
1 t. baking soda

Bring butter, water and cocoa to a boil. Remove from heat and add flour, sugar and salt, mixing well. Beat in eggs, sour cream and baking soda and pour into a greased 15"x10" jelly-roll pan. Bake at 375 degrees for 20 to 22 minutes or until a wooden pick inserted in center comes out clean. Immediately spread Frosting over cake. Serves 12.

Frosting:

½ c. butter
¼ c. baking cocoa
6 T. milk
16-oz. pkg. powdered sugar
1 t. vanilla extract
1 c. walnuts, chopped

Combine butter, cocoa and milk in a medium saucepan; bring to a boil. Remove from heat and stir in remaining ingredients, beating until spreading consistency.

Tami Bowman
Gooseberry Patch

" *This has been my husband's birthday cake every year since he was little!* " —Tami

Easy Pumpkin Roll

This fall favorite is so pretty,...and oh-so simple to make.

1 c. sugar
3 eggs, beaten
⅔ c. canned pumpkin
¾ c. biscuit baking mix
2 t. cinnamon
1 t. pumpkin pie spice
½ c. chopped pecans
1½ c. powdered sugar, divided
8-oz. pkg. cream cheese, softened
⅓ c. butter, softened
1 t. vanilla extract

Combine sugar and eggs in a large bowl; beat at medium speed with an electric mixer 5 minutes. Add pumpkin, baking mix and spices. Spread pumpkin mixture evenly into a greased 15"x10" jelly-roll pan lined with greased wax paper. Sprinkle with pecans. Bake at 375 degrees for 13 to 15 minutes. Sift ½ cup powdered sugar into a 15-inch by 10-inch rectangle on a clean tea towel. Turn cake onto sugared towel; carefully peel off wax paper. Starting at narrow end, roll up cake and towel together and cool completely on a wire rack, seam-side down.

Blend cream cheese and butter at medium speed with an electric mixer until creamy; add remaining powdered sugar and vanilla, blending well. Carefully unroll cake; spread with cream cheese mixture and reroll without the towel. Place on a serving plate, seam-side down; cover and chill at least 2 hours. Serves 12 to 15.

Lenise Sulin
Chapel Hill, NC

Easy Pumpkin Roll

Chocolate-Cappuccino
Cheesecake

Chocolate-Cappuccino Cheesecake

This makes an absolutely delicious gift...if you can bear to give it away!

1½ c. pecans, finely chopped
1½ c. chocolate wafer cookies, crushed
⅓ c. butter, melted
½ c. semi-sweet chocolate chips, melted

Combine pecans, cookies and butter; press into bottom and up sides of a greased 9" springform pan. Drizzle with chocolate; chill until chocolate is firm.

Pour Filling into crust; bake at 300 degrees for one hour and 10 minutes. Cool completely. Cover and chill 8 hours. Spread Topping over cake. Remove sides of pan. Serves 12.

Filling:

2 8-oz. pkgs. cream cheese, softened
1½ c. semi-sweet chocolate chips, melted and cooled
1 c. brown sugar, packed
4 eggs, beaten
1 c. sour cream
⅓ c. cold coffee
2 t. vanilla extract

Combine all ingredients; blend until smooth.

Topping:

⅔ c. whipping cream
¼ c. sugar
½ c. semi-sweet chocolate chips

In a saucepan, heat whipping cream and sugar over low heat, whisking constantly. Add chocolate chips, whisking until smooth.

Sandy Stacy
Medway, OH

Peaches & Cream Cheesecake

This will disappear like magic!

¾ c. all-purpose flour
½ c. milk
1 egg
3.4-oz. pkg. instant vanilla pudding mix
3 T. butter, softened
1 t. baking powder
½ t. salt
15-oz. can sliced peaches, drained and juice reserved
8-oz. pkg. cream cheese, softened
½ c. plus 1 T. sugar, divided
1 t. cinnamon

Beat flour, milk, egg, pudding mix, butter, baking powder and salt at medium speed with an electric mixer 2 minutes. Pour into a greased 9" springform pan; arrange peaches over flour mixture. In a separate bowl, beat cream cheese, 3 tablespoons reserved juice and ½ cup sugar at medium speed with an electric mixer 2 minutes. Spoon over peaches. Combine remaining sugar and cinnamon; sprinkle on top. Bake at 350 degrees for 30 to 35 minutes or until set. Let cool in pan on a wire rack. Refrigerate at least 4 hours. Remove sides of pan. Serves 6 to 8.

Betty Rowland
Hillsboro, OH

picture perfect

Display old photos in a new way. Look for 2 clear drinking glasses; one needs to be slightly smaller in diameter than the other. Place the smaller glass inside the larger one and then slip photos in the open space between...very clever!

Chocolate Icebox Cake

This is best made the day before you plan to serve it.

2 4-oz. pkgs. sweet baking chocolate, chopped
½ c. butter
3 T. hot water
2 T. powdered sugar
4 eggs, separated
½ t. vanilla extract
12 to 18 ladyfingers

Combine chocolate, butter and hot water in a medium saucepan over medium heat; cook, stirring constantly, until smooth. Stir in sugar; let mixture cool. Add egg yolks, one at a time, beating well after each addition. Beat egg whites at high speed with an electric mixer until stiff peaks form; fold into chocolate mixture. Stir in vanilla; set aside.

Line bottom and sides of a lightly greased 8"x8" baking pan with a layer of ladyfingers; pour half of the chocolate mixture over the top. Cover with another layer of ladyfingers; pour remaining chocolate mixture over top. Freeze at least 12 hours. Serves 6 to 8.

Brenda Flowers
Olney, IL

toppings galore!

The individual cups in a muffin pan make it perfect for holding a variety of ice-cream toppings...just spoon assorted flavors of sprinkles or mini candy into each muffin cup.

Triple Chocolate– Sour Cream Cake

A chocolate lover's dream!

1 c. all-purpose flour
1 t. baking powder
½ t. baking soda
½ t. salt
2 1-oz. sqs. unsweetened baking chocolate, chopped
1¼ c. sugar
1 T. baking cocoa
⅓ c. boiling water
2 eggs
¾ c. butter, softened
½ c. sour cream
1 t. vanilla extract

Combine flour, baking powder, baking soda and salt in a mixing bowl; set aside. In a food processor or blender, mix chocolate, sugar and cocoa; process until crumbly. Add boiling water to chocolate mixture. Blend until chocolate melts. Break eggs into food processor and mix well. Add butter, sour cream and vanilla; process again. Place flour mixture into food processor, pulsing until all ingredients are well-blended. Lightly grease and flour an 8" springform pan; pour batter into pan. Bake at 350 degrees for one hour or until cake begins to pull away from sides of pan. Remove cake from oven; let cool on a wire rack. Remove cake from pan. Frost cooled cake with Icing. Serves 10.

Icing:

½ c. whipping cream
6 1-oz. sqs. bittersweet baking chocolate, chopped

Heat cream in a saucepan over medium heat (do not boil). Add chocolate and stir for one minute. Remove pan from heat and stir until chocolate is completely melted. Cool icing to a warm temperature, then spread on cake. Refrigerate cake to allow icing to set before serving.

Pumpkin Cheesecake with Ginger Cream Topping

This will become a "must-have-every-year" recipe for your holiday meal.

¾ c. sugar, divided
¾ c. brown sugar, packed and divided
¾ c. graham cracker crumbs
½ c. pecans, finely chopped
¼ c. butter, melted
15-oz. can pumpkin
1 t. vanilla extract
1 T. all-purpose flour
1½ t. cinnamon
½ t. ground ginger
½ t. nutmeg
¼ t. salt
3 8-oz. pkgs. cream cheese, softened
3 eggs
Garnish: chopped pecans

Combine ¼ cup sugar, ¼ cup brown sugar, graham cracker crumbs, pecans and butter; press in bottom and one inch up sides of a lightly greased 9" springform pan. Cover and chill one hour.

Combine remaining sugar, brown sugar, pumpkin, vanilla and next 5 ingredients; set aside. Beat cream cheese at medium speed until creamy. Add pumpkin mixture, beating well. Add eggs, one at a time, beating after each addition. Pour mixture into prepared crust. Bake at 350 degrees for 55 minutes. Cool completely in pan on a wire rack.

Spoon Ginger Cream Topping over cheesecake. Cover and chill at least 8 hours. To serve, carefully remove sides of springform pan; garnish with pecans. Serves 16.

Ginger Cream Topping:

1 c. whipping cream
1 c. sour cream
2 T. sugar
¼ c. crystallized ginger, minced
3 T. dark rum or 1 t. rum extract
½ t. vanilla extract

Combine first 3 ingredients in a bowl; beat at high speed until soft peaks form. Fold in ginger, rum or rum extract and vanilla.

Pumpkin Cheesecake with Ginger Cream Topping

Chocolate & Marshmallow Cupcakes

Chocolate & Marshmallow Cupcakes

These are super for the kids' Christmas parties!

8-oz. pkg. unsweetened dark baking chocolate,
   chopped
1 c. butter, softened
4 eggs, beaten
1 c. sugar
¾ c. all-purpose flour
1 t. salt
½ c. mini semi-sweet chocolate chips
Garnish: ½ c. mini marshmallows

   Place chocolate and butter in a microwave-safe bowl; microwave at high just until melted. Cool until just warm.

   Blend together eggs and sugar until light and foamy. Add flour and salt; mix well. Pour in chocolate mixture; blend until smooth. Spoon batter into 12 paper-lined muffin cups; sprinkle chocolate chips evenly over tops. Bake at 350 degrees for 15 minutes or until a wooden pick inserted in center comes out clean. Remove from oven; arrange several mini marshmallows on top of each cupcake. Broil just until marshmallows turn golden. Remove from oven and let stand 5 minutes to cool slightly. Makes one dozen.

Kathy Grashoff
Fort Wayne, IN

Black Forest Cupcakes

I like to top these with rich, dark chocolate frosting, but cream cheese or old-fashioned vanilla frosting is just as good.

1 c. all-purpose flour
½ t. baking powder
½ t. baking soda
½ t. salt
6 T. butter, softened
1 c. sugar
2 eggs
2 1-oz. sqs. unsweetened baking chocolate, melted
   and cooled
1 t. vanilla extract
½ c. milk
16-oz. can chocolate frosting
21-oz. can cherry pie filling

   Whisk flour, baking powder, baking soda and salt together; set aside. Beat butter on high speed with an electric mixer until fluffy; gradually blend in sugar. Continue blending until light and fluffy; beat in eggs, one at a time. Add melted chocolate and vanilla. Add flour mixture alternately with milk until just mixed. Spoon batter into paper-lined muffin tins, filling ⅔ full; bake at 350 degrees for 15 to 20 minutes. Cool 15 minutes on a wire rack before removing from pan; spread with frosting and top with a tablespoonful of cherry pie filling. Makes one dozen.

Mary Murray
Gooseberry Patch

Aunt Mayme's Rhubarb Custard Pie

If fresh rhubarb isn't in season, you can substitute frozen. Just be sure to thaw it thoroughly.

2 T. plus 2 t. butter
1¼ c. sugar
3 c. rhubarb, chopped
¼ c. cornstarch
6 T. water, divided
2 egg yolks, beaten
1 t. vanilla extract
9-inch refrigerated pie crust, baked
Garnish: whipped topping

Melt butter in a saucepan; add sugar and rhubarb. Cook over medium heat until sugar is dissolved and rhubarb is tender. Combine cornstarch and 3 tablespoons water in a separate small bowl. Add to rhubarb mixture in pan. Combine egg yolks and remaining water; gradually add to rhubarb mixture in pan. Cook, stirring constantly, over low heat until thickened; stir in vanilla. Pour into pie crust; cool completely. Garnish with whipped topping. Chill until ready to serve. Serves 6 to 8.

Mary Terdich
Crystal Lake, IL

A delightful family recipe handed down from my husband's aunt. It's smooth, creamy and delicious! —Mary

Strawberry Pizza

With a sugar cookie crust, a cream cheese "sauce" and fresh strawberry topping, what's not to like about this dessert pizza? Be creative and add your favorite fruit toppings like kiwi, banana slices or even chocolate curls.

18-oz. tube refrigerated sugar cookie dough
8-oz. pkg. cream cheese, softened
2 c. frozen whipped topping, thawed
1 t. vanilla extract
1 c. powdered sugar
12¾-oz. pkg. strawberry glaze
16-oz. pkg. strawberries, hulled and sliced

Roll out dough onto a greased 12" pizza pan; bake according to package directions. Let cool.

Mix together cream cheese, whipped topping, vanilla and powdered sugar; spread over crust. Top with glaze and strawberries. Serves 6 to 8.

Micki Stephens
Marion, OH

quick, easy...clean!

To clean strawberries, place them in a sink filled with water and gently wash with the sprayer nozzle on the sink. The water from the nozzle will toss and turn the berries, giving them a thorough cleaning.

Strawberry Pizza

Sour Cherry Pie

Sour Cherry Pie

2 9-inch refrigerated pie crusts
4 c. sour cherries, pitted and ½ c. juice
   reserved
1 c. sugar
1 T. all-purpose flour
2½ T. cornstarch
zest and juice of one lime
2 T. butter, diced
1 egg, beaten
2 T. whipping cream

Roll out one crust; place in a 9" pie plate. Wrap with plastic wrap and chill. Roll out remaining crust to ⅛-inch thickness. Cut as many one-inch-wide strips as possible to make a lattice; cut any leftover crust into leaf shapes with a mini cookie cutter. Place lattice strips and leaves on a parchment paper-lined baking sheet; cover with plastic wrap and chill.

Combine cherries and juice in a large bowl. Sprinkle with sugar, flour, cornstarch, lime zest and juice. Toss well and pour into pie crust; dot with butter. Weave lattice strips over filling. Arrange leaves in a decorative pattern on lattice. Whisk together egg and cream; brush over lattice and edges of crust. Bake at 400 degrees for about 50 minutes, shielding after 30 minutes, if needed. Cool slightly before cutting. Serves 6 to 8.

Sharon Demers
Dolores, CO

When I was a little girl my father would sing to me, 'Can you bake a cherry pie, Sharon girl, Sharon girl?' My reply would always be a giggle and then a big 'Nooo!' Well, I can finally make a cherry pie and only wish that my dad were still with us so I could serve him a big piece. —Sharon

Fresh Peach Pie

It's a tradition for my mom and me to make fruit pies when she visits. While making the pies, I have the pleasure of Mom's company as well as her help; then we share this family favorite with my husband and daughter.

1 c. sugar
2 T. plus 1½ t. cornstarch
¼ t. salt
½ c. water
4 to 5 c. peaches, pitted, peeled and sliced
1 T. lemon juice
Optional: milk

Combine sugar, cornstarch and salt in a large saucepan. Add water and peaches. Bring to a boil; boil for one minute, stirring constantly. Cool; stir in lemon juice. Pour cooled peach mixture into a 9" pie plate lined with half of Standard Pie Crust. Roll remaining pie crust dough and fit over top. Seal edges well and cut vents in top. Bake on lower shelf of oven at 425 degrees for 50 minutes. If desired, brush milk on top of crust to aid in browning. Serves 6 to 8.

Standard Pie Crust:
2 c. all-purpose flour, sifted
1 t. salt
¾ c. shortening
¼ c. cold water

Combine flour and salt in a large bowl. Cut in shortening as follows: For a tender crust, cut in about ⅔ of shortening with a pastry blender or 2 forks until mixture resembles coarse meal. For a flaky crust, cut in remaining shortening until mixture is the size of large peas. Add water, one tablespoon at a time, to flour mixture. Mix thoroughly with fork until all particles cling together and form dough. Using your hands, work dough into a smooth ball. Roll out on a floured board or cloth. Makes enough dough for a double-crust pie.

Susan Brzozowski
Ellicott City, MD

Perfect Pecan Pie

For a quick variation, try walnut halves in place of pecans.

3 eggs, beaten
½ c. sugar
¼ t. salt
3 T. butter, melted
1 c. dark corn syrup
1 t. vanilla extract
2 c. pecan halves
9-inch refrigerated pie crust
Optional: vanilla ice cream

Whisk together eggs and next 5 ingredients until thoroughly blended. Stir in pecans. Fit pie crust into a 9" pie plate. Fold edges under and crimp. Pour filling into pie crust. Bake at 350 degrees on lower rack of oven 40 minutes or until pie is set, covering edges with aluminum foil after 15 minutes. Cool completely on a wire rack. Serve with vanilla ice cream, if desired. Serves 6.

sweet offering
For an oh-so pretty gift, top pies with an inverted pie plate and secure both together with a bandanna.

Perfect Pecan Pie

Caramel Crunch Apple Pie

9-inch refrigerated pie crust
24 caramels
2 T. water
4 c. apples, peeled, cored and sliced
¾ c. all-purpose flour
⅓ c. sugar
⅓ t. cinnamon
⅓ c. butter
½ c. chopped walnuts

Fit pie crust into a 9" pie plate according to package directions. Melt caramels in water in a heavy saucepan over low heat, stirring frequently, until smooth. Spoon apples into crust; top with caramel sauce. Mix together flour, sugar and cinnamon; cut in butter until mixture resembles coarse crumbs. Add walnuts; sprinkle over apples. Bake at 375 degrees for 40 minutes or until apples are tender. Serves 6 to 8.

DeNeane Deskins
Indian Harbor Beach, FL

Fresh Blueberry Pie

¾ c. sugar
3 T. cornstarch
½ t. cinnamon
⅛ t. salt
4 c. blueberries
2 9-inch refrigerated pie crusts
1 T. lemon juice
2 T. butter, sliced

Combine first 4 ingredients in a bowl; sprinkle over blueberries. Line a 9" pie plate with one crust; pour berry mixture in crust. Sprinkle with lemon juice and dot with butter. Roll out remaining pie crust to fit top; crimp and flute edges. Cut vents in top. Bake at 425 degrees for 45 minutes or until crust is golden. Serves 6 to 8.

Jo Ann
Gooseberry Patch

Frosty Butter Pecan Crunch Pie

2 c. graham cracker crumbs
½ c. butter, melted
2 3.4-oz. pkgs. instant vanilla pudding mix
2 c. milk
1 qt. butter pecan ice cream, slightly softened
8-oz. container frozen whipped topping, thawed
2 1.4-oz. chocolate-covered toffee candy bars, crushed

Combine graham cracker crumbs and melted butter in a medium bowl; pat into an ungreased 13"x9" baking pan. Freeze until firm.
In a large bowl, beat pudding mix and milk at medium speed with an electric mixer until blended, about one minute. Fold in ice cream and whipped topping; spoon over chilled crust. Sprinkle with candy bar pieces; freeze. Remove from freezer 20 minutes before serving. Serves 12 to 15.

Lisa Johnson
Hallsville, TX

giftable goodies
Store all dry ingredients for your favorite pie recipe inside plastic zipping bags. Tuck bags inside a homespun-lined spongeware pie plate along with the recipe. Bring the corners of the homespun together and tie with strands of raffia…a delicious gift!

Peanut Butter Strudel Pie

The best peanut butter pie! Topped with meringue, it's wonderful!

¾ c. powdered sugar
¼ c. creamy peanut butter
9-inch refrigerated pie crust, baked
⅔ c. plus 6 T. sugar, divided
⅓ c. all-purpose flour
¼ t. salt
2 c. milk
3 eggs, separated
2 T. butter
½ t. vanilla extract
¼ t. cream of tartar

In a small bowl, combine powdered sugar and peanut butter to resemble coarse crumbs. Spread over bottom of pie crust, reserving one tablespoon for topping.

In a 2-quart saucepan, stir together ⅔ cup sugar, flour and salt; gradually add milk. Bring mixture to a boil over medium heat, stirring constantly; cook and stir 5 minutes or until thickened. Remove from heat and set aside.

Beat egg yolks and blend in a small amount of milk mixture; stir well. Return egg mixture to hot mixture in pan; cook and stir over low heat for 3 minutes. Remove from heat and stir in butter and vanilla. Cover and set filling aside.

Beat egg whites and cream of tartar until foamy. Gradually beat in remaining sugar, one tablespoon at a time, beating until stiff peaks form. Reheat filling over medium heat, stirring constantly, just until hot. Pour hot filling over peanut butter crumbs in pie crust. Spread meringue over pie, being sure to touch edges of crust to seal. Sprinkle reserved peanut butter crumbs over meringue. Bake at 325 degrees for 25 minutes or until meringue is golden. Cool completely before serving. Serves 6 to 8.

Phyllis Laughrey
Mt. Vernon, OH

Peanut Butter Strudel Pie

Lemon Meringue Pie

So often I would come home from school and Mom would have made this pie...it would be cooling on the counter and I could barely wait to have a bite. Now I make it for my girls, and they love it too!

14-oz. can sweetened condensed milk
½ c. lemon juice
3 eggs, separated and egg whites reserved
9-inch graham cracker pie crust
15 to 20 vanilla wafers

Whisk together condensed milk and lemon juice in a large mixing bowl; add egg yolks, whisking until blended. Pour mixture into pie crust and cover with Meringue. Line edge of pie with vanilla wafers, sticking each halfway into pie. Bake at 325 degrees for 10 to 15 minutes or until top is golden. Serves 6 to 8.

Meringue:
3 egg whites
¼ t. cream of tartar
¼ c. to ½ c. sugar

Beat together egg whites and cream of tartar until soft peaks form; add sugar, beating until stiff peaks form.

Marilyn Williams
Westerville, OH

meringue magic
Spreading meringue so it touches the edges of the pie crust is the secret to keep it from shrinking...works every time!

Crustless Coconut Pie

This recipe makes 2 pies...one to keep and one to give away! (Pictured on page 208)

4 eggs
1¾ c. sugar
2 c. milk
¼ c. butter, melted
½ c. self-rising flour
1 t. vanilla extract
1 c. sweetened flaked coconut, divided

Beat eggs at medium speed with an electric mixer until frothy. Add sugar and next 4 ingredients; beat well. Place ½ cup coconut in each of 2 shallow, lightly greased 9" pie plates; pour half of filling mixture into each pie plate, stirring gently to distribute coconut. Bake at 350 degrees for 25 to 30 minutes or until golden. Makes 2 pies; each serves 6.

Glenda Geohagen
DeFuniak Springs, FL

Key Lime Pie

1½ c. vanilla wafers, crushed
¼ c. butter, melted
8-oz. pkg. cream cheese, softened
14-oz. can sweetened condensed milk
1 T. lime zest
⅓ c. lime juice
2 to 3 drops green food coloring
8-oz. container frozen whipped topping, thawed

Mix wafer crumbs with butter; pat into a 9" pie plate. Bake at 350 degrees for 10 minutes; cool. Blend together cream cheese and condensed milk. Add lime zest, lime juice and green coloring. Fold in whipped topping; pour into crust and chill for 30 minutes. Serves 6.

Michelle Elliott
Loveland, CO

German Chocolate Pie

This is a quick & easy recipe for family gatherings.

2 1-oz. sqs. sweet baking chocolate
1 c. butter
3 eggs
2 T. all-purpose flour
1 c. sugar
1 t. vanilla extract
1 c. pecans, chopped
½ c. coconut
Garnish: whipped cream, shaved
    chocolate, pecans

Melt chocolate and butter over low heat until smooth; let cool. Beat eggs, flour, sugar and vanilla for 3 minutes at high speed with an electric mixer until blended. Pour chocolate mixture over egg mixture and beat 3 more minutes. Stir in pecans and coconut. Pour into a well-greased 9" pie plate. Bake at 350 degrees for 28 minutes. Cool just before serving. Garnish with whipped cream, shaved chocolate and pecans. Serves 6.

Pauline Raens
Abilene, TX

Mocha Pecan Mud Pie

Two store-bought ice creams pack lots of flavor into this frozen dessert. (Pictured on page 208)

12 chocolate sandwich cookies,
    crumbled
3 T. butter, melted
1 egg white, lightly beaten
1¼ c. chopped pecans
¼ c. sugar
1 pt. coffee ice cream, softened
1 pt. chocolate ice cream, softened
12 chocolate sandwich cookies,
    coarsely chopped and divided
Optional: frozen whipped topping,
    thawed, additional cookies and
    pecans, coarsely chopped

Stir together cookie crumbs and butter. Press into a 9" pie plate. Brush with egg white. Bake at 350 degrees for 5 minutes. Cool on a wire rack.

Place pecans on a lightly greased baking sheet; sprinkle with sugar. Bake at 350 degrees for 8 to 10 minutes. Cool.

Stir together ice creams, one cup coarsely chopped cookies and one cup pecans; spoon into crust. Freeze 10 minutes. Press remaining coarsely chopped cookies and pecans on top. Cover and freeze at least 8 hours. Top with whipped topping and additional chopped cookies and pecans, if desired. Serves 8.

consider having a pie night
Invite family and friends to bring their favorite pie to share. And don't forget copies of the recipes...someone's sure to ask!

Chocolate Chess Pie

½ c. butter
1½ 1-oz. sqs. unsweetened baking chocolate,
    chopped
1 c. brown sugar, packed
½ c. sugar
2 eggs, beaten
1 T. milk
1 t. all-purpose flour
1 t. vanilla extract
9-inch refrigerated pie crust
Garnish: whipped cream

   Melt butter and chocolate in a small saucepan
over low heat; set aside. Combine sugars, eggs,
milk, flour and vanilla in a medium bowl. Gradually
add chocolate mixture, beating constantly. Fit pie
crust into 9" pie plate according to package directions. Pour into pie crust; bake at 325 degrees for
40 to 45 minutes. Let cool before serving. Garnish
with whipped cream. Serves 6 to 8.

Heidi Jo McManaman
Grand Rapids, MI

Mom's Blackberry Crisp

Be sure to heap the berries on because they'll cook down.
(Pictured on page 208)

¾ c. sugar, divided
¾ c. plus 1 T. all-purpose flour, divided
1 t. cinnamon, divided
5 to 6 c. blackberries
⅛ t. salt
⅓ c. butter
¼ c. chopped walnuts
Optional: ¼ t. orange or lemon zest

   Combine ¼ cup sugar, 4 to 5 tablespoons
flour and ½ teaspoon cinnamon; gently fold into
berries. Spread in a greased 9" pie plate. Combine
remaining sugar, flour and cinnamon; add salt.
Cut in butter a little at a time with a fork or pastry
blender until crumbly. Add chopped nuts and zest,
if desired. Sprinkle topping over berries. Bake at
400 degrees for about 20 minutes or until golden.
Serves 4 to 6.

Pat Gilmer
West Linn, OR

Chocolate Chess Pie

Simple Scottish
Shortbread (page 244)

Buckeye Brownies (page 257)

Candy Cane Puffs
(page 261)

Grandma Miller's
Nutmeg Logs (page 248)

COOKIES & CANDIES

*All-time favorite handheld treats
to satisfy your sweet tooth*

Watermelon
Slice Cookies

Watermelon Slice Cookies

These red and green treats are sure to be a hit at any summertime get-together.

¾ c. butter, softened
¾ c. sugar
1 egg
½ t. almond extract
2 c. all-purpose flour
¼ t. baking powder
½ t. salt
red and green gel food coloring
⅓ c. mini semi-sweet chocolate chips
1 t. sesame seed

Beat butter and sugar in a large mixing bowl at medium speed with an electric mixer. Beat in egg and extract; set aside. Combine flour, baking powder and salt; gradually add to butter mixture, beating well. Set aside one cup dough. Tint remaining 1⅓ cups dough with red food coloring and shape into a 3½-inch long log; wrap in plastic wrap. Tint ⅓ cup reserved dough with green food coloring; wrap in plastic wrap. Wrap remaining plain dough and refrigerate all 3 doughs 2 hours or until firm. On a lightly floured surface, roll plain dough into an 8-inch by 3½-inch rectangle. Place red dough log on the end of one short side of rectangle; roll up.

Roll green dough into a 10-inch by 3½-inch rectangle. Place red-and-white dough log on the end of one short side of rectangle; roll up. Wrap in plastic wrap; refrigerate overnight. Unwrap and cut into 36 one-inch thick slices. Place 2 inches apart on ungreased baking sheets. Place chocolate chips and sesame seed on red part of dough to resemble watermelon seeds. Bake at 350 degrees for 9 to 11 minutes or until firm. Immediately slice cookies in half. Makes 3 dozen.

Kay Barg
Sandy, UT

Chocolate Refrigerator Cookies

My mom rarely uses a recipe when she cooks, but she found this one in a cookbook that I gave her 30 years ago and has been making them ever since.

1¼ c. butter, softened
1½ c. powdered sugar
1 egg
3 c. cake flour
½ c. baking cocoa
¼ t. salt

Beat butter and sugar until light and fluffy; add egg, beating well. Blend in flour, cocoa and salt. Cover and chill for one hour. Divide dough in half. Shape each half into a roll 1½ inches in diameter. Wrap and chill at least 8 hours. Cut rolls into ⅛-inch slices. If dough crumbles while cutting, let warm slightly. Place one inch apart on ungreased baking sheets. Bake at 400 degrees for about 8 minutes. Immediately transfer to wire racks to cool. Frost with Fudge Frosting. Makes 8 dozen.

Fudge Frosting:
¼ c. shortening
⅓ c. milk
1 c. sugar
2 1-oz. sqs. unsweetened baking chocolate, melted
¼ t. salt
1 t. vanilla extract

Bring all ingredients except vanilla to a boil in a saucepan, stirring occasionally. Boil one minute without stirring. Place pan in a bowl of ice and water. Beat until frosting is cooled and thickened. Stir in vanilla.

Judy Kelly
St. Charles, MO

Lemon Slice Cookies

These also make a great gift!

1 c. butter, softened
1 c. brown sugar, packed
½ c. sugar
1 egg
1 T. lemon zest
2 T. lemon juice
2 c. all-purpose flour
¼ t. baking soda
½ t. salt

Beat butter and sugars until light and fluffy; blend in egg, lemon zest and lemon juice. Combine flour, baking soda and salt; add to butter mixture and mix until just blended. Divide dough in half; with floured hands, shape each half into a 10-inch long log. Wrap each in plastic wrap; refrigerate until firm. Cut each roll into ¼-inch thick slices; arrange on greased baking sheets. Bake at 400 degrees for 8 to 10 minutes; cool on a wire rack. Makes about 3 dozen.

sweet surprise!
Tie a stack of 3 big cookies together with a length of jute and arrange them in the middle of a dinner plate or inside a lunchbox.

Double Peanut Butter Cookies

Enjoy these soft, chewy, peanut-buttery cookies warm from the oven.

1½ c. all-purpose flour
½ c. sugar
½ t. baking soda
¼ t. salt
½ c. shortening
¾ c. creamy peanut butter, divided
¼ c. light corn syrup
1 T. milk

Combine flour, sugar, baking soda and salt. Blend in shortening and ½ cup peanut butter until mixture resembles coarse meal. Blend in syrup and milk. Form into a roll 2 inches thick; cover and chill at least 30 minutes. Cut into ⅛-inch thick to ¼-inch thick slices. Arrange half the slices on ungreased baking sheets; spread each with ½ teaspoon peanut butter. Top with remaining slices; seal edges with a fork. Bake at 350 degrees for 12 minutes, or until golden. Makes about 2 dozen.

Shari Miller
Hobart, IN

When I was in first grade, I got an Easy-Bake Oven for Christmas...I was so excited! My friends would come over and we would bake and bake. —Shari

Double Peanut Butter Cookies

Simple Scottish Shortbread

1 c. butter, softened
½ c. powdered sugar
½ t. vanilla extract
2¼ c. all-purpose flour

Beat together butter, powdered sugar and vanilla until well blended. Add flour, one cup at a time, to butter mixture, blending well. On a floured surface, roll out dough to ¼ to ½-inch thickness. With a sharp knife, cut dough into 2-inch squares or cut into 1¾-inch rounds with a cookie cutter. Place on ungreased baking sheets and prick top of cookies with a fork. Bake at 325 degrees for 20 minutes or until bottoms are golden and tops are light in color. Cool on wire racks. Store in airtight containers. Makes about 4 dozen.

Simple Scottish Shortbread

Dazzling Neapolitan Cookies

These cookies only seem difficult but are really easy to make.

1 c. butter, softened
1 c. sugar
1 egg
1 t. vanilla extract
2½ c. all-purpose flour
1½ t. baking powder
½ t. salt
1-oz. sq. sweet baking chocolate, melted
⅓ c. chopped pecans
⅓ c. sweetened flaked coconut
½ t. almond extract
¼ c. chopped candied cherries, diced
2 drops red food coloring

Beat butter and sugar until light and fluffy; add egg and vanilla. Gradually blend in flour, baking powder and salt; divide dough into thirds. Place each third in a separate mixing bowl. Stir chocolate and pecans into one third; set aside. Stir coconut and almond extract into another third; set aside. Stir cherries and red food coloring into remaining third; set aside. Line an ungreased 8"x8" baking pan with plastic wrap; press chocolate mixture evenly to cover bottom of pan. Layer with coconut mixture and then cherry mixture, pressing gently; cover and refrigerate for 8 hours. Lift dough from pan; cut into 5 equal sections. Carefully cut each section into ⅛-inch thick slices; arrange on ungreased baking sheets. Bake at 375 degrees for 8 to 10 minutes; remove to wire racks to cool. Makes 8 dozen.

Peppery Molasses Cookies

These are really spicy...the black pepper gives them a kick! (Pictured on page 13)

¾ c. butter, softened
¾ c. sugar
1 egg
¼ c. molasses
2 c. all-purpose flour
2 t. baking soda
1½ t. pepper
1 t. cinnamon
½ t. salt
additional sugar

Beat butter and sugar in a large bowl until fluffy. Beat in egg; add molasses. Combine flour and next 4 ingredients. Gradually add to butter mixture; mix well. Form into one-inch balls and roll in sugar. Place cookies on ungreased baking sheets 2 inches apart. Bake at 350 degrees for 12 to 15 minutes. Remove and cool on wire racks. Makes 3½ to 4 dozen.

Lisa Ashton
Aston, PA

a delightful hostess gift
Fill a pretty drinking glass with Dazzling Neapolitan Cookies, cover the top with a dainty handkerchief and secure with a ribbon.

Maple Drop Cookies

1 c. butter, softened
¾ c. sugar
2 c. all-purpose flour
¼ t. salt
1½ t. maple flavoring
Optional: pecan halves

Beat butter and sugar until light and fluffy; blend in remaining ingredients except pecan halves. Drop dough by teaspoonfuls onto greased baking sheets; place a pecan half on top of each cookie, if desired. Bake at 350 degrees for 12 to 15 minutes. Makes about 3 dozen.

Debi DeVore
Dover, OH

Pineapple-Nut Cookies

I've enjoyed these cookies for years. I began making them when my children were small, and now I make them for my grandkids.

½ c. butter, softened
1 c. brown sugar, packed
1 egg
2½ c. all-purpose flour
1 t. baking soda
½ t. salt
½ c. pecans, chopped
8-oz. can crushed pineapple, drained
½ t. vanilla extract

Beat butter and sugar until light and fluffy; blend in egg. Combine flour, baking soda and salt. Add to butter mixture; blend well. Stir in pecans, pineapple and vanilla; drop by teaspoonfuls onto ungreased baking sheets. Bake at 375 degrees for 10 to 12 minutes. Cool on wire racks. Makes about 3½ dozen.

Norma Longnecker
Lawrenceville, IL

Raisin-Oatmeal Cookies

Soaking the raisins in hot water plumps them nicely.

½ c. golden raisins
⅓ c. hot water
17½-oz. package oatmeal cookie mix
½ c. butter, softened
1 egg
1 T. vanilla extract

Combine raisins and hot water. Let stand 5 minutes; drain.

Stir together cookie mix and next 3 ingredients. Add raisins and stir until blended. Dough will be stiff. Drop dough by tablespoonfuls 2 inches apart onto lightly greased baking sheets.

Bake, in batches, at 375 degrees for 10 minutes or until golden. Cool on baking sheets on wire racks one minute; remove from pans to wire racks to cool completely. Makes about 3 dozen.

handy helper
Cookie scoops are handy for measuring dough...they scoop dough into a uniform size to help divide out the perfect amount needed.

Raisin-Oatmeal
Cookies

Grandma Miller's Nutmeg Logs

You'll want more than just one!

1 c. butter, softened
¾ c. sugar
1 egg, beaten
2 t. vanilla extract
2 t. rum extract
3 c. all-purpose flour
1 t. nutmeg
Garnish: ¼ t. nutmeg

In a large bowl, blend together butter and sugar; add egg. Stir in vanilla and rum extracts. Mix flour and nutmeg into butter mixture. Divide dough into 52 portions. Roll each portion into a one-inch wide log and cut into a 1½-inch length.

Place on ungreased baking sheets. Since cookies don't spread during cooking, they can be placed close together. Bake at 350 degrees for 10 to 15 minutes. Let cool. Spread Frosting on cookies. Run tines of a fork across frosting to resemble a log. Sprinkle with nutmeg. Makes 52.

Frosting:

3 T. butter, softened
½ t. vanilla extract
1 t. rum extract
2½ c. powdered sugar
3 T. milk

Mix first 4 ingredients together; add milk, stirring until desired consistency.

Thais Menges
Three Rivers, MI

Date-Filled Cookies

A recipe handed down from my grandmother; it's a family favorite!

1⅓ c. sugar
⅔ c. shortening
¼ c. milk
1 t. vanilla extract
2 eggs
3⅔ c. all-purpose flour
2½ t. baking powder
½ t. salt

Blend sugar and shortening until light and fluffy; add milk, vanilla and eggs. Combine flour, baking powder and salt. Add to sugar mixture; blend well. Divide dough in half; wrap and chill at least one hour.

Roll out dough and cut into 2-inch rounds with a cookie cutter or glass. Place half of dough rounds on baking sheet, fill with ¼ teaspoon Date Filling, top with remaining dough rounds and press edges together with a fork. Bake at 400 degrees for 8 to 10 minutes or until slightly browned. Remove from pans to wire racks to cool. Makes about 3½ dozen.

Date Filling:
1 T. all-purpose flour
½ c. sugar
1 c. dates, finely chopped
½ c. water

Combine flour and sugar in a medium saucepan; stir in dates and water. Cook over low heat, stirring constantly, until mixture thickens. Makes about ¾ cup.

Adele Peterman
Austin, TX

Chocolate Chip Cookies

No cookie jar is complete without this all-time favorite!

1 c. butter, softened
¼ c. sugar
¾ c. brown sugar, packed
2 eggs
1 t. vanilla extract
2⅓ c. all-purpose flour
5.1-oz. pkg. instant vanilla pudding mix
1 t. baking soda
12-oz. pkg. semi-sweet chocolate chips

Beat butter and sugars until light and fluffy; blend in eggs and vanilla. Combine flour, pudding mix and baking soda. Add to butter mixture, blending well. Stir in chocolate chips. Drop dough by teaspoonfuls onto ungreased baking sheets. Bake at 375 degrees for 8 to 10 minutes or until golden. Remove to wire racks to cool. Makes 2 to 3 dozen.

Becky Rowland
Belpre, OH

Whoopie Pies

Not pies at all, but soft, chocolatey cookies!

2 c. sugar
½ c. shortening
2 eggs
1 t. vanilla extract
4 c. all-purpose flour
½ c. baking cocoa
2 t. baking soda
½ t. salt
1 c. milk
1 T. vinegar
1 c. warm water

Blend together sugar, shortening, eggs and vanilla; set aside. Sift together flour, cocoa, baking soda and salt; set aside. Combine milk and vinegar; stir to blend and set aside. Add flour mixture to sugar mixture alternately with milk mixture and warm water. Drop by heaping teaspoonfuls onto lightly greased baking sheets. Bake at 425 degrees for 7 to 10 minutes; let cool. Spread Filling on bottom of half of cookies; top with remaining halves of cookies, flat side down, to make a sandwich. Makes 3 dozen.

Filling:
1½ c. milk
½ c. plus 1½ t. all-purpose flour
2 c. powdered sugar
¾ c. shortening
½ c. butter, softened
1 t. salt
1 t. vanilla extract

Combine milk and flour in a saucepan; heat, stirring until thickened. Refrigerate until chilled. In a mixing bowl, combine chilled milk mixture and remaining ingredients. Beat until fluffy.

Brenda Doak
Delaware, OH

Snowcap Cookies

These look just like mini mountain peaks and are a great make-ahead gift because they freeze so well.

¾ c. butter, softened
1 c. sugar
3 eggs
1 t. vanilla extract
6 1-oz. sqs. white baking chocolate,
    melted and cooled
3½ c. all-purpose flour
1 t. baking powder
1 t. salt
⅛ t. nutmeg
1½ c. chopped walnuts, toasted
powdered sugar

Beat butter and sugar until light and fluffy; add eggs, one at a time, mixing well after each addition. Stir in vanilla; add melted chocolate, blending for 30 seconds. Set mixture aside. Combine flour, baking powder, salt and nutmeg; gradually add to butter mixture. Fold in walnuts. Drop by table-spoonfuls onto greased baking sheets. Bake at 350 degrees for 10 to 12 minutes; remove from pans and cool on wire racks. Sprinkle with powdered sugar. Makes 3 to 4 dozen.

> ## snowcaps in a snow cap!
> Wrap a batch of Snowcap Cookies in clear plastic wrap, then tuck inside a woolly toboggan...add a package of cocoa mix to really chase away the chills.

Magic Bars

You've probably seen many variations of this recipe and each is as wonderful as the other. So put together some magic of your own with this tasty treat.

½ c. butter, melted
1⅓ c. graham cracker crumbs
14-oz. can sweetened condensed milk
1½ c. semi-sweet chocolate chips
1½ c. chopped walnuts

Stir together butter and graham cracker crumbs; press into a greased 13"x9" baking pan. Pour milk over crumb mixture; sprinkle with chocolate chips and walnuts. Bake at 350 degrees for 25 minutes or until edges are golden and bubbly. Cut into bars. Makes 2 dozen.

Melanie Heffner
Beaverton, OR

Magic Bars

Blackberry Lemon
Squares

Blackberry Lemon Squares

2¼ c. all-purpose flour, divided
½ c. powdered sugar
1 c. cold butter, cut into pieces
4 eggs
2 c. sugar, divided
2 t. lemon zest
½ c. fresh lemon juice
1 t. baking powder
¼ t. salt
2 c. blackberries
Garnish: powdered sugar

Line bottom and sides of a 13"x9" baking pan with heavy-duty aluminum foil, allowing 2 to 3 inches to extend over sides; lightly grease foil.

Pulse 2 cups flour, ½ cup powdered sugar and butter in a food processor 5 to 6 times or until mixture is crumbly. Press mixture onto bottom of prepared pan. Bake at 350 degrees on an oven rack one-third up from bottom of oven 25 minutes or just until golden.

Whisk together eggs, 1½ cups sugar, lemon zest and juice in a large bowl until blended. Combine baking powder, salt and remaining flour; whisk into egg mixture until blended. Pour mixture into prepared crust.

Pulse blackberries and remaining sugar in a food processor 3 to 4 times or until blended. Transfer mixture to a small saucepan. Cook over medium-low heat, stirring often, 5 to 6 minutes or until thoroughly heated. Pour through a fine wire-mesh strainer into a bowl, gently pressing blackberry mixture with back of a spoon; discard solids. Drizzle over mixture in pan.

Bake at 350 degrees on middle oven rack 30 to 35 minutes or until filling is set. Let cool in pan on a wire rack 30 minutes. Lift from pan onto wire rack, using foil sides as handles, and let cool 30 minutes or until completely cool. Remove foil, and cut into 2-inch squares; sprinkle with powdered sugar. Makes 2 dozen.

Mom's Italian Biscotti

These biscotti have all of the great flavors of the traditional version but they take much less time to make!

5½ c. all-purpose flour
1½ c. sugar
¾ c. butter, softened
1 T. plus 2 t. baking powder
6 eggs, beaten
zest and juice of 2 lemons
3½ c. powdered sugar

Blend together flour, sugar, butter and baking powder; form a well in center. Add eggs and zest; knead until dough is smooth. Shape dough into 2-inch balls on a floured surface; roll each into a 7-inch rope. Twist into knots; place on lightly greased baking sheets. Bake at 350 degrees for 15 to 18 minutes. Cool on a wire rack. Combine lemon juice and powdered sugar; drizzle over cookies. Makes 3 dozen.

Jeanette Toscano
Pomona, NY

My parents emigrated from Italy in the 1960s and brought this biscotti recipe with them. These cookies have a buttery-light texture with a hint of lemon. On Christmas Eve, children of all ages look forward to dunking them in milk, coffee or tea. —Jeanette

Black-Bottom Banana Bars

Bananas and chocolate are a terrific combination!

½ c. butter, softened
I c. sugar
I egg
I t. vanilla extract
1½ c. bananas, mashed
1½ c. all-purpose flour
I t. baking powder
I t. baking soda
½ t. salt
¼ c. baking cocoa

Beat butter and sugar. Add egg and vanilla. Blend well. Mix in bananas; set aside. Combine flour, baking powder, baking soda and salt; blend into banana mixture. Divide batter in half; add cocoa to one half. Pour vanilla batter into a greased 13"x9" baking pan; spoon chocolate batter on top. Swirl with a knife to make a marble appearance; bake at 350 degrees for 25 minutes. Cut into bars to serve. Makes 2½ to 3 dozen.

Barbara Buckley
Edwards, MS

the right mix
Be sure to let your butter soften before beating with the sugar so no lumps will form. You'll get perfect results every time!

Fudgy Oatmeal Bars

I like to tuck these into my daughters' lunchboxes.

2 c. brown sugar, packed
I c. plus 2 T. butter, softened and divided
2 t. vanilla extract, divided
2 eggs
2½ c. all-purpose flour
I t. baking soda
I t. salt, divided
3 c. quick-cooking oats, uncooked
14-oz. can sweetened condensed milk
12-oz. pkg. semi-sweet chocolate chips
I c. walnuts, chopped

Beat brown sugar and one cup butter until light and fluffy; blend in one teaspoon vanilla and eggs. Sift together flour, baking soda and ½ teaspoon salt; stir in oats and add to egg mixture. Reserve a third of oats mixture; press remaining oats mixture into a greased jelly-roll pan. Heat remaining butter, condensed milk and chocolate chips over low heat, stirring constantly until chocolate is melted; remove from heat. Stir in nuts, remaining vanilla and salt. Spread over oats mixture in pan. Drop reserved oats mixture by rounded teaspoonfuls onto chocolate mixture. Bake at 350 degrees for 25 to 30 minutes or until golden. Cut into bars while warm. Makes 32.

Becky Sykes
Gooseberry Patch

Pumpkin Spice Bars

18¼-oz. pkg. spice cake mix
½ c. plus 1 T. butter, melted and divided
½ c. pecans, finely chopped
1 T. plus 1 t. vanilla extract, divided
8-oz. pkg. cream cheese, softened
⅓ c. light brown sugar, packed
1 c. canned pumpkin
1 egg
½ c. white baking chocolate, finely chopped
⅓ c. long-cooking oats, uncooked
Optional: powdered sugar

Combine cake mix, ½ cup melted butter, pecans and one tablespoon vanilla, mixing well with a fork. Reserve one cup crumbs for streusel topping. Press remaining crumbs into a lightly greased 13"x9" baking pan. Bake at 350 degrees for 13 to 15 minutes or until puffy and set. Cool in pan on a wire rack 20 minutes.

Beat cream cheese at medium speed with an electric mixer 30 seconds or until creamy. Add brown sugar, pumpkin, egg and remaining vanilla; beat until blended. Pour filling over baked crust.

Stir white chocolate, remaining melted butter and oats into reserved streusel. Sprinkle over filling.

Bake at 350 degrees for 30 minutes or until edges begin to brown and center is set. Cool completely in pan on a wire rack. Sprinkle with powdered sugar, if desired. Cut into bars. Serve at room temperature or chilled. Makes 2 dozen.

Pumpkin Spice Bars

The Best Blondies

The Best Blondies

For an extra-special dessert, serve each square topped with a scoop of ice cream and caramel sauce...delicious!

1 c. butter, melted
2 c. brown sugar, packed
2 eggs, beaten
2 t. vanilla extract
2 c. all-purpose flour
½ t. baking powder
¼ t. salt
1 c. chopped pecans
1 c. white chocolate chips
¾ c. toffee or caramel baking bits

Line a 13"x9" baking pan with parchment paper. Spray sides of pan with non-stick vegetable spray and set aside. In a large bowl, mix together butter and brown sugar. Beat in eggs and vanilla until mixture is smooth. Stir in flour, baking powder and salt; mix in pecans, chocolate chips and toffee or baking bits. Pour into prepared pan and spread evenly. Bake at 375 degrees for 30 to 40 minutes or until set in the middle. Allow to cool in pan before cutting into squares. Makes one dozen.

Elizabeth Cisneros
Chino Hills, CA

Buckeye Brownies

Buckeye Brownies

Chocolate and peanut butter...tastes just like buckeye candies.

19½-oz. pkg. brownie mix
2 c. powdered sugar
½ c. plus 6 T. butter, softened and divided
1 c. creamy peanut butter
6-oz. pkg. semi-sweet chocolate chips

Prepare and bake brownie mix in a greased 13"x9" baking pan according to package directions. Let cool.

Mix together powdered sugar, ½ cup butter and peanut butter; spread over cooled brownies. Chill one hour.

Melt together chocolate chips and remaining butter in a saucepan over low heat, stirring occasionally. Spread over brownies. Let cool; cut into squares. Makes 2 to 3 dozen.

Heather Prentice
Mars, PA

---

flea-market find

If you see a vintage cake pan with its own slide-on lid at a tag sale, snap it up! Not only is it indispensable for toting frosted bar cookies to a party, it also makes a clever lap tray for kids to carry along crayons and coloring books on car trips.

Meringue Kisses

*Try piping these out in different holiday shapes...
snowmen are cute with chocolate chips for eyes
and buttons, and cherries for their noses!*

3 egg whites, at room temperature
½ t. cream of tartar
⅔ c. sugar
½ c. mini semi-sweet chocolate chips
½ t. peppermint extract
several drops red or green food coloring

Beat egg whites with an electric mixer on high
speed until foamy; beat in cream of tartar. Slowly
beat in sugar, one tablespoon at a time until dissolved and stiff peaks form. Fold in chocolate
chips, extract and food coloring. Drop mixture
by teaspoonfuls onto parchment paper-lined
baking sheets. Bake at 275 degrees for 30 minutes;
turn off oven and leave overnight. Store in an
airtight container at room temperature. Makes
2 to 3 dozen.

Candy Hannigan
Monument, CO

Butterscotch Candy

Looking for a sweet treat? This will hit the spot!

2 c. sugar
¼ c. butter
¼ c. water
1 T. white vinegar

Combine ingredients in a heavy saucepan; cook
over medium heat until mixture reaches soft-crack
stage, or 270 to 290 degrees on a candy thermometer. Pour into a buttered 15"x10" jelly-roll pan;
set aside to cool. Cut into squares to serve. Makes
about one pound.

Caramel-Coffee Tassies

In a word...delectable!

½ c. butter, softened
3-oz. pkg. cream cheese, softened
1 c. all-purpose flour
14-oz. pkg. caramels
¼ c. evaporated milk
1½ t. coffee liqueur or brewed coffee

Beat butter and cream cheese together until
well blended; stir in flour. Form into a ball; chill
for one hour or overnight.
Shape dough into ½-inch balls; press each into
an ungreased mini muffin cup. Bake at 350 degrees
for 10 to 15 minutes or until golden. Let cool.
Combine caramels and evaporated milk in a
saucepan over medium heat. Stir frequently until
melted. Remove from heat; stir in liqueur or
coffee. Spoon caramel filling into baked shells;
let cool. Pipe Frosting onto caramel filling.
Makes about 2 dozen.

Frosting:
½ c. shortening
⅓ c. sugar
⅓ c. evaporated milk, chilled
½ t. coffee liqueur or brewed coffee

Blend shortening and sugar until fluffy; add
evaporated milk and liqueur or coffee. Beat at
medium-high speed with an electric mixer for 7 to
10 minutes until fluffy.

Staci Meyers
Cocoa, FL

Caramel-Coffee Tassies

Marshmallow Pops

Marshmallow Pops

Keep a variety of candy sprinkles on hand for this super quick & easy lunchbox or after-school treat!

10-oz. pkg. marshmallows
12 white craft sticks
12-oz. pkg. semi-sweet chocolate chips
2 T. shortening
Garnish: candy sprinkles, toasted
    coconut, chopped nuts

Thread 2 marshmallows onto each craft stick; set aside. Melt chocolate chips and shortening in a heavy saucepan over low heat, stirring constantly. Dip marshmallows into chocolate; sprinkle with favorite garnish. Cool on wax paper; store in refrigerator. Makes one dozen.

Judi Gause
Jacksonville Beach, FL

County Fair Taffy

An old-fashioned favorite that's fun to give… and fun to make!

1 c. molasses
1 c. sugar
2 t. white vinegar
2 T. butter
½ t. baking soda
⅛ t. salt

Combine molasses, sugar and vinegar in a large saucepan; cook to hard-ball stage, or 250 to 265 degrees on a candy thermometer. Remove from heat and stir in butter, baking soda and salt; stir until foaming stops. Pour into a buttered 13"x9" baking pan; allow to cool. With buttered hands, pull taffy back and forth until taffy loses shine. Roll taffy into long ropes and cut into desired pieces with scissors. Wrap individually in wax paper. Makes 4 dozen.

Candy Cane Puffs

Just right for giving, these look so pretty in a Christmas tin.

2½ c. all-purpose flour
¼ t. salt
½ c. butter, softened
1 c. powdered sugar
1 egg
1 t. vanilla extract
½ t. peppermint extract
11-oz. pkg. white chocolate chips
½ c. peppermint candies, crushed

Combine flour and salt; set aside.
Blend together butter and sugar; beat in egg and extracts. Mix into flour mixture using low speed of an electric mixer. Wrap dough in plastic wrap; refrigerate for one hour.
Shape dough into walnut-size balls; place on lightly greased baking sheets. Bake at 375 degrees for 10 to 12 minutes; cool. Melt white chocolate chips in a double boiler; dip cooled cookies into melted chocolate. Roll in crushed peppermint candy; set on wax paper until hardened. Makes about 3 dozen.

Kristine Marumoto
Sandy, UT

Candy Cane Puffs

Peanut Butter Fudge

This is easy to make and so creamy! It's a great gift for friends.

4½ c. sugar
1⅔ c. evaporated milk
½ c. butter
2 c. crunchy peanut butter
1 c. creamy peanut butter
8 oz. marshmallow creme
2 t. vanilla extract

Combine sugar, milk and butter in a large saucepan. Bring to a boil over medium heat; cook for 8 minutes, stirring constantly. Remove from heat and stir in peanut butter, marshmallow creme and vanilla. Pour into a buttered 13"x9" pan. Let cool in pan. Cut into squares, wrap individually and box for gifts, or store and cut as needed. Makes 5 pounds.

Judy Kelly
St. Charles, MO

Never-Fail Caramels

2 c. sugar
1 c. brown sugar, packed
1 c. corn syrup
1 c. evaporated milk
2 c. whipping cream
1 c. butter
1½ t. vanilla extract

Combine all ingredients except vanilla in a heavy saucepan. Cook over medium-high heat, stirring constantly, until caramel reaches firm-ball stage, or 244 to 248 degrees on a candy thermometer. Remove from heat and stir in vanilla. Pour mixture into a buttered 15"x10" jelly-roll pan; cool. Cut caramel into small squares and wrap individually in wax paper. Makes 4 to 5 dozen.

Martha Washingtons

You'll absolutely love this old-fashioned chocolate candy that's chock-full of coconut, nuts and creamy milk...yum!

1 c. butter, melted and cooled
14-oz. can sweetened condensed milk
2 c. powdered sugar
2 c. pecans or walnuts, chopped
14-oz. pkg. sweetened flaked coconut
20-oz. pkg. melting chocolate, chopped

Combine all ingredients except chocolate; mix well and chill overnight. Roll into balls the size of marbles; set on wax paper-lined baking sheets or trays. Microwave chocolate in a microwave-safe bowl at high for one to 2 minutes, stirring every 30 seconds until smooth. Dip balls into chocolate and return to wax paper to cool. Makes about 6 dozen.

Renee Velderman
Hopkins, MI

Even if my mom doesn't make any other Christmas candy, she must make this one to please her children. –Renee

Martha
Washingtons

Chocolate Granola Brittle

The beauty of this recipe is that you can make a decadent brittle in the microwave in half the time it takes to make the traditional candy.

1 c. sugar
½ c. light corn syrup
⅛ t. salt
1 c. pecans, coarsely chopped
1 T. butter
1 t. vanilla extract
1 t. baking soda
¾ c. chocolate granola
3 1-oz. sqs. semi-sweet baking chocolate
1½ T. shortening

Combine first 3 ingredients in a 2-quart glass bowl. Microwave at high 5 minutes. Stir in pecans. Microwave 1½ minutes. Stir in butter and vanilla. Microwave one minute and 45 seconds or until candy is the color of peanut butter. Stir in baking soda; mixture will bubble.

Quickly pour candy onto a lightly greased rimless baking sheet. Pour as thinly as possible without spreading candy. Cover brittle quickly with parchment paper and use a rolling pin to thin out candy; peel off paper. Sprinkle granola over brittle. Replace paper and use rolling pin to press granola into brittle; peel off paper. Cool brittle completely; break into pieces.

Place chocolate squares and shortening in a small bowl. Microwave at high 1½ to 2 minutes, stirring after one minute. Dip each piece of brittle halfway into chocolate mixture. Place dipped brittle on parchment paper to harden. Store in an airtight container. Makes about one pound.

helpful tip
If you want to make more than one pound, don't double the recipe...it won't give you the same result. Just make it twice.

Chocolate Granola Brittle

Chocolate Truffles

Keep plenty on hand for drop-in guests or wrap up several for the newspaper and letter carriers.

8 1-oz. sqs. unsweetened baking chocolate
⅓ c. plus 2 T. half-and-half, divided
⅓ c. butter-flavored shortening
3 egg yolks
⅓ c. powdered sugar
⅔ c. finely chopped pecans

In a medium saucepan, melt chocolate over low heat, stirring constantly. Gradually stir ⅓ cup half-and-half into melted chocolate; stir until smooth. Add shortening; stir until melted. Remove from heat. Stir one tablespoon chocolate mixture into egg yolks; add yolk mixture, powdered sugar and remaining half-and-half to saucepan. Beat with an electric mixer at high speed until well blended. Refrigerate for 2 hours or until firm. Shape into one-inch balls; roll in nuts. Refrigerate until serving time. Makes 2 to 2½ dozen.

Margaret Hanson-Maddox
Montpelier, IN

candy chemistry

For candy making at high altitudes, keep in mind that for every 500 feet above sea level, you'll need to decrease the temperature by one degree. For example, if you live at 3500 feet and the recipe calls for cooking candy to 234 degrees, simply cook it to 227 degrees.

Nutty Maple Candy

Cut into leaves with mini cookie cutters for a fall celebration.

12-oz. pkg. semi-sweet chocolate chips
11-oz. pkg. butterscotch chips
12-oz. jar creamy peanut butter
1 c. butter
½ c. evaporated milk
3-oz. pkg. cook & serve vanilla pudding mix
1½ T. maple flavoring
2 t. vanilla extract
2-lb. pkg. powdered sugar
3 c. chopped peanuts

Combine chocolate and butterscotch chips in a microwave-safe bowl. Microwave at high one to 2 minutes, stirring every 30 seconds until smooth. Add peanut butter, stirring until smooth. Spread 1¾ cups mixture into a buttered 15"x10" jelly-roll pan; refrigerate until firm. Set aside remaining mixture.

Melt butter in a heavy saucepan; stir in milk and pudding mix. Heat over medium heat until thickened; remove from heat. Add maple flavoring and vanilla; stir in powdered sugar. Spread over chilled chocolate mixture; return to refrigerator. Reheat remaining chocolate mixture in microwave, if necessary; stir in peanuts. Carefully spread over pudding mixture; refrigerate until firm. Cut into squares. Makes about 5 dozen.

Mint Petites

¼ c. sugar
1 c. butter, softened
¼ to ½ t. peppermint extract
½ t. vanilla extract
2 c. all-purpose flour
Garnish: vanilla or chocolate frosting,
    peppermint or chocolate
    mint candies

In a large bowl, blend sugar and butter together until fluffy. Add extracts; mix well. Stir in flour and blend well. Shape into one-inch balls; place on ungreased baking sheets and flatten slightly. Bake at 375 degrees for 12 minutes or until lightly golden. Let cool. Frost and sprinkle with crushed peppermint candies, or top with chocolate mints cut into triangles. Makes 2 to 3 dozen.

Debbie Pecore
Charlton, MA

Angel Candy

24-oz. pkg. white or chocolate
    melting chocolate, broken
2 c. sweetened corn & oats cereal
2 c. stick pretzels, broken into
    small pieces
2 c. roasted peanuts or pecans

Heat chocolate in a large saucepan over very low heat until melted, stirring constantly. Remove from heat; add remaining ingredients, stirring until well coated. Drop mixture by tablespoonfuls onto wax paper-lined baking sheets. Let cool; store in an airtight container. Makes 3 to 4 dozen.

Vickie Lowrey
Fallon, NV

Salty Chocolate-Pecan Candy

This crunchy candy will soften slightly while at room temperature.

1 c. pecans, coarsely chopped
3 4-oz. bars bittersweet chocolate
    baking bars
3 4-oz. white chocolate
    baking bars
1 t. coarse sea salt or or ¾ t. kosher salt

Place pecans in a single layer on a baking sheet. Bake at 350 degrees for 8 to 10 minutes or until toasted. Reduce oven temperature to 225 degrees.

Line a 17"x12" jelly-roll pan with parchment paper. Break each chocolate bar into 8 equal squares, making 48 squares total. Arrange in a checkerboard pattern in pan, alternating white and dark chocolate. (Pieces will touch.)

Bake at 225 degrees for 5 minutes or just until chocolate is melted. Remove pan to a wire rack. Swirl chocolates into a marble pattern using a wooden pick. Sprinkle evenly with toasted pecans and salt.

Chill one hour or until firm. Break into pieces. Store in an airtight container in refrigerator up to one month. Makes 1¾ pounds.

good neighbor surprise
Make a cone shape from pretty scrapbook paper. Glue in place. Punch a hole in each side of the cone and slide ribbon or rick rack through to make a handle; tie each end to secure. Place a bag filled with your favorite homemade candy into cone and leave on the doorknob for your neighbor to find!

Salty Chocolate-Pecan Candy

No-Knead
Oatmeal Bread
(page 275)

Chocolate Buttermilk
Biscuits (page 295)

Jumbo Quiche Muffins
(page 292)

Maple Nut Twist (page 275)

BOUNTIFUL BREADS

Sweet & savory rolls, muffins,
quick breads and more

That Yummy Bread

That Yummy Bread

1 c. milk
2 T. sugar
¼ c. shortening
2½ t. salt
1 c. warm water (110 to 115 degrees)
2 envs. active dry yeast
7 c. all-purpose flour, divided
2 eggs, beaten and divided
1 to 2 T. butter, melted

In a saucepan, heat milk just to boiling; stir in sugar, shortening and salt. Cool to lukewarm and set aside. Combine water and yeast, stirring to dissolve, and add to milk mixture. Pour into a bowl and add 4 cups flour; stir and beat. Gradually add remaining flour; stir. Let dough rest 10 minutes; turn dough out onto a floured surface and knead until smooth. Place dough in a greased bowl, turning to coat. Cover and let rise in a warm place (85 degrees), free from drafts, until double in bulk. Punch down dough; shape into 2 balls. Roll each ball into a ¼-inch thick 15-inch by 9-inch rectangle. Brush with one egg, reserving remainder for filling. Spread Herb Filling to one inch from edges of dough; roll up jelly-roll style, starting at short edge. Pinch edges to seal; place in 2 greased 9"x5" loaf pans, seam-side down. Brush with butter; cover and let rise in a warm place 55 minutes, until double in bulk. Slash tops of loaves with a knife; bake at 375 degrees for one hour. Let cool on a wire rack before slicing. Makes 2 loaves.

Herb Filling:
2 c. fresh parsley, chopped
2 c. green onions, chopped
1 clove garlic, minced
2 T. butter
¾ t. salt
pepper and hot pepper sauce to taste

Sauté parsley, onions and garlic in butter; cool slightly. Add reserved egg from main recipe. Add salt, pepper and hot pepper sauce.

Francie Stutzman
Dayton, OH

Butterscotch Banana Bread

3½ c. all-purpose flour
4 t. baking powder
1 t. baking soda
1 t. cinnamon
1 t. nutmeg
2 c. bananas, mashed
1½ c. sugar
½ c. butter, melted
2 eggs
½ c. milk
11-oz. pkg. butterscotch chips, melted

Combine first 6 ingredients in a large bowl; set aside. Beat sugar and butter in a large mixing bowl, beating at medium speed with an electric mixer until light and fluffy; add eggs. Gradually add flour mixture to sugar mixture alternately with milk, beginning and ending with flour mixture, until blended. Fold in butterscotch chips; pour batter evenly into 2 greased and floured 9"x5" loaf pans. Bake at 350 degrees for one hour to one hour and 10 minutes or until a wooden pick inserted in center comes out clean. Cool in pans 15 minutes; remove from pans to wire racks to cool. Serve warm or cold. Makes 2 loaves.

Claire McGeough
Lebanon, NJ

Autumn Spice Bread

When I was growing up, my mother made this every Thanksgiving and Christmas. The smell of it lingering throughout the house would be a sure sign fall was in the air and would have our family lining up at the oven door! Now my sister and I carry on this scrumptious tradition for our families.

3½ c. all-purpose flour
2 t. baking soda
2 t. cinnamon
1 t. salt
1 t. nutmeg
½ t. ground ginger
½ t. ground cloves
1 c. butter, softened
2 c. sugar
2 c. canned pumpkin
4 eggs, beaten
1½ c. semi-sweet chocolate chips
2 c. chopped walnuts, divided

Grease two, 9"x5" loaf pans; set aside. Combine flour and next 6 ingredients. Beat butter, sugar and pumpkin until light and fluffy; blend in eggs. Add flour mixture to egg mixture, beating at low speed with an electric mixer until blended. Stir in chocolate chips and one cup walnuts. Pour into loaf pans and sprinkle with ½ cup walnuts. Bake at 350 degrees for one to 1½ hours. Let cool in pans for 5 minutes. Remove from pans to a wire rack. Spread Spice Glaze over warm loaves. Sprinkle with remaining walnuts. Makes 2 loaves.

Spice Glaze:
1 c. powdered sugar
¼ t. nutmeg
¼ t. cinnamon
2 to 3 t. whipping cream or milk

Combine dry ingredients; blend in cream or milk until mixture is desired consistency.

Lisa Lepak
Suamico, WI

Chocolate Bread

1¼ c. milk
½ c. water
1 env. active dry yeast
4½ c. all-purpose flour, divided
½ c. baking cocoa
¼ c. sugar
1 t. salt
1 egg
2 T. butter, softened
2 4-oz. semi-sweet chocolate baking bars, chopped
1½ T. turbinado sugar

Heat milk and water until warm (110 to 115 degrees). Combine milk, water and yeast in a large bowl; whisk until smooth. Let stand 5 minutes. Stir 2 cups flour, cocoa, sugar and salt into yeast mixture; beat at medium speed with an electric mixer until smooth. Beat in egg, butter and 2 cups flour until a soft dough forms.

Turn dough out onto a floured surface. Knead until smooth and elastic, about 6 minutes, adding remaining ½ cup flour, one tablespoon at a time as needed, to prevent dough from sticking. Fold in chopped chocolate during last minute of kneading.

Place dough in a large, lightly greased bowl, turning to coat top. Cover with plastic wrap; let rise in a warm place (85 degrees), free from drafts, one hour and 40 minutes or until double in bulk.

Punch down dough. Divide dough in half; gently shape each portion into an 8-inch by 4-inch oval. Place dough in 2 lightly greased 8½"x4½" loaf pans. Cover and let rise 1½ hours or until double in bulk.

Sprinkle loaves with turbinado sugar. Bake at 375 degrees for 25 minutes or until loaves sound hollow when tapped. Remove from pans. Let cool on a wire rack. Makes 2 loaves.

Chocolate Bread

No-Knead
Oatmeal Bread

No-Knead Oatmeal Bread

Spread peanut butter or softened butter on this slightly sweet and so-yummy favorite.

2 envs. active dry yeast
½ c. warm water (110 to 115 degrees)
1 c. quick-cooking oats, uncooked
½ c. light molasses
⅓ c. shortening
1½ c. boiling water
1 T. salt
6¼ c. all-purpose flour, divided
2 eggs, beaten

In a small bowl, dissolve yeast in warm water; let stand about 5 minutes. In a large bowl, combine oats, molasses, shortening, boiling water and salt; stir until shortening is melted. Cool until lukewarm. Stir in 2 cups flour; add eggs and beat well. Stir in yeast mixture. Add remaining flour, 2 cups at a time, mixing well after each addition until a stiff dough forms. Beat vigorously until smooth, about 10 minutes. Place dough in a lightly greased bowl, turning to coat top. Cover tightly; place in refrigerator at least 2 hours to overnight. Turn dough out onto a floured surface. Form into 2 loaves; place seam-side down in greased 8"x4" loaf pans. Cover; let rise in a warm place (85 degrees), free from drafts, 2 hours or until double in bulk. Bake at 375 degrees for about 40 minutes. If top begins to brown too fast, cover with aluminum foil during last half of baking time. Makes 2 loaves.

Hattie Douthit
Crawford, NE

"I've been making this bread since I was a little girl. –Hattie

Maple Nut Twist

(Pictured on page 268)

½ c. milk
½ c. butter, divided
1 env. active dry yeast
¼ c. warm water (110 to 115 degrees)
⅓ c. plus 3 T. sugar, divided
1½ t. salt
2 eggs, beaten
3¼ to 3½ c. plus 2 T. all-purpose flour, divided
½ c. brown sugar, packed
½ c. chopped walnuts
¼ c. maple syrup
½ t. cinnamon
½ t. maple extract
1 c. powdered sugar
1 to 2 T. water

In a saucepan, heat milk and ¼ cup butter until butter is melted. In a large bowl, dissolve yeast in warm water. Add 3 tablespoons sugar, salt, eggs and 2 cups flour; beat until smooth. Blend in milk mixture. Add 1¼ to 1½ cups flour until dough forms; knead until smooth. Cover and let rise in a warm place (85 degrees), free from drafts, 2 hours or until double in bulk. In a medium bowl, combine brown sugar, walnuts, remaining sugar, maple syrup, remaining softened butter, remaining 2 tablespoons flour and cinnamon; set aside. Punch dough down and divide in half; roll out each half into a 14-inch by 8-inch rectangle. Spread walnut filling over each rectangle. Starting at long side, roll up dough jelly-roll style. With a sharp knife, cut down the center of the jelly-roll lengthwise; twist 2 pieces together to form a rope braid. Turn ends under and shape braid into a ring. Place dough in a greased 9" pie plate and let rise in a warm place one hour or until double in bulk. Bake at 350 degrees for 30 minutes or until golden. Mix together remaining ingredients; drizzle over warm bread. Serves 16 to 20.

Gay Snyder
Deerfield, OH

Zucchini Bread

4 eggs
2 c. sugar
1 c. applesauce
2 t. oil
2 t. water
3 c. all-purpose flour
2 c. zucchini, shredded
1 c. chopped pecans
2 t. baking soda
1½ t. salt
1 t. cinnamon
1 t. vanilla extract
½ t. baking powder

Beat eggs, sugar, applesauce, oil and water together in a mixing bowl. Add remaining ingredients and mix well. Pour batter into 2 greased and floured 9"x5" loaf pans. Bake at 350 degrees for 45 minutes to one hour or until a wooden pick inserted in center comes out clean. Cool on a wire rack. Makes 2 loaves.

Michelle Hawkins
Radcliff, KY

pretty planter
Reuse a butter dish as a windowsill planter. Simply turn over the lid, set it on the dish and plant with a tiny, low-growing herb like thyme.

Pull-Apart Pizza Bread

12-oz. tube refrigerated flaky biscuits, quartered
1 T. olive oil
12 slices pepperoni, quartered
¼ c. shredded mozzarella cheese
¼ c. grated Parmesan cheese
1 onion, chopped
1 t. Italian seasoning
¼ t. garlic salt

Brush biscuits with oil; set aside. Combine remaining ingredients in a bowl; add biscuits. Toss well; arrange in a Bundt® pan lined with well-greased aluminum foil. Bake at 400 degrees for 15 minutes. Pull bread apart to serve. Makes about 2 dozen.

Sallyann Cortese
Sewickley, PA

Irish Soda Bread

3½ c. all-purpose flour
¼ c. sugar
4 t. baking powder
1 t. baking soda
1 t. salt
2 T. butter, melted
1 egg
2 c. buttermilk
8-oz. pkg. raisins
3 T. caraway seed

Combine flour, sugar, baking powder, baking soda and salt in a mixing bowl. Add butter, egg and buttermilk; stir until well combined. Mix in raisins and caraway seed. Pour into a greased 8" round cake pan or 8"x4" loaf pan. Bake at 325 degrees for 55 minutes to one hour or until top is cracked and golden. Cool on a wire rack. Makes one loaf.

Michelle Murphy
Madison, CT

Fiesta Cornbread

Anadama Bread

A hearty brown bread with a crunchy crust but soft inside.

½ c. cornmeal
2 c. boiling water
2 T. shortening
½ c. molasses
I t. salt
I env. active dry yeast
½ c. warm water (110 to 115 degrees)
6 c. all-purpose flour

Stir cornmeal slowly into boiling water; mix well. Add shortening, molasses and salt; set aside to cool. Dissolve yeast in warm water; let stand 5 minutes. Add yeast mixture to cornmeal mixture alternately with flour until blended. Knead until smooth and elastic and place in large greased bowl, turning to coat top. Cover and let rise in a warm place (85 degrees), free from drafts, until double in bulk. Punch down dough; turn dough out onto a floured surface and divide in half. Knead and shape into 2 loaves. Place in greased 9"x5" loaf pans; cover and let rise again until double in bulk. Bake at 375 degrees for one hour. Cool on a wire rack. Makes 2 loaves.

April Hale
Kirkwood, NY

Fiesta Cornbread

If you'd like, shred Pepper Jack cheese and substitute for the Cheddar...it will add more kick!

I c. cornmeal
I c. buttermilk
8-oz. can creamed corn
2 jalapeño peppers, chopped
½ t. salt
¾ t. baking soda
2 eggs, beaten
I onion, chopped
¼ c. oil
I c. shredded Cheddar cheese, divided

Combine first 8 ingredients; set aside. Heat oil in an 8" to 10" cast-iron skillet; pour in half the batter. Sprinkle with half the cheese; pour remaining batter over top. Sprinkle with remaining cheese; bake at 400 degrees for 30 minutes. Serves 6 to 9.

Kathryn Harris
Lufkin, TX

kid-friendly project
The kids can make homemade butter in no time...wonderful on still-warm slices of bread! Just fill a jar with heavy cream, add a tight-fitting lid and roll or shake until the butter forms.

Orange Coffee Rolls

1 env. active dry yeast
¼ c. warm water (110 to 115 degrees)
1 c. sugar, divided
2 eggs
½ c. sour cream
¼ c. plus 2 T. butter, melted
1 t. salt
2¾ to 3 c. all-purpose flour
2 T. butter, melted and divided
1 c. sweetened flaked coconut,
    toasted and divided
2 T. orange zest

Combine yeast and warm water in a bowl; let stand 5 minutes. Add ¼ cup sugar and next 4 ingredients; beat at medium speed with an electric mixer until blended. Gradually stir in enough flour to make a soft dough. Turn dough out onto a well-floured surface; knead until smooth and elastic, about 5 minutes. Place in a well-greased bowl, turning to coat top. Cover and let rise in a warm place (85 degrees), free from drafts, 1½ hours or until double in bulk. Punch dough down and divide in half. Roll one portion into a 12-inch circle; brush with one tablespoon melted butter. Combine remaining sugar, ¾ cup coconut and orange zest; sprinkle half of mixture over dough. Cut into 12 wedges; roll up each wedge, beginning at wide end. Place in a greased 13"x9" baking pan, point side down. Repeat with remaining dough, butter and coconut mixture. Cover and let rise in a warm place, free from drafts, 45 minutes or until double in bulk. Bake at 350 degrees for 25 to 30 minutes or until golden. Cover with aluminum foil after 15 minutes to prevent excessive browning, if necessary. Spoon warm Glaze over warm rolls; sprinkle with remaining coconut. Makes 2 dozen.

Glaze:
¾ c. sugar
½ c. sour cream
¼ c. butter
2 t. orange juice

Combine all ingredients in a small saucepan; bring to a boil. Boil 3 minutes, stirring occasionally. Let cool slightly. Makes 1⅓ cups.

Blueberry & Cheese Coffee Cake

½ c. plus 2 T. butter, softened and
 divided
1¾ c. sugar, divided
2 eggs
2½ c. all-purpose flour, divided
1 t. baking powder
1 t. salt
¾ c. milk
¼ c. water
2 c. fresh blueberries
8-oz. pkg. cream cheese, cut into
 ¼-inch cubes
2 T. lemon zest

Beat ½ cup butter at medium speed with an electric mixer until creamy; gradually add 1¼ cups sugar, beating well. Add eggs, one at a time, beating until blended after each addition.

Combine 2 cups flour, baking powder and salt; stir well. Combine milk and water; stir well. Add flour mixture to butter mixture alternately with milk mixture, beginning and ending with flour mixture. Mix at low speed after each addition until mixture is blended. Gently stir in blueberries and cream cheese. Pour batter into a greased 9"x9" baking pan.

Combine remaining flour, remaining sugar, lemon zest and remaining butter; stir well with a fork. Sprinkle mixture over batter. Bake at 375 degrees for 55 minutes or until golden. Serve warm or let cool completely on a wire rack. Serves 16.

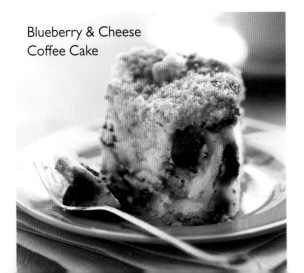

Blueberry & Cheese
Coffee Cake

Nan's Cinnamon Rolls

This recipe was handed down to me nearly fifty years ago by my sister-in-law, who got the recipe from her mother, my mother-in-law. These cinnamon rolls are always the most requested by my family & friends at Christmastime.

3 c. all-purpose flour
2½ t. baking powder
1 c. sugar, divided
2 eggs, beaten
½ c. milk
½ c. butter, softened
1 T. cinnamon

Sift together flour and baking powder; add ½ cup sugar. In a separate bowl, mix eggs, milk and butter. Add egg mixture to flour mixture; mix and knead together to form a soft dough. On a floured surface, roll out dough to ¼-inch thickness into a 15-inch by 10-inch rectangle. In a small bowl, combine cinnamon and remaining sugar; sprinkle over dough. Roll up dough jelly-roll style; slice ½-inch thick. Place on ungreased baking sheets. Bake at 350 degrees for 15 to 20 minutes, or until golden. Serve warm. Makes 2 dozen.

Ann Lyons
Ontario, Canada

tasty trivia
The American tradition of serving coffee and sweet cake along with gossip actually evolved from the tradition of English tea.

Soft Bread Pretzels

These are a very easy project for kids of all ages...
try shaping them into long bread sticks or even letter
shapes. Be creative!

1 env. active dry yeast
1 T. sugar
1½ c. warm water (110 to 115 degrees)
4 c. all-purpose flour
1 t. salt
1 egg, beaten
coarse salt to taste

Dissolve yeast and sugar in water in a mixing bowl; let stand 5 minutes. Blend in flour and salt. Turn dough out onto a lightly floured surface; knead until smooth. Cut dough into 10 to 12 pieces. Roll each into a long rope. Twist into pretzel shape or desired shape. Arrange pretzels on a greased baking sheet. Brush tops with egg. Sprinkle coarse salt on top. Bake at 425 degrees for about 15 minutes or until golden. Makes 10 to 12.

Lisa Cook
Amherst, WI

flavored butter
Stir together softened butter and your favorite chopped herbs from the garden or, for a sweet variety, stir in cinnamon sugar or honey. Everyone will love this extra treat to spread on homemade rolls!

Old-Fashioned Potato Rolls

Soft, delicious rolls...great for dinner or split for
sandwiches.

1 env. active dry yeast
3 T. sugar, divided
⅓ c. warm water (110 to 115 degrees)
1 c. potatoes, cooked and mashed
⅔ c. sour cream
6 T. butter, divided, melted and cooled
2 t. salt
2 eggs
4 to 4½ c. all-purpose flour

Combine yeast and one tablespoon sugar in warm water in a large bowl; let stand 5 to 10 minutes until foamy. Mix together mashed potatoes, sour cream, ¼ cup butter, remaining sugar, salt and eggs; stir into yeast mixture. Add flour to yeast mixture, ½ cup at a time, beating at low speed with an electric mixer until a stiff dough forms. Place dough on a lightly floured surface and knead 5 to 10 minutes. Place dough in a large greased bowl, turning to coat top. Cover loosely with a cloth and let rise in a warm place (85 degrees), free from drafts, about one hour or until double in bulk. Punch down dough and roll into a long rope; cut rope in 12 equal pieces. Roll each piece into a ball and place balls of dough in a greased 13"x9" baking pan. Brush tops of rolls with remaining melted butter; cover and let rise in a warm place 45 minutes or until double in bulk. Bake at 375 degrees for 20 minutes or until golden. Makes one dozen.

Geneva Rogers
Gillette, WY

Golden Butter Rolls

1 c. milk
1¼ c. butter, divided
1 env. active dry yeast
½ c. plus 1 t. sugar, divided
½ c. warm water (110 to 115 degrees)
1 t. salt
3 eggs, beaten
1 c. whole-wheat flour
3½ to 4 cups all-purpose flour

In a heavy saucepan, heat milk and ½ cup butter. Remove from heat and cool. In a small bowl, dissolve yeast and one teaspoon sugar in warm water. When mixture foams, add to a large mixing bowl with remaining sugar, salt, eggs and flours. Add the cooled milk mixture and blend until smooth. Turn dough out onto a lightly floured surface; knead until smooth and elastic. Place in a large greased bowl, turning to coat top; brush top of dough with ¼ cup softened butter. Cover and let rise in a warm place (85 degrees), free from drafts, until double in bulk. Divide dough into 3 portions. Roll each portion into a ½-inch thick circle. Cut each circle into 10 to 12 pie-shaped wedges. Roll up each wedge beginning at wide end and place one inch apart on a greased baking sheet. Brush tops of each roll with ¼ cup softened butter; let rise until double in bulk. Bake at 375 degrees for 15 to 20 minutes or until golden. Remove and brush with remaining butter while rolls are still warm. Makes 2½ to 3 dozen.

Susan Ingersoll
Cleveland, OH

Golden Butter Rolls

Whole-Wheat
Popovers

Whole-Wheat Popovers

Also called Laplanders and puff pops, popovers are considered an American version of England's Yorkshire pudding.

½ c. all-purpose flour
½ c. whole-wheat flour
¼ t. salt
1 c. 2% reduced-fat milk
2 eggs
2 egg whites
1 T. oil

Combine first 3 ingredients in a medium bowl. Whisk together remaining ingredients. Whisk milk mixture into flour mixture, whisking until smooth. Place a popover pan or six 8-ounce custard cups heavily coated with non-stick vegetable spray on a baking sheet. Place in a 425-degree oven 3 minutes or until hot. Remove baking sheet from oven and fill cups ½ full with batter.

Bake at 425 degrees for 30 minutes. Turn oven off; remove pan from oven. Cut a small slit in top of each popover; return to oven. Let popovers stand in closed oven 3 minutes. Serve immediately. Makes 6.

Lemon Fans

For a little variety…try using orange zest instead of lemon zest!

2 envs. active dry yeast
¼ c. warm water (110 to 115 degrees)
1 c. milk
2 eggs
⅓ c. sugar
2 t. lemon zest
1½ t. salt
4 to 4½ c. all-purpose flour
¼ c. butter, melted and divided

In a large bowl, dissolve yeast in water. Let stand about 5 to 10 minutes or until foamy. In a small bowl, mix together milk and eggs. Stir milk mixture, sugar, lemon zest and salt into yeast mixture. Using a heavy-duty electric mixer fitted with a paddle attachment and set on low speed, beat in flour, ½ cup at a time, until a dough forms. Turn dough out onto a floured surface. Knead until smooth and elastic, about 5 to 10 minutes, adding more flour to prevent sticking. Place dough in a large greased bowl, turning to coat top. Cover loosely with a damp cloth; let rise in a warm place (85 degrees), free from drafts, about one hour or until double in bulk. Divide dough in half. On a floured surface, using a floured rolling pin, roll each dough half into ⅛-inch thick rectangle. Brush with 2 tablespoons butter. Cut each rectangle crosswise into 1½-inch wide strips. Stack 6 strips on top of each other. Cut each stack crosswise into twelve, 1½-inch squares. To prepare rolls, place 6 dough squares, cut-side down, in each greased muffin cup. Brush tops with remaining butter. Cover; let rise in a warm place about 20 minutes or until almost double in bulk. Bake at 400 degrees for 10 to 15 minutes or until golden. Transfer pans to wire racks to cool slightly. Remove rolls and cool completely on wire racks. Makes 2 dozen.

Cindy Neel
Gooseberry Patch

Herb Biscuits Supreme

You'll never make biscuits any other way once you've tried these!

1½ c. all-purpose flour
3 t. baking powder
¼ t. salt
¼ t. cream of tartar
1 t. sugar
½ t. dill weed
1½ t. dried chives
1 c. whipping cream

Combine flour, baking powder, salt, cream of tartar and sugar; stir in dill weed and chives. Add cream; stir with a fork until just moistened. Turn dough out onto a floured surface; knead 3 or 4 times. Roll out to a ¾-inch thickness; cut into rounds with a biscuit cutter. Place side by side on an ungreased baking sheet. (Dough rounds should touch.) Bake at 450 degrees for 10 to 12 minutes or until lightly golden. Makes 8.

La Verne Fang
Delavan, IL

easy how-to
Making biscuits and there's no biscuit cutter handy? Try Mom's little trick... just grab a glass tumbler or the open end of a clean, empty soup can.

Pimento Cheese Biscuits

1 c. shredded sharp Cheddar cheese
2¼ c. self-rising flour
½ c. chilled butter, cut into ¼-inch thick slices
1 c. buttermilk
4-oz. jar diced pimentos, drained
additional self-rising flour
2 T. butter, melted

Combine cheese and 2¼ cups flour in a large bowl. Sprinkle butter slices over cheese mixture; toss gently. Cut butter into flour with a pastry blender until crumbly and mixture resembles small peas. Cover and chill 10 minutes.

Combine buttermilk and diced pimentos; add buttermilk mixture to flour mixture, stirring just until dry ingredients are moistened.

Turn dough out onto a lightly floured surface; knead 3 or 4 times, gradually adding additional flour as needed. With floured hands, press or pat dough into a ¾-inch thick rectangle about 9-inch by 5-inch. Sprinkle top of dough with additional flour. Fold dough over onto itself in 3 sections, starting with one short end. (Fold dough rectangle as if folding a letter-size piece of paper.) Repeat procedure 2 more times, beginning with pressing into a ¾-inch thick dough rectangle (about 9-inch by 5-inch).

Press or pat dough to ½-inch thickness on a lightly floured surface. Cut with a 2-inch round cutter; place side by side on a parchment paper-lined or lightly greased 15"x10" jelly-roll pan. Dough rounds should touch.

Bake at 450 degrees for 13 to 15 minutes, or until lightly golden. Remove from oven and brush with melted butter. Makes 2½ dozen.

Pimento Cheese
Biscuits

Mom's Sweet Potato Biscuits

Serve these biscuits with ham...delicious!

2 c. self-rising flour
3 T. brown sugar, packed
¼ t. cinnamon
⅛ t. ground allspice
3 T. shortening
¼ c. plus 2 T. butter, divided
1 c. canned sweet potatoes, drained and mashed
6 T. milk

Combine first 5 ingredients and ¼ cup butter with a fork until crumbly. Add sweet potatoes and milk, stirring just until moistened. Turn dough out onto a floured surface and knead several times. Roll out dough to ½-inch thickness on a floured surface; cut with a 2-inch round biscuit cutter. Place biscuits on an ungreased baking sheet. Melt remaining butter; brush over biscuits. Bake at 400 degrees for 10 to 12 minutes, or until golden. Makes about 1½ dozen.

Nancy Wise
Little Rock, AR

Mom's Sweet
Potato Biscuits

Buttermilk Hushpuppies

Perfect for a barbecue or fish fry!

2 c. cornmeal
1 c. all-purpose flour
1 T. sugar
1 T. baking powder
½ t. baking soda
1½ t. salt
1 t. pepper
1 egg
1 t. hot pepper sauce
1½ c. buttermilk
1 c. onion, minced
1 c. corn
oil for deep frying

Combine first 7 ingredients in a medium mixing bowl; set aside. Whisk egg and hot pepper sauce together; stir in buttermilk. Add to cornmeal mixture; stir until just moistened. Fold in onion and corn; drop by tablespoonfuls into hot oil. Cook until golden, turning once; drain on paper towels. Makes 3 dozen.

Liz Plotnick-Snay
Gooseberry Patch

Cheddar-Apple Biscuits

Apples and cheese taste great together...especially when paired with brown sugar and cinnamon.

⅓ c. brown sugar, packed
2 T. all-purpose flour
½ t. cinnamon
10-oz. tube refrigerated buttermilk biscuits
1 c. shredded Cheddar cheese
2 apples, cored, peeled and sliced into rings
1 T. butter, melted

Combine first 3 ingredients in a small bowl; set aside. Press each biscuit into a 3-inch circle. Place on lightly greased baking sheets; sprinkle each with cheese and top with an apple ring. Sprinkle with sugar mixture and drizzle with melted butter. Bake at 350 degrees for 15 minutes, or until golden. Makes 10.

Tammie Jones
Lincolnton, NC

---

make it special
Cookie cutters make breakfast a treat... use them to cut out biscuit dough, shape pancakes or cut shapes from the centers of French toast. Use mini cutters to make the sweetest pats of butter!

Parmesan Bread Sticks

A must-have with spaghetti or lasagna and a tossed salad.

⅓ c. butter, melted
1 t. dried rosemary, crushed
1 clove garlic, minced
2¼ c. all-purpose flour
2 T. grated Parmesan cheese
1 T. sugar
3½ t. baking powder
1 c. milk

Pour butter into a 13"x9" baking pan, tilting to coat. Sprinkle with rosemary and garlic; set aside. Combine flour, cheese, sugar and baking powder; stir in milk. Turn dough out onto a floured surface; knead until smooth. Roll into a 12-inch by 6-inch rectangle; cut into one-inch strips. Twist each strip 6 times; place in butter mixture. Bake at 400 degrees for 20 to 25 minutes. Makes one dozen.

Mary Murray
Mt. Vernon, OH

Blue Cheese Cut-Out Crackers

You'll love these delicate cheese wafers with a touch of hot pepper!

1 c. all-purpose flour
¼ c. plus 3 T. butter, softened
¼ c. plus 3 T. crumbled blue cheese
½ t. dried parsley
1 egg yolk
¼ t. salt
4 t. whipping cream
¼ t. cayenne pepper

Mix all ingredients together; let stand 30 minutes. Turn dough out onto a floured surface and roll to about ⅛-inch thickness. Use your favorite cookie cutters (flowers, teacups, wedding bells) to cut out the crackers. Place on ungreased baking sheets; bake at 400 degrees for 8 to 10 minutes, or just until golden. Cool completely on baking sheets. Carefully remove the delicate crackers when cool. Makes 1½ to 2 dozen.

tag sale treasure
Snap up stoneware butter crocks when you find them at flea markets. They're just the right size for serving party spreads and dips as well as butter.

Blue Cheese
Cut-Out Crackers

Rosemary-Lemon Scones

Wonderful served warm with butter and jam.

2 c. all-purpose flour
2 T. sugar
1 T. baking powder
2 t. fresh rosemary, chopped
2 t. lemon zest
¼ t. salt
¼ c. butter
2 eggs, beaten
½ c. whipping cream
1 t. cinnamon

Combine flour, sugar, baking powder, rosemary, lemon zest and salt. Using a pastry blender or 2 forks, cut in butter until mixture is crumbly; set aside. In a medium bowl, combine eggs and whipping cream; add to flour mixture and stir well. Dough will be sticky. Turn dough out onto a well-floured surface. Knead dough gently 10 times; shape into an 8-inch circle about one-inch thick. Cut circle into equal wedges and place on a lightly greased baking sheet. Sprinkle cinnamon over scones and bake at 400 degrees for 15 minutes, or until golden. Cool on a wire rack. Makes 8.

effortless entertaining
For a pretty table accent, tuck cheery red potted geraniums in lunch-size paper bags.

Ginger Scones

Ginger Scones

2¾ c. all-purpose flour
2 t. baking powder
½ t. salt
½ c. sugar
¾ c. butter
⅓ c. crystallized ginger, chopped
1 c. milk

Combine first 4 ingredients in a large bowl; cut in butter with a pastry blender or 2 forks until mixture is crumbly. Stir in ginger. Add milk, stirring just until dry ingredients are moistened. Turn dough out onto a lightly floured surface and knead 10 to 15 times. Pat or roll dough to ¾-inch thickness; shape into a round and cut dough into 8 wedges. Place wedges on a lightly greased baking sheet.
Bake at 400 degrees for 18 to 22 minutes, or until scones are lightly golden. Cool on a wire rack. Makes 8.

Vickie
Gooseberry Patch

Strawberry Scones

2 c. all-purpose flour
⅓ c. sugar
2 t. baking powder
¼ t. salt
⅓ c. butter
I egg, beaten
I t. vanilla extract
¼ c. whipping cream
¼ c. buttermilk
I c. strawberries, hulled and sliced
Optional: sugar

Combine flour, sugar, baking powder and salt in a large mixing bowl; cut in butter with a pastry blender or 2 forks until crumbly. Form a well in center; set aside. Whisk together egg, vanilla, cream and buttermilk; add to dry ingredients, stirring until just moistened. Fold in strawberries; turn dough out onto a lightly floured surface and knead until smooth, about 10 seconds. Pat into a 7-inch circle about one-inch thick; slice into 8 wedges. Arrange on a parchment paper-lined baking sheet; brush with Glaze and sprinkle with additional sugar, if desired. Bake at 375 degrees for 15 minutes, or until golden. Cool on a wire rack. Makes 8.

Glaze:
I egg, beaten
I T. whipping cream

Whisk egg and cream together.

Jennifer Wickes
Pine Beach, NJ

Gingerbread Muffins

When measuring molasses, coat your measuring cup with non-stick vegetable spray. The molasses won't stick!

2 eggs
⅔ c. oil
I c. molasses
½ c. sugar
3 c. all-purpose flour
2 t. baking soda
2 t. salt
I t. cinnamon
I t. ground cloves
I t. ground ginger
I c. boiling water
Garnish: sugar

In a medium bowl, beat eggs, oil, molasses and sugar, mixing well. Sift together dry ingredients in a large bowl and add egg mixture. Stir in boiling water, mixing well. Fill greased or paper-lined muffin cups ⅔ full. Sprinkle tops lightly with sugar. Bake at 350 degrees for 20 to 25 minutes. Makes about 2 dozen.

Anne Daigle
Augusta, ME

Gingerbread muffins are so heart-warming, from the spicy aroma wafting from the oven as they bake to the delicious taste. I make them on special occasions like Christmas, for weekend guests, and as a cure for homesickness. They travel well and have gone to college with my two daughters and been shipped to my son stationed in Korea. —Anne

Focaccia

Perfect served with pasta!

4 to 4¼ c. all-purpose flour, divided
1 env. fast-rising yeast
1 T. dried basil
1 t. dried thyme
2 cloves garlic, pressed
½ t. salt
1½ c. warm water (120 to 130 degrees)
1 t. honey
2 T. olive oil, divided

Sift together 2 cups flour, yeast, basil, thyme, garlic and salt. Combine water and honey; blend into yeast mixture. Add enough remaining flour so that dough is smooth and not sticky. Turn dough out onto a lightly floured surface and knead for 8 to 10 minutes. Cover and let rise in a warm place (85 degrees), free from drafts, until double in bulk. Spread one tablespoon oil on a baking sheet and transfer dough to baking sheet; pat into a 14-inch by 10-inch rectangle. Brush dough with remaining olive oil; let rise 5 minutes. Bake at 375 degrees for 30 minutes or until golden. Serves 8 to 10.

Elizabeth Ramicone
Columbus, Ohio

Jumbo Quiche Muffins

These handheld breakfast treats are perfect to tote along when rushing out the door before school. The kids will love them!

16.3-oz. tube refrigerated flaky buttermilk
    biscuits
½ c. cream cheese, softened
4 eggs, beaten
¼ t. seasoned salt
¼ t. pepper
6 slices bacon, crisply cooked and
    crumbled
½ c. shredded Cheddar cheese

Place each biscuit into a greased jumbo muffin cup; press to form a well. Combine cream cheese, eggs, salt and pepper. Spoon 3 tablespoons egg mixture into each biscuit well; sprinkle with bacon and top with cheese. Bake at 375 degrees for 15 minutes. Makes 8.

Debra Alf
Robbinsdale, MN

These oversized muffins are always a breakfast hit. —Debra

Jumbo Quiche Muffins

Chocolate
Buttermilk Biscuits

Chocolate Buttermilk Biscuits

3 T. sugar, divided
⅛ t. cinnamon
2 c. all-purpose flour
1 T. baking powder
⅓ c. butter
¾ c. buttermilk
½ c. semi-sweet chocolate chips
¼ c. butter, melted

Combine 2 tablespoons sugar and cinnamon; set aside. Combine flour, baking powder and remaining sugar; cut in butter with a pastry blender or 2 forks until mixture is crumbly. Add buttermilk and chocolate chips, stirring just until dry ingredients are moistened. Turn dough out onto a lightly floured surface; knead 3 or 4 times. Roll dough to ½-inch thickness; cut with a 2¼-inch round cookie or biscuit cutter. Arrange biscuits on a lightly greased baking sheet; sprinkle with sugar mixture. Bake at 425 degrees for 15 minutes or until golden. Brush with melted butter. Makes one dozen.

Kathy Grashoff
Fort Wayne, IN

Sugar-Topped Muffins

18¼-oz. pkg. white cake mix
1 c. milk
2 eggs
½ t. nutmeg
⅓ c. sugar
½ t. cinnamon
¼ c. butter, melted

Blend cake mix, milk, eggs and nutmeg at low speed with an electric mixer until just moistened; beat at high speed 2 minutes. Fill paper-lined muffin cups ⅔ full. Bake at 350 degrees until golden, about 15 to 18 minutes. Cool 5 minutes. Combine sugar and cinnamon on a small plate. Brush muffin tops with butter; roll in sugar and cinnamon mixture. Serve warm. Makes 2 dozen.

Raspberry Streusel Muffins

The aroma of these muffins is a wonderful wake-up call for your family or overnight guests!

1¾ c. all-purpose flour, divided
¼ c. sugar
1 c. brown sugar, packed and divided
2 t. baking powder
¼ t. salt
2 t. cinnamon, divided
1 egg, beaten
½ c. plus 2 T. unsalted butter, melted and divided
½ c. milk
1¼ c. raspberries
2 t. lemon zest, divided
½ c. chopped pecans
1 c. powdered sugar
1 T. lemon juice

Sift together 1½ cups flour, sugar, ½ cup brown sugar, baking powder, salt and one teaspoon cinnamon. Mix in egg, ½ cup butter and milk with a wooden spoon. Gently stir in raspberries and one teaspoon lemon zest. Grease 12 muffin cups and fill ⅔ full.

Blend together pecans and remaining flour, brown sugar, cinnamon, butter and zest. Sprinkle topping over batter. Bake at 350 degrees for 20 to 25 minutes. Mix together powdered sugar and lemon juice; drizzle over warm muffins. Makes one dozen.

Carol Jones
Twin Falls, ID

clever totes
Check with your local orchard or at the farmers' market to find some wooden fruit crates and bushel baskets…they make easy work of toting breakfast fixin's from the car to the church kitchen!

Mom's Applesauce Muffins

½ c. butter, softened
1 c. sugar
1 c. applesauce
1 egg, beaten
2 c. all-purpose flour
1 t. baking soda
1 t. cinnamon
½ t. ground cloves
¼ t. salt
1 c. raisins

Combine butter, sugar, applesauce and egg. In a separate bowl, combine flour, baking soda, cinnamon, cloves and salt; stir into butter mixture just until moistened. Stir in raisins. Fill paper-lined muffin cups ¾ full; sprinkle with Crumb Topping. Bake at 350 degrees for 25 to 30 minutes. Makes 12 to 16.

Crumb Topping:

½ c. butter, softened
¾ c. all-purpose flour
¾ c. quick-cooking oats, uncooked
½ c. brown sugar, packed
2 t. cinnamon

Blend all ingredients until crumbly.

Emily Johnson
Pocatello, ID

Mom's Applesauce
Muffins

to molly
from jane

Coconut Cream Muffins

These are even better right out of the oven with a little lemon curd spread on them.

1¼ c. all-purpose flour
1 t. baking powder
¼ t. salt
1½ t. vanilla extract
¼ t. almond extract
⅔ c. half-and-half
½ c. butter, softened
¾ c. sugar
2 eggs
1¾ c. sweetened flaked coconut

Blend together flour, baking powder and salt in a small bowl. Stir extracts into half-and-half. Beat butter in a large bowl at high speed with an electric mixer for one minute. Gradually add sugar and beat until fluffy. Reduce mixer speed to medium and beat in eggs until blended. Reduce mixer speed to low. Add flour mixture to butter mixture alternately with half-and-half mixture, beginning and ending with flour mixture just until blended. Stir in coconut. Fill greased muffin cups ⅔ full. Bake at 350 degrees for 18 to 20 minutes, or until a wooden pick inserted in center of muffins comes out clean. Cool in pan for 5 minutes. Remove to a wire rack and cool completely. Makes one dozen.

Stephanie Moon
Boise, ID

" *I have many recipes tucked away, but this favorite is one I wanted to share.* " —Stephanie

S'mores Muffins

Enjoy a campfire favorite anytime!

1 c. shortening
4 eggs
1 c. sour cream
2 c. sugar
¼ c. baking cocoa
2 t. salt
3 c. all-purpose flour
2 t. baking soda
1 t. cinnamon
1 c. graham crackers, crushed
1 c. mini marshmallows
1 c. chocolate chips
Garnish: marshmallow creme,
  graham cracker crumbs

Combine shortening, eggs, sour cream and sugar; set aside. Mix together remaining ingredients except garnish in a separate mixing bowl; add shortening mixture to cocoa mixture. Fill greased muffin tins ¾ full and bake at 325 degrees for 30 to 40 minutes. Cool in pan 20 minutes; remove muffins from pans. Garnish muffins with marshmallow creme and graham cracker crumbs. Makes 2 dozen.

Brenda Huey
Geneva, IN

POTLUCK PLEASERS

*Comforting classics to tote
to gatherings with family & friends*

Chicken Lasagna with
Roasted Red Pepper Sauce

Chicken Lasagna with Roasted Red Pepper Sauce

4 c. cooked chicken, finely chopped
2 8-oz. containers chive-and-onion
   cream cheese
10-oz. pkg. frozen chopped spinach,
   thawed and well drained
1 t. seasoned pepper
¾ t. garlic salt
9 no-boil lasagna noodles, uncooked
2 c. shredded Italian 3-cheese blend

Stir together first 5 ingredients.
Layer a lightly greased 11"x7" baking pan with a third of Roasted Red Pepper Sauce, 3 noodles, a third of chicken mixture and a third of cheese. Repeat layers twice. Place baking pan on a baking sheet.
Bake, covered, at 350 degrees for 50 to 55 minutes, or until hot and bubbly. Uncover and bake 15 more minutes. Serves 6 to 8.

Roasted Red Pepper Sauce:

12-oz. jar roasted red peppers, drained
16-oz. jar creamy Alfredo sauce
¾ c. grated Parmesan cheese
½ t. red pepper flakes

Process all ingredients in a food processor until smooth, stopping to scrape down sides. Makes 3½ cups.

Jo Ann
Gooseberry Patch

"There's nothing like a hot pan of lasagna on a cold winter's night!" —Jo Ann

Creamed Chicken & Mushrooms

This is one of those hearty meals best served with mashed potatoes, green beans and big, fluffy biscuits!

6 T. butter
6 T. all-purpose flour
1 t. salt
⅛ t. pepper
10½-oz. can condensed chicken broth
12-oz. can evaporated milk
1 to 2 c. cooked chicken, chopped
4-oz. can mushrooms, drained
¼ c. dry white wine or chicken broth

In a 4-quart saucepan, melt butter and add flour, salt and pepper. Remove from heat and stir in broth and evaporated milk. Bring to a boil; cook one minute, stirring constantly. Stir in chicken, mushrooms and wine or broth; heat through. Serves 6 to 8.

Tammy McCartney
Oxford, OH

Easy Chicken Pot Pie

Ready-made pie crusts make this homestyle dish extra easy.

2 9-inch refrigerated pie crusts
6¾-oz. can chicken, chopped
16-oz. can mixed vegetables,
    drained
10¾-oz. can cream of chicken
    soup
½ t. celery flakes
¼ t. pepper
¼ t. poultry seasoning

Fit one pie crust into a 9" pie plate. Combine remaining ingredients in a bowl; pour into pie crust.
Moisten edges of bottom crust with water; top with remaining crust. Fold edges under and crimp; cut slits in top. Bake at 400 degrees for 45 to 50 minutes; let stand 10 minutes before serving. Serves 8.

Wanda White
Kings Mountain, NC

kitchen tip
In this recipe, a 10-ounce package of frozen oven-roasted diced chicken, thawed, and a 16-ounce package of frozen vegetables can be substituted for canned chicken and vegetables.

Chicken Tex-Mex Bake

Chicken Tex-Mex Bake

2 12½-oz. cans chicken, drained and shredded
2 10-oz. cans mild red enchilada sauce
10¾-oz. can cream of chicken soup
4½-oz. can diced green chiles
14½-oz. can diced tomatoes
2½ c. shredded Mexican-blend cheese, divided
1 c. sour cream
½ c. onion, diced
½ t. pepper
10 flour tortillas, cut into one-inch squares
    and divided
½ c. sliced black olives

Combine first 5 ingredients and half the cheese; mix well. Blend in sour cream, onion and pepper; set aside. Arrange half the tortillas over the bottom of a greased 13"x9" baking pan. Spoon half the chicken mixture over tortillas. Repeat layers, ending with chicken mixture on top. Sprinkle with remaining cheese; top with olives. Cover loosely with aluminum foil; bake at 350 degrees for 40 minutes or until hot and bubbly. Serves 8.

Jenny Flake
Gilbert, AZ

Mandy's Easy Cheesy Chicken Casserole

3 to 4 cooked chicken breasts, chopped
16-oz. pkg. wide egg noodles, cooked
24-oz. container sour cream
2 10¾-oz cans cream of chicken soup
8-oz. pkg. shredded Cheddar cheese
8-oz. pkg. shredded mozzarella cheese
1 sleeve round buttery crackers, crushed
¼ c. butter, melted
2 T. poppy seed

Combine chicken, noodles, sour cream, soup and cheeses in a large bowl. Pour into a lightly greased 13"x9" baking pan. Mix together cracker crumbs and butter; sprinkle over top. Sprinkle poppy seed over cracker crumbs. Bake, uncovered, at 350 degrees for 25 to 30 minutes, or until crackers are crispy and golden and cheese is melted. Serves 8 to 10.

Mandy Wheeler
Ashland, KY

Mandy's Easy Cheesy
Chicken Casserole

Turkey & Wild Rice Casserole

Turkey & Wild Rice Casserole

It's easy to double or even triple this tasty recipe, and it can be made ahead and refrigerated...terrific for the holiday season when guests may drop in.

2 c. cooked turkey, diced
6-oz. pkg. cooked long-grain and wild rice
10¾-oz. can cream of mushroom soup
6-oz. jar sliced mushrooms, drained
1 c. celery, thinly sliced
1 c. red pepper, chopped

Combine all ingredients in a large bowl. Spread in a lightly greased 11"x7" baking pan. Cover and bake at 350 degrees for 30 to 40 minutes. Serves 4 to 6.

Margaret Scoresby
Mosinee, WI

simple side

Broiled tomatoes are perfect alongside this recipe. Pulse a couple of slices of bread with some fresh Parmesan cheese in the food processor and stir together with some melted butter. Sprinkle halved tomatoes with salt and pepper and top with the crumb mixture. Pop them under the broiler for a few minutes until golden.

Deep-Dish Taco Squares

Full of flavor, but not too hot and spicy.

2 c. biscuit baking mix
½ c. water
1 lb. ground beef
1 green pepper, chopped
1 onion, chopped
⅛ t. garlic powder
8-oz. can tomato sauce
1¼-oz. pkg. taco seasoning mix
1 c. shredded Cheddar cheese
1 c. sour cream
⅓ c. mayonnaise-type salad dressing
¼ t. paprika
Garnish: sour cream, chopped tomatoes, chopped lettuce, chopped onion

Combine biscuit baking mix and water; spread in a lightly greased 13"x9" baking pan. Bake at 375 degrees for 9 minutes; remove from oven and set aside. Brown ground beef, green pepper, onion and garlic powder; drain. Stir in tomato sauce and taco seasoning. Spread mixture over crust. Stir together cheese, sour cream and salad dressing; spoon over beef mixture and sprinkle with paprika. Bake, uncovered, at 375 degrees for 25 more minutes. Cut into squares; top with sour cream, tomatoes, lettuce and onion. Serves 12 to 15.

Jody Bolen
Ashland, OH

Mom's Stuffed Cabbage Rolls

*Every year we look forward to fall when we get
the huge heads of cabbage that have perfect leaves for
these rolls.*

3 qts. plus ½ c. water, divided
3½-lb. head cabbage, leaves removed
1 lb. ground beef
½ c. instant rice, uncooked
1 onion, minced
2 eggs, beaten
1 c. mushrooms, chopped
2 t. salt, divided
⅛ t. pepper
⅛ t. ground allspice
1 onion, sliced into rings
16-oz. can tomato sauce
28-oz. can diced tomatoes
⅓ c. lemon juice
¼ c. brown sugar, packed

Bring 3 quarts water to a boil in a large stockpot;
add cabbage leaves and simmer 2 to 3 minutes or
until leaves are pliable. Remove cabbage and drain.
Place 12 of the largest leaves to the side. Combine
beef, rice, onion, eggs, mushrooms, one teaspoon
salt, pepper, allspice and ¼ cup water; mix until well
blended. Place ¼ cup beef mixture into the center
of each leaf; roll up, beginning at the thick end of
each leaf. Place a few remaining cabbage leaves in
bottom of a Dutch oven; arrange rolls seam-side
down on leaves and top with sliced onions.

In a large mixing bowl, combine remaining salt,
tomato sauce, tomatoes, lemon juice and remaining water; pour over cabbage rolls. Bring to a boil
over medium heat; sprinkle with brown sugar.
Remove from heat; cover and bake at 350 degrees
for 1½ hours. Uncover and bake for 1½ more
hours. Serves 12.

Megan Pepping
Coshocton, OH

Company Baked Ziti

*Layers of sour cream and three types of cheese...
this pasta classic is extra rich and cheesy.*

1 lb. ground beef
1 lb. sweet Italian ground pork sausage
1 onion, chopped
2 26-oz. jars spaghetti sauce
16-oz. pkg. ziti pasta, cooked
6-oz. pkg. sliced provolone cheese
1 c. sour cream
1½ c. shredded mozzarella cheese
½ c. grated Parmesan cheese

Brown beef, sausage and onion in a skillet over
medium heat; drain. Stir in sauce; reduce heat to
low and simmer 15 minutes. Layer in a greased
13"x9" baking pan as follows: half the pasta, provolone cheese, sour cream, half the sauce mixture,
remaining pasta, mozzarella cheese and remaining
sauce. Top with Parmesan cheese. Cover and bake
at 350 degrees for 30 minutes, or until hot and
bubbly and cheeses are melted. Serves 6 to 8.

Colleen Leid
Narvon, PA

*Oh-so simple to put together, yet everyone
loves it!* —Colleen

Company Baked Ziti

Cheryl's Country-Style Ribs

Cheryl's Country-Style Ribs

Serve these ribs with coleslaw and corn on the cob.

7 to 8 lbs. country-style pork ribs, sliced
   into serving-size portions
salt to taste
2 onions, sliced
½ c. brown sugar, packed

Place ribs in an ungreased large roasting pan; sprinkle lightly with salt. Top ribs with onion slices, brown sugar and 3⅓ cups Barbecue Sauce. Cover and bake at 350 degrees for 2 hours.

Uncover and add remaining sauce. Increase heat to 400 degrees; bake 30 more minutes. Serves 12 to 15.

Barbecue Sauce:

2 c. catsup
1 c. water
½ c. sugar
½ c. vinegar
½ c. Worcestershire sauce
2 T. smoke-flavored cooking sauce
1 t. garlic powder
1 t. salt

Combine all ingredients and mix well. Keep refrigerated. Makes 4½ cups.

Cheryl Tesar
DeWitt, NE

"A family favorite...so delicious, there are rarely any leftovers!" —Cheryl

Whole Baked Ham

12 to 14-lb. fully cooked boneless or
   bone-in ham
12 whole cloves
1½ c. pineapple juice
½ c. maple-flavored syrup
6 slices canned pineapple
1 c. water
¾ c. brown sugar, packed
3 T. mustard

Place ham, fat-side up, in a shallow roasting pan. Press cloves into top of ham. Stir together pineapple juice and syrup; pour over ham.

Arrange pineapple slices on ham. Bake, uncovered, at 325 degrees for 1½ hours. Add water and bake 1½ hours more. Remove from oven; remove pineapple slices. Mix together brown sugar and mustard; spread over ham. Bake 30 more minutes. Serves 18 to 20.

Jacqueline Kurtz
Reading, PA

Whole Baked Ham

Gruyère Rolls

Rich, nutty-tasting Gruyère cheese delicately flavors these rolls.

3 c. all-purpose flour, divided
1 pkg. active dry yeast
3 c. shredded Gruyère cheese
1½ t. salt
¼ t. sugar
1¼ c. warm water (110 to 115 degrees)
Optional: melted butter

Combine 2¾ cups flour, yeast and next 3 ingredients in a large mixing bowl. Gradually add water to flour mixture, beating at high speed with an electric mixer until combined. Beat 2 more minutes at medium speed. Gradually stir in enough remaining flour to make a soft dough.

Turn dough out onto a floured surface and knead until smooth and elastic (about 10 minutes). Place in a well-greased bowl, turning to coat top. Cover and let rise in a warm place (85 degrees), free from drafts, one hour or until double in bulk.

Punch dough down; turn out onto a lightly floured surface and knead lightly 4 or 5 times. Divide dough in half. Shape each portion into 8 balls; roll each ball in flour.

Place rolls 2 inches apart on a greased baking sheet. Cover and let rise in a warm place, free from drafts, 30 minutes or until double in bulk. Bake at 425 degrees for 5 minutes. Reduce oven temperature to 350 degrees; continue to bake, 13 minutes or until golden. Brush with butter, if desired. Makes 16.

Honey-Butter Rolls

Golden and light, these never last long!

1½ c. whole-wheat flour
3¼ c. all-purpose flour, divided
2 envs. active dry yeast
2 t. salt
½ t. baking soda
1½ c. plain yogurt
½ c. water
3 T. butter
2 T. honey
Optional: melted butter

Combine whole-wheat flour, ½ cup all-purpose flour, yeast, salt and baking soda in a mixing bowl. In a saucepan over low heat, heat yogurt, water, butter and honey to 110 to 115 degrees; pour over dry ingredients, blending well. Beat at medium speed with an electric mixer for 3 minutes. Add enough remaining flour to form a soft dough. Turn out onto a floured surface; knead until smooth and elastic, about 6 to 8 minutes. Place in a greased bowl, turning to coat top. Cover and let rise in a warm place (85 degrees), free from drafts, one hour or until double in bulk. Punch down dough; divide into 24 pieces. Roll each piece into a 9-inch rope. To form S-shaped rolls, coil each end of rope toward center in opposite directions. Place 3 inches apart on greased baking sheets. Cover and let rise until double in bulk. Bake at 400 degrees for 15 minutes, or until golden. Brush tops with melted butter, if desired. Makes 2 dozen.

Zoe Bennett
Columbia, SC

a special gift to a new bride
Pass down Grandma's rolling pin, along with some of her favorite recipes.

Sour Cream Corn Muffins

1 c. yellow cornmeal
1 c. all-purpose flour
¼ c. sugar
2 t. baking powder
1 t. salt
½ t. baking soda
1 c. sour cream
2 eggs
¼ c. butter, melted

In a large bowl, combine cornmeal, flour, sugar, baking powder, salt and baking soda. In a small bowl, combine sour cream, eggs and butter; add to cornmeal mixture, stirring until moistened. Spoon batter into a greased 12-cup muffin pan and bake at 425 degrees for 15 to 20 minutes until golden. Makes one dozen.

Kathy Moberg
Saline, MI

Parmesan-Garlic Bread

1 cup whipping cream
¼ c. mayonnaise
9 cloves garlic, minced
¾ c. plus 2 T. grated Parmesan cheese, divided
1 loaf French bread
paprika to taste

Beat whipping cream until thickened; blend in mayonnaise. Add garlic and ¾ cup Parmesan cheese; stir well. Slice French bread in half lengthwise; generously spread garlic mixture on each half. Sprinkle with remaining Parmesan cheese and paprika. Place loaf halves on an ungreased baking sheet; bake at 400 degrees for 15 to 20 minutes, or until garlic topping turns golden. Cut into one-inch slices. Makes about 2 dozen.

Roxanne Bixby
West Franklin, NH

Southern-Style Spoonbread

For Southerners, this is a must-have brunch dish. Not one bite will be left.

3 c. milk
1½ c. yellow cornmeal
½ c. butter, softened
2 t. baking powder
5 eggs, separated
1 c. cooked country ham, diced

Bring milk to a slow boil in a saucepan; gradually add cornmeal, stirring constantly. Reduce heat to low and cook, stirring constantly, 10 minutes or until thickened. Remove from heat; add butter and baking powder and stir until butter is melted. Let cool and set aside. In a small bowl, use a fork to beat egg yolks until light; stir into cooled cornmeal mixture. Add ham and mix until blended; set aside. Beat egg whites at medium speed with an electric mixer until stiff peaks form; fold into cornmeal mixture until well combined. Pour into a greased 2-quart casserole dish. Bake at 350 degrees for about 40 minutes, or until a wooden pick inserted in center comes out clean. Serves 6 to 8.

Sharon Tillman
Hampton, VA

Southern-Style Spoonbread

Old-Fashioned Potato Salad

You can also make this with new red potatoes and tiny, just-shelled peas.

1 c. mayonnaise-type salad dressing
⅔ c. sugar
1 t. mustard
1 T. vinegar
1 onion, chopped
1 stalk celery, chopped
2 eggs, hard-boiled, peeled and chopped
8 potatoes, peeled, boiled and cubed
salt and pepper to taste

Combine salad dressing, sugar, mustard and vinegar. Stir in onion, celery, eggs and cooled potatoes. Add salt and pepper to taste. Cover and chill. Serves 6 to 8.

Tina Langseth
Springfield, MN

Scalloped Potatoes with Ham

1 onion, chopped
1 T. oil
3 cloves garlic, finely chopped
2 sweet potatoes, peeled and cut into
   ¼-inch slices
2 potatoes, peeled and cut into ¼-inch slices
½ c. all-purpose flour
1 t. salt
¼ t. pepper
2 c. cooked ham, chopped
2 c. shredded Gruyère cheese, divided
1¾ c. whipping cream
2 T. butter, cut into pieces

Sauté onion in oil in a saucepan over medium-high heat 5 minutes or until tender. Add garlic; cook 30 seconds. Remove from heat and set aside. Place potatoes in a large bowl.

Combine flour, salt and pepper; sprinkle over potatoes, tossing to coat. Arrange half of potato mixture in a greased 13"x9" baking pan or 3-quart casserole dish. Top with onion mixture, ham and one cup cheese. Top with remaining potato mixture. Pour cream over potato mixture. Dot with butter; cover with aluminum foil.

Bake at 400 degrees for 50 minutes. Uncover, top with remaining one cup cheese and bake 20 more minutes or until potatoes are tender and cheese is golden. Let stand 10 minutes before serving. Serves 6.

Squash & Zucchini Casserole

1½ lbs. yellow squash, cut into ¼-inch slices
1 lb. zucchini, cut into ¼-inch slices
1 sweet onion, chopped
2½ t. salt, divided
1 c. carrots, peeled and grated
10¾-oz. can cream of chicken soup
8-oz. container sour cream
8-oz. can water chestnuts, drained and chopped
8-oz. pkg. herb-flavored stuffing mix
½ c. butter, melted

Place squash and zucchini in a Dutch oven.
Add chopped onion, 2 teaspoons salt and water
to cover. Bring to a boil over medium-high heat
and cook 5 minutes; drain well.

Stir together carrots, next 3 ingredients and
remaining salt in a large bowl; fold in squash
mixture. Stir together stuffing mix and melted
butter; spoon half of stuffing mixture into bottom of a lightly greased 13"x9" baking pan. Spoon
squash mixture over stuffing mixture and top with
remaining stuffing mixture.

Bake at 350 degrees for 30 to 35 minutes or until
bubbly and golden, covering with aluminum foil
after 20 to 25 minutes to prevent excessive browning, if necessary. Let stand 10 minutes before
serving. Serves 8.

Vickie
Gooseberry Patch

Fourth of July Beans

1 lb. bacon, diced
1 lb. ground beef
1 lb. hot ground pork sausage
1 c. onion, chopped
28-oz. can pork & beans
15-oz. can ranch-style beans
15-oz. can maple-flavored baked beans
16-oz. can kidney beans, drained and rinsed
½ c. barbecue sauce
½ c. catsup
½ c. brown sugar, packed
1 T. mustard
2 T. molasses
1 t. salt
½ t. chili powder

In a large Dutch oven over medium-high heat,
cook bacon until crisp; drain, discarding drippings.
Remove bacon from pan and set aside. In same
pan, cook beef, sausage and onion until meat is
browned; drain. Transfer to a greased 13"x9" baking
pan. Stir in bacon and remaining ingredients;
mix well. Cover and bake at 350 degrees for
45 minutes. Uncover and bake for 15 more
minutes. Serves 10 to 12.

Laurie Lightfoot
Hawthorne, NV

Wild Rice Stuffing

Wild Rice Stuffing

Dates and crunchy almonds make this stuffing recipe special!

1⅓ c. wild rice, uncooked
2 T. butter
2 c. onion, chopped
1 c. carrots, peeled and grated
1 c. green pepper, chopped
6 c. herb-seasoned stuffing mix
1 c. slivered almonds
½ c. fresh parsley, chopped
10-oz. pkg. dates, chopped
1½ t. dried rosemary
1½ t. dried thyme
1½ t. dried sage
3 c. chicken broth

Prepare rice according to package directions; set aside. Combine butter, onion, carrots and pepper in a medium skillet over medium-high heat and sauté until onion is tender; remove from heat. Blend in remaining ingredients; stir in rice. Spoon stuffing into a greased 3-quart casserole dish. Bake, covered, at 325 degrees for 45 minutes. Uncover and bake 15 more minutes. Serves 10 to 12.

Southern Macaroni Salad

Everyone always wants seconds of this tasty salad!

2 green peppers, chopped
3 tomatoes, chopped
1 onion, chopped
3 T. vinegar
¼ c. sugar
1¾ T. celery seed
1⅛ t. salt
1 c. mayonnaise
2 16-oz. pkgs. cooked elbow macaroni

Combine first 7 ingredients in a large bowl; let stand for 30 minutes. Stir in mayonnaise and macaroni; cover and chill. Serves 12.

Wendy Lee Paffenroth
Pine Island, NY

fun idea
Don't toss away those old rubber boots... they make clever planters! Trim them with stripes or dots cut from colored craft tape, then fill with soil and potted flowers.

Ripe Tomato Tart

Fresh plum tomatoes are available year-round so you can enjoy this summery-tasting pie anytime.

9-inch refrigerated pie crust
1½ c. shredded mozzarella cheese, divided
4 plum tomatoes, cut into wedges
¾ c. fresh basil, chopped
4 cloves garlic, minced
½ c. mayonnaise
½ c. grated Parmesan cheese
⅛ t. white pepper

Line an ungreased 9" tart pan with pie crust; press crust into fluted sides of pan and trim edges. Bake at 450 degrees for 5 to 7 minutes; remove from oven. Sprinkle with ½ cup mozzarella cheese; let cool on a wire rack. Combine remaining ingredients; mix well and spoon into crust. Reduce heat to 375 degrees; bake for about 20 minutes or until bubbly. Serves 6.

Darlene Lohrman
Chicago, IL

guiding light
Light a welcoming path for guests...wind twinkling mini lights along the walk to your front door.

Layered Cornbread & Turkey Salad

Smoked turkey, Swiss cheese, vegetables, crumbled cornbread and crisp bacon make a colorful layered salad to serve in a clear bowl or dish.

6-oz. pkg. buttermilk cornbread mix
12-oz. bottle Parmesan-peppercorn salad dressing
½ c. mayonnaise
¼ c. buttermilk
9-oz. pkg. romaine lettuce, shredded
2½ c. cooked smoked turkey, chopped
2 yellow peppers, chopped
2 tomatoes, seeded and chopped
1 red onion, chopped
1 c. celery, diced
2 c. shredded Swiss cheese
10 slices bacon, crisply cooked and crumbled
Garnish: 2 green onions, sliced

Prepare and bake cornbread according to package directions; cool and crumble. Set aside.
Stir together salad dressing, mayonnaise and buttermilk until blended.
Layer half each of crumbled cornbread, shredded lettuce and remaining ingredients except garnish in a large glass bowl; spoon half of dressing mixture evenly over top. Repeat layers, ending with dressing mixture. Cover and chill at least 8 hours or up to 24 hours. Sprinkle with green onions just before serving. Serves 6.

Layered Cornbread
& Turkey Salad

Three-Layer Ruby Red Salad

3.4-oz. pkg. raspberry gelatin mix
2 c. boiling water, divided
12-oz. pkg. frozen raspberries in syrup
1 c. sour cream
3-oz. pkg. cream cheese, softened
2 T. sugar
½ c. pecans, chopped
3.4-oz. pkg. cherry gelatin mix
8-oz. can crushed pineapple, drained
14-oz. can whole-berry cranberry sauce
spinach or lettuce leaves
Garnish: fresh raspberries

For bottom layer, dissolve raspberry gelatin in one cup boiling water. Add frozen raspberries and stir until thawed and separated. Pour into a 9"x9" baking pan. Place in refrigerator for gelatin to thicken. For middle layer, combine sour cream, cream cheese, sugar and pecans; carefully spread on top of thickened raspberry gelatin. Chill. For top layer, dissolve cherry gelatin in remaining one cup boiling water. Stir in pineapple and cranberry sauce. Let thicken slightly at room temperature. Carefully spoon over sour cream mixture. Chill until firm. Cut into squares and serve on spinach or lettuce leaves. Garnish with fresh raspberries. Serves 9.

Three-Layer Ruby Red Salad

Creamy Garden Coleslaw

Save time by picking up a package of shredded coleslaw mix.

1 head cabbage, shredded
1 zucchini, shredded
1 c. carrots, peeled and grated
½ c. green pepper, chopped
¾ c. mayonnaise
2 T. sugar
2 t. lemon juice
1 t. celery seed
½ t. salt

Combine all ingredients in a large bowl; toss lightly. Cover and chill for about 15 to 20 minutes. Serves 12.

Jackie Crough
Salina, KS

packing a tossed salad?

Put the dressing in the bottom of your container, topped with greens and veggies. At meal time, just stir or shake for a crisp salad every time!

Picnic Salad Skewers

What a fun way to pack a salad! For a meal-in-one version, slide on some cubes of Cheddar cheese and cold cuts, too.

8 redskin potatoes
8 pearl onions, peeled
1 green pepper, cut into one-inch squares
1 red or yellow pepper, cut into one-inch squares
16 cherry tomatoes
1 zucchini, sliced ¼-inch thick
8 wooden skewers
Optional: 4-oz. container crumbled feta cheese

Cover potatoes with water in a saucepan; bring to a boil over medium heat. Cook 10 to 13 minutes, adding onions after 5 minutes; drain and cool. Thread all vegetables alternately onto skewers.

Arrange skewers in a large shallow plastic container. Drizzle with Vinaigrette. Cover and refrigerate at least one hour, turning frequently. Sprinkle with cheese, if desired, before serving. Serves 8.

Vinaigrette:

⅔ c. olive oil
⅓ c. red wine vinegar
2 cloves garlic, minced
1 T. dried oregano
1 t. salt
¼ t. pepper

Whisk together all ingredients. Makes about one cup.

Pam James
Delaware, OH

Granny's Shoofly Pie

My children love it when we go to Granny's house and she has just pulled a shoofly pie out of the oven!

1 t. baking soda
1 c. hot water
½ c. brown sugar, packed
3 eggs, beaten
1 c. molasses
9-inch refrigerated pie crust

Dissolve baking soda in hot water in a mixing bowl. Add remaining ingredients except pie crust. Pour half the mixture into pie crust; sprinkle with ¼ cup Crumb Topping. Pour remaining molasses mixture over crumbs; sprinkle with remaining Crumb Topping. Bake at 400 degrees for 10 minutes. Reduce heat to 375 degrees and bake for 50 more minutes. Serves 8.

Crumb Topping:

2½ c. all-purpose flour
1 c. brown sugar, packed
½ c. shortening

Combine flour and brown sugar; mix well. Cut in shortening with a pastry blender or 2 forks until crumbly.

Kristi Boyle
Easton, MD

Apple Brown Betty

8 slices white bread, torn
½ c. butter, melted
1 t. cinnamon, divided
2½ lbs. Granny Smith apples, peeled, cored
    and sliced
⅔ c. light brown sugar, packed
2 T. lemon juice
1 t. vanilla extract
¼ t. nutmeg

Place bread slices in a 15"x10" jelly-roll pan. Bake at 400 degrees for 15 minutes or until lightly toasted, stirring occasionally. Grease a 2-quart casserole dish; set aside. Combine butter, ½ teaspoon cinnamon and bread in a medium bowl; toss gently until evenly moistened. In a large mixing bowl, combine apples, brown sugar, lemon juice, vanilla, nutmeg and remaining cinnamon. Place ½ cup bread pieces in a casserole dish; top with half the apple mixture. Layer with one cup bread pieces and remaining apple mixture. Toss remaining bread over apple mixture, leaving a one-inch border around the edge. Cover with aluminum foil and bake for 40 minutes. Uncover and bake 10 more minutes. Let stand 10 minutes before serving. Serves 8.

Tina Stidam
Ashley, OH

winter warmer
Set up a table with slow cookers of chocolatey cocoa or warm spiced cider...a welcome way to warm up on a chilly night.

Cider

Some of my fondest memories are from when I was a little girl spending time with my grandparents. Every Sunday, Granny would fix a feast when the family gathered together. This recipe is one of many I absolutely loved! —Tina

Bread Pudding

*Day-old bread is best for soaking up the liquid in
this oh-so decadent dessert.*

4 eggs
1½ c. sugar
3 12-oz. cans evaporated milk
½ c. butter, melted
1 T. vanilla extract
2 t. cinnamon
6 c. French bread, torn into pieces and packed
1 Granny Smith apple, peeled, cored and chopped
1½ c. walnuts, coarsely chopped and toasted
1 c. golden raisins

Whisk eggs in a large bowl. Whisk in sugar
and next 4 ingredients. Fold in remaining ingredients, stirring until bread is moistened. Pour into a
greased 13"x9" baking pan.

Bake, uncovered, at 350 degrees for 50 minutes,
or until set. Cut into squares. Serve warm with
warm Rum Sauce. Serves 12.

Rum Sauce:
2 14-oz. cans sweetened condensed milk
2 T. dark rum or 1 t. rum extract
1 T. vanilla extract

Pour condensed milk into a small saucepan;
cook over medium heat until hot, stirring often.
Remove from heat; stir in rum or rum extract and
vanilla. Makes 2½ cups.

Creamy Banana Pudding

1½ c. cream cheese, softened
1½ 5.1-oz. pkgs. instant vanilla pudding mix
4½ c. milk, divided
1½ t. vanilla extract
12-oz. container frozen whipped topping, thawed
12-oz. pkg. vanilla wafers, coarsely crushed
4 bananas, sliced
Optional: additional whipped topping and vanilla wafers, broken into large pieces

Process cream cheese, pudding mix, 2½ cups milk and vanilla in a food processor or blender until smooth. Pour into a large bowl; whisk in remaining milk.

Whisk whipped topping into pudding mixture. Layer crushed vanilla wafers, banana slices and pudding mixture in a 4-quart casserole dish. Top with additional whipped topping and vanilla wafers, if desired. Chill at least 4 hours before serving. Serves 10 to 12.

Elizabeth Cox
Lewisville, TX

Creamy Banana Pudding

Pioneer Blueberry Buckle

Simple to make, feeds a crowd and tastes so good! Use fresh blueberries for this dessert.

5 c. all-purpose flour, divided
1½ c. sugar
½ c. butter, softened
2 eggs
1 c. milk
4 t. baking powder
1 t. salt
4 c. blueberries

Combine 4 cups flour and remaining ingredients except blueberries; mix well and set aside. Gently toss blueberries with remaining flour; discard any remaining flour. Add blueberry mixture to flour mixture. Spread into a greased and floured 13"x9" baking pan. Sprinkle evenly with Topping. Bake at 375 degrees for about one hour, or until golden and a wooden pick inserted in center comes out clean. Serves 20.

Topping:

1 c. sugar
1 c. brown sugar, packed
1⅓ c. all-purpose flour
2 t. cinnamon
1 c. butter, softened
Optional: 1 c. chopped nuts

Mix together sugars, flour and cinnamon; cut in butter with a pastry blender or 2 forks until crumbly. Stir in nuts, if desired.

Michelle Fareri
Haddon Heights, NJ

Lemon Trifle

Wonderful as a finale to a summer meal when you want a special dessert!

14-oz. can sweetened condensed milk
8-oz. container lemon yogurt
1 T. lemon zest
8-oz. container frozen whipped topping, thawed
1 angel food cake, cut into bite-size pieces
⅓ c. lemon juice
2 c. strawberries, hulled and sliced
1 c. blueberries
1 c. raspberries
½ c. sweetened flaked coconut, lightly toasted

Combine first 3 ingredients in a mixing bowl; fold in whipped topping. Combine angel food cake cubes and lemon juice. Layer a third of cake cubes in a trifle bowl. Spoon a third of condensed milk mixture over cake; top with strawberries. Layer a third of remaining cake cubes over strawberries, a third of condensed milk mixture and blueberries. Repeat with remaining cake, condensed milk mixture and raspberries. Sprinkle with coconut. Cover and chill for at least 8 hours. Serves 8.

Nancy Girard
Chesapeake, VA

going...going...gone!
Enjoy the fun of an old-fashioned pie or cake auction! Bidding on sweet treats made by the youth group is a terrific fundraiser for summer camp.

Fresh Peach Ice Cream

(Pictured on page 298)

5 c. milk, divided
4 egg yolks
8 peaches, peeled, pitted and mashed
2 T. lemon juice
2½ T. vanilla extract
½ t. ground ginger
½ t. almond extract
2 14-oz. cans sweetened condensed milk

Combine 2½ cups milk and egg yolks in a heavy saucepan and whisk well. Cook over medium heat, stirring constantly, about 10 minutes or until mixture thickens and coats a spoon. Do not boil. Combine egg mixture with remaining milk, peaches and remaining ingredients in a large bowl and stir well. Cover and chill. Pour mixture into the container of an electric ice cream freezer. Freeze according to manufacturer's directions. Spoon into a container with a tight-fitting lid and freeze one hour or until completely firm. Makes about one gallon.

Grandma & Katie's Frozen Dessert

Refreshing during the summer, or any time of year, this tasty treat can be made ahead of time.

½ c. creamy peanut butter
½ c. light corn syrup
2 c. crispy rice cereal
2 c. chocolate-flavored crispy rice cereal
½ gal. vanilla ice cream, softened
½ to 1 c. Spanish peanuts, coarsely chopped
Garnish: chocolate syrup

Blend together peanut butter and corn syrup in a large bowl.

Add cereals; stir until coated. Press into the bottom of an ungreased 13"x9" baking pan. Spread ice cream over cereal mixture; sprinkle with peanuts. Swirl chocolate syrup over top. Cover with foil; freeze at least 4 hours before serving. Cut into squares to serve. Serves 15 to 18.

Jennifer Brown
Garden Grove, CA

Vanilla Wafer Cake

1 c. butter
2 c. sugar
6 eggs
12-oz. pkg. vanilla wafers, crushed
1 c. pecans, chopped
½ c. milk
1 t. vanilla extract

Beat butter and sugar until light and fluffy. Add eggs, one at a time, beating well after each addition. Add vanilla wafers, pecans, milk and vanilla. Pour into greased and floured Bundt® pan. Bake at 325 degrees for 1½ hours. Let cool in pan; remove from pan and cool completely on a wire rack. Serves 12 to 16.

Margie Scott
Winnsboro, TX

Chow Mein Cookies

Here's a tasty butterscotch cookie with a twist... chow mein noodles!

2 6-oz. pkgs. semi-sweet chocolate chips
11-oz. pkg. butterscotch chips
2 3-oz. cans chow mein noodles
½ c. cashew pieces

Melt together chocolate and butterscotch chips over low heat in a saucepan; blend well. Stir in chow mein noodles and cashews. Drop by teaspoonfuls onto wax paper-lined baking sheets. Let stand until set. Makes 2 to 3 dozen.

Mary Freireich
Dublin, OH

Red Velvet Cake

18¼-oz. pkg. fudge marble cake mix
1 t. baking soda
1½ c. buttermilk
2 eggs, beaten
1-oz. bottle red food coloring
1 t. vanilla extract

Combine cake mix, fudge marble packet and baking soda in a medium bowl; add remaining ingredients. Beat at low speed with an electric mixer until moistened. Beat at high speed for 2 minutes. Pour batter into 2 greased and floured 9" round cake pans. Bake at 350 degrees for 30 to 35 minutes or until a wooden pick inserted in center comes out clean. Cool in pans for 10 minutes; remove from pans to wire racks to cool completely. Wrap layers individually in aluminum foil and freeze layers overnight to make cake easier to frost. Spread Vanilla Frosting between layers and on top and sides of cake. Serves 10 to 12.

Vanilla Frosting:

5 T. all-purpose flour
1 c. milk
1 c. butter, softened
1 c. sugar
2 t. vanilla extract

Whisk flour and milk in a saucepan over medium-low heat until smooth. Bring to a boil, cook, stirring constantly, for 2 minutes or until thickened. Cover and refrigerate until chilled.
In a medium bowl, blend butter and sugar; add chilled milk mixture. Beat for 8 minutes or until fluffy; stir in vanilla.

Angela Miller
Jefferson City, MO

Red Velvet Cake

Festive Cranberry
Honey (page 331)

Mini Pumpkin Spice
Loaves (page 334)

Lemon Delights
(page 354)

Toffee Peanuts
(page 338)

GIFTS FROM
THE KITCHEN

Handcrafted goodies made from the heart

Ultimate Fudge Sauce

1 c. whipping cream
¾ c. sugar
8 oz. unsweetened baking chocolate,
   finely chopped
⅓ c. corn syrup
¼ c. butter
1½ t. vanilla extract
⅛ t. salt

Combine whipping cream and sugar in a heavy saucepan. Place over medium heat and cook, stirring constantly, until sugar dissolves. Stir in chocolate, corn syrup and butter. Cook over medium-low heat, stirring occasionally, until chocolate melts and ingredients are blended. Remove from heat; stir in vanilla and salt. Let cool to room temperature. Transfer sauce to jars with tight-fitting lids. Store in refrigerator. To serve, spoon sauce into a microwave-safe bowl and microwave on high in 20-second intervals until pourable. Makes 2½ cups.

Vickie
Gooseberry Patch

Norma's BBQ Sauce

My mother, Norma, was head cook at the Pine Street Café in the 1950s and she shared this favorite recipe with me.

6 c. onion, chopped
3 c. butter, melted
2¾ c. all-purpose flour
6 c. vinegar
¼ c. hot pepper sauce
4 qts. water
1¼ c. Worcestershire sauce
2½ t. pepper
8 qts. catsup
1 c. chili powder
1½ lbs. brown sugar, packed
1 c. mustard
13 1-quart catsup bottles and lids, sterilized

Cook onions in melted butter in a large stock-pot until soft; whisk in flour. Add remaining ingredients except catsup bottles; heat until boiling. Pour into sterilized catsup bottles; wipe rims. Secure with sterilized lids; set aside to cool to room temperature. Makes 13 bottles.

Nancy Price
Dublin, OH

all hands on deck
Canning is more fun assembly-line style with a group of friends sharing the process and the yummy rewards!

Pumpkin Butter

When fall rolls around, it's time for this spicy, sweet recipe.

29-oz. can pumpkin
¾ c. apple juice
2 t. ground cloves
1½ c. sugar
2 t. cinnamon
1 t. nutmeg
5 ½-pint canning jars and lids, sterilized

Combine first 6 ingredients in a large heavy saucepan; stir well. Bring mixture to a boil; reduce heat and simmer until thickened, about 30 minutes, stirring frequently. Spoon into hot jars, leaving ½-inch headspace. Wipe rims; secure with lids and rings. Process in a boiling-water bath for 10 minutes; set jars on a towel to cool. Check for seals. Makes 5 jars.

Bonnie Zeilenga
DeMotte, IN

Apricot & Almond Chutney

Bursting with flavor!

1 c. cider vinegar, divided
1 c. sugar
12 apricots, pitted and chopped
2 red peppers, chopped
2 onions, chopped
1 clove garlic, chopped
1 orange, seeded and chopped
1 lemon, seeded and chopped
½ c. crystallized ginger, chopped
½ t. salt
½ c. raisins
½ c. chopped almonds
1 t. ground ginger
2 1-pint canning jars and lids, sterilized

Pour ¾ cup vinegar into a saucepan; add sugar. Cook over low heat until sugar is dissolved; bring mixture to a boil and simmer for 5 minutes. Add fruits, vegetables and crystallized ginger to sugar mixture; simmer over medium heat for 30 minutes, stirring constantly. Add salt, raisins, almonds, ginger and remaining vinegar; simmer 30 more minutes or until chutney is reduced and thickened. Spoon into hot jars, leaving ½-inch headspace; wipe rims and secure lids and rings. Process in a boiling-water bath for 10 minutes. Makes 2 jars.

Carrot Cake Jam

This is a wonderful jam that tastes just like Grandma's carrot cake!

1½ c. carrots, peeled and shredded
1½ c. pears, peeled, cored and chopped
2 8-oz. cans crushed pineapple
3 T. lemon juice
1½ t. cinnamon
1 t. nutmeg
1 t. ground cloves
3-oz. pouch liquid pectin
6½ c. sugar
6 ½-pint canning jars and lids, sterilized

Mix all ingredients except pectin, sugar and jars in a large saucepan. Bring to a boil over medium heat. Reduce heat to medium-low; simmer for 20 minutes, stirring occasionally. Add pectin and return to a boil. Stir in sugar; bring to a full, rolling boil, stirring constantly. Remove from heat. Pour into hot jars, leaving ½-inch headspace. Secure with lids. Cool and store in refrigerator up to 3 weeks. Makes 6 jars.

Teri Johnson
North Ogden, UT

> **outdoor fun**
> When the temperature rises, treat a friend who loves to cook outdoors to a grilling-themed basket. Stock it with skewers, oven mitts, tongs, tasty condiments and a jar of Apricot & Almond Chutney.

Festive Cranberry Honey

This recipe makes enough to give several gifts.

3 14-oz. cans whole-berry cranberry sauce
12-oz. jar orange marmalade
1½ c. honey
7 to 8 1-pint canning jars and lids, sterilized

Place cranberry sauce and marmalade in a large microwave-safe bowl. Microwave on high 2 minutes or until melted. Stir in honey until well blended. Spoon into hot jars. Wipe rims and secure with with lids and rings. Store in the refrigerator. Serve with breads or use as a glaze for meat. Makes about 7 to 8 jars.

Savory Rice Mix

4 c. long-cooking rice, uncooked
¼ c. dried, minced onion
1 env. from a 2-oz. pkg. onion soup mix
1 T. dried parsley
¼ t. garlic salt
¼ t. salt

Combine all ingredients; store in an airtight container for up to 4 months. Attach instructions. Makes about 4 cups mix.

Instructions: Combine one cup mix with 2 cups beef broth in a 2-quart saucepan; add one tablespoon butter. Bring to a rolling boil; reduce heat. Simmer, covered, until liquid is absorbed, about 20 to 25 minutes. Serves 4.

Crispy Sweet Pickles

A wonderful recipe found in my mother's 50-year-old cookbook. If you can't find slaked lime at your grocery, look for pickling lime...it's the same ingredient with a different name.

7 lbs. cucumbers, sliced
2 gal. water
2 c. slaked lime
2 qts. white vinegar
4½ lbs. sugar
3 T. canning salt
1 t. celery seed
1 t. whole cloves
1 t. mixed pickling spice
3-inch cinnamon stick
14 1-pint canning jars and lids, sterilized

Combine first 3 ingredients in a large mixing bowl; cover and set aside for 24 hours, stirring occasionally. Drain and rinse until water runs clear; soak cucumbers in ice water for 3 hours; drain. Mix together remaining ingredients except jars; pour over cucumbers. Let stand overnight. Pour cucumber mixture into a large stockpot; bring to a boil. Reduce heat and simmer for 35 minutes, stirring often. Pack in hot jars, leaving ½-inch headspace; wipe rims. Secure with lids and rings; process in a boiling-water bath for 10 minutes. Set jars on a towel to cool; check for seals. Makes 14 jars.

Ann Brown
Winnsboro, TX

Green Tomato Relish

The wife of my husband's Army buddy in Kentucky shared this wonderful relish recipe. It takes care of the supply of green tomatoes at the end of summer's gardening season!

17 green tomatoes
1 c. salt
1 head cabbage
6 green peppers
5 red peppers
6 onions
3 qts. vinegar
8 c. sugar
2 T. celery seed
2 T. mustard seed
1 T. whole cloves
12 1-pint canning jars and lids, sterilized

Place tomatoes and salt in a food processor; pulse until coarsely chopped. Let stand overnight. Drain. Place cabbage, peppers and onions in a food processor; pulse until chopped. Mix all vegetables together in a large Dutch oven; add remaining ingredients, except jars. Cook over medium heat until onions are tender. Spoon into hot jars, leaving ½-inch headspace. Wipe rims; secure with lids and rings. Process in boiling-water bath for 10 minutes; set jars on a towel to cool. Check for seals. Makes 12 jars.

Phyllis Peters
Three Rivers, MI

Berry-Delicious Country Muffin Mix

1½ c. all-purpose flour
1 c. quick-cooking oats, uncooked
¼ c. brown sugar, packed
1 T. baking powder
½ t. cinnamon

Combine all ingredients in a large mixing bowl; place in a large plastic zipping bag. Attach instructions.

Instructions: Pour muffin mix in a large bowl; add one cup milk, one beaten egg and 3 tablespoons oil, stirring just until dry ingredients are moistened. Gently fold in 2¼ cup berries. Fill paper-lined muffin cups ⅔ full. Bake at 425 degrees until tops are golden, about 25 to 30 minutes. Makes one dozen.

luscious lemon butter
Whip up some lemon butter to give with Berry-Delicious Country Muffin Mix. Just stir a pinch of sugar and lemon zest to taste into softened butter...delightful on warm muffins.

Mini Pumpkin Spice Loaves

(Pictured on page 326)

¾ c. butter, softened
3 c. sugar
3 eggs
3 c. all-purpose flour
2 t. baking powder
1 t. baking soda
½ t. salt
1 t. cinnamon
1 t. ground cloves
¼ t. nutmeg
1 c. chopped pecans, toasted
¾ c. golden raisins
2 c. canned pumpkin
1 t. vanilla extract

Beat butter at medium speed with an electric mixer until creamy. Gradually add sugar, beating well. Add eggs, one at a time, beating just until blended after each addition. Combine flour and next 6 ingredients in a medium bowl. Add pecans and raisins, tossing to coat. Add flour mixture to butter mixture alternately with pumpkin, beginning and ending with flour mixture. Stir in vanilla. Spoon batter into 12 greased and floured 5"x3" mini loaf pans. Bake at 325 degrees for 45 minutes or until a wooden pick inserted in center comes out clean. Cool in pans on wire racks 10 minutes; remove from pans and let cool completely. Frost loaves with Cream Cheese Icing. Makes 12 mini loaves.

Cream Cheese Icing:
3-oz. pkg. cream cheese, softened
3 T. butter, softened
½ t. vanilla extract
2¾ c. powdered sugar
2 T. milk

Beat first 3 ingredients at medium speed with an electric mixer until creamy; gradually add powdered sugar, beating until smooth. Add milk, one tablespoon at a time, beating until thick. Makes 1¾ cups.

Cranberry-Pecan Coffee Cakes

½ c. butter, softened
1 c. sugar
2 eggs
2 c. all-purpose flour
2 t. baking powder
½ t. baking soda
½ t. salt
8-oz. container sour cream
1 t. almond extract
1 t. vanilla extract
14-oz. can whole-berry cranberry sauce
1 c. coarsely chopped pecans

Beat butter at medium speed with an electric mixer until creamy. Gradually add sugar, beating well. Add eggs, one at a time, beating until blended after each addition.

Combine flour and next 3 ingredients. Add flour mixture to butter mixture alternately with sour cream, beginning and ending with flour mixture. Stir in extracts.

Spoon ½ cup batter into four greased and floured 5"x3" mini loaf pans. Gently stir cranberry sauce; spoon 3 tablespoons over batter in each pan and spread lightly to edges. Sprinkle 2 tablespoons pecans over cranberry sauce in each pan. Repeat layers in each pan using remaining batter, cranberry sauce and pecans.

Bake at 350 degrees for 48 to 50 minutes or until a wooden pick inserted in center comes out clean. Cool in pans on a wire rack 15 minutes; remove from pans and let cool completely on wire rack. Drizzle Almond Cream Glaze over cooled cakes. Makes 4 mini coffee cakes.

Almond Cream Glaze:
¾ c. powdered sugar
2 T. whipping cream
½ t. almond extract

Stir together all ingredients. Makes ⅓ cup.

Cranberry-Pecan
Coffee Cakes

Spiced
Christmas
Cashews

Spiced Christmas Cashews

These well-seasoned cashews are sweet, salty and oh-so snackable! Everybody raves about them. I often make ten to twelve batches for gifts during the holiday season…maybe even more!

1 egg white
1 T. water
2 9¾-oz. cans salted cashews
⅓ c. sugar
1 T. chili powder
2 t. salt
2 t. ground cumin
½ t. cayenne pepper

Whisk together egg white and water in a large bowl. Add cashews; toss to coat. Transfer to a colander; drain for 2 minutes. In a separate bowl, combine sugar and spices; add cashews and toss to coat. Arrange in a single layer on a greased 15"x10" jelly-roll pan. Bake, uncovered, at 250 degrees for one hour and 15 minutes, stirring once. Cool in pan on a wire rack. Store in an airtight container. Makes about 3½ cups.

Paula Marchesi
Lenhartsville, PA

Savory Popcorn Topper

Keep an eye out for vintage jadite salt and pepper shakers…fill 'em with this mix and tie a ribbon around the top with a gift tag.

1 c. dried vegetable mix
2 t. dried oregano
2 t. dried basil
1 T. dried parsley
1 T. peppercorns
1 T. lemon zest
1 T. citric acid
1 t. garlic powder
¼ t. celery seed
2 sun-dried tomatoes, thinly sliced

Combine all ingredients in a food processor; blend until finely ground. Store in an airtight container. Makes about ½ cup.

instant cheer
Tuck a shaker filled with Savory Popcorn Topper along with a bag of microwave popcorn into an old-fashioned popcorn container, or ask for an extra tub at the local movie theater. Deliver with a favorite movie to a friend who may be feeling under the weather.

Cayenne Cheddar Crackers

2 c. all-purpose flour
1 t. salt
¼ t. cayenne pepper
¼ t. dry mustard
¾ c. chilled butter
½ c. shredded Cheddar cheese
6 to 8 T. cold water

Combine first 4 ingredients in a mixing bowl; cut in butter with a pastry blender or 2 forks until crumbly. Stir in cheese and just enough water to hold dough together; shape into a ball and wrap in plastic wrap. Refrigerate dough for at least 30 minutes. Roll dough out onto a lightly floured surface into a 16-inch by 12-inch rectangle; cut into 3-inch by 1-inch strips using a sharp knife or pizza cutter. Place on parchment paper-lined baking sheets; bake at 350 degrees for 10 to 12 minutes. Cool; store in airtight containers. Makes 4 dozen.

Chili Seasoning Mix

2 T. chili powder
1 T. dried, minced onion
1 T. dried, minced garlic
2 t. sugar
2 t. ground cumin
2 t. dried parsley
2 t. salt
1 t. red pepper flakes
1 t. dried basil
¼ t. pepper

Mix together all ingredients; store in an airtight container. Use 2 tablespoons per pound of ground beef for chili. Makes about ½ cup mix, or enough for 2 to 4 batches of chili.

Jill Carr
Carlock, IL

Toffee Peanuts

Use this recipe method to candy-coat any mix of nuts, such as blanched almonds, whole cashews, walnut halves or a combination of the three.

1½ c. sugar
¼ c. butter
½ c. water
4 c. raw peanuts, shelled
½ t. salt
¼ t. cinnamon

Lightly grease a large 15"x10" jelly-roll pan; set aside.
Stir together sugar, butter and ½ cup water in a large deep skillet over medium heat; cook, stirring constantly, 3 minutes or until butter melts and sugar dissolves.
Increase heat to medium-high; add peanuts and cook, stirring often, 15 minutes or until mixture becomes dry. Reduce heat to medium; cook, stirring often, 6 to 9 minutes or until sugar melts, is golden and coats nuts. (Do not stir constantly.) Sprinkle with salt and cinnamon; stir well. Spread nuts in a single layer on prepared pan. Cool completely; break nuts apart. Store in an airtight container up to 2 weeks. Makes 7 cups.

Toffee Peanuts

Caramel-Pecan
Popcorn Crunch

Caramel-Pecan Popcorn Crunch

These crisp, buttery popcorn clusters with toasted pecans rival any sweet popcorn snack you can buy at the store.

2 c. pecan halves
2 3½-oz. pkgs. natural-flavored microwave popcorn, popped
2 c. light brown sugar, packed
½ c. butter
½ c. corn syrup
2 t. vanilla extract
½ t. almond extract
½ t. salt
½ t. baking soda

Bake pecans in a single layer in a shallow pan at 350 degrees for 8 to 10 minutes, or until lightly toasted and fragrant.

Reduce oven temperature to 250 degrees. Combine popcorn and pecans in a lightly greased 16"x12" roasting pan.

Combine brown sugar, butter and corn syrup in a 2½-quart heavy saucepan. Bring to a boil over medium-high heat, stirring until butter melts. Wash down sides of pan with a brush dipped in hot water. Cook mixture until it reaches the hard-ball stage, or 250 to 265 degrees on a candy thermometer, about 4 minutes. Do not stir.

Remove from heat; stir in remaining ingredients. Gradually pour brown sugar mixture over popcorn and nuts, stirring gently to coat well, using a long-handled spoon.

Bake at 250 degrees for 1½ hours, or until dry, stirring occasionally. Cool completely in pan. Break into clusters and store in an airtight container up to 2 weeks. Makes 25 cups.

Confetti Snack Mix

A fruit-filled snack that packs a punch!

12 c. popped popcorn
½ c. sweetened flaked coconut, toasted
½ c. chopped almonds, toasted
½ c. dried apricots, chopped
½ c. dried cherries, chopped
¼ c. butter
2 T. strawberry jam
2 T. brown sugar, packed
½ t. cinnamon

Combine popcorn, coconut, almonds, apricots and cherries in a large mixing bowl; set aside. Melt butter with remaining ingredients in a heavy saucepan over medium heat; cook until mixture reaches soft-ball stage, or 234 to 240 degrees on a candy thermometer. Pour over popcorn mixture; toss to coat. Makes about 12 cups.

clever party favor
Fill empty cardboard tubes with this fruit mix, then wrap each tube in colorful tissue paper. Secure open ends with curling ribbon.

Mocha-Almond Popcorn

A crispy-crunchy snack mix that's perfect for movie night.

½ c. brewed coffee
½ c. corn syrup
¼ c. butter
1 c. brown sugar, packed
1 T. baking cocoa
12 c. popped popcorn
1 c. chopped almonds, toasted

Combine first 5 ingredients in a heavy saucepan; heat to soft-crack stage, or 270 to 290 degrees on a candy thermometer. Remove from heat; set aside. Mix popcorn and almonds together in a large bowl; pour brown sugar mixture on top, tossing to coat. Makes about 12 cups.

Candy Corn-Popcorn Balls

These fun treats are perfect to hand out to trick-or-treaters at Halloween.

2 c. sugar
1 c. corn syrup
½ t. cream of tartar
1 T. butter
½ t. baking soda
24 c. popped popcorn
1 to 1½ c. candy corn

Heat first 4 ingredients in a heavy saucepan until it reaches the hard-ball stage, or to 265 degrees on a candy thermometer; remove from heat. Carefully stir in baking soda. Pour over popped popcorn; toss to coat. When just cool enough to handle, mix in candy corn and form into 3-inch balls using buttered hands. Set aside to cool completely. Wrap individually in plastic wrap or cellophane; store in an airtight container. Makes 16 balls.

Megan Tkacik
New Castle, PA

These delicious popcorn balls are sweetened with candy corn! —Megan

take-away treats
Package treats, such as candied nuts, fudge, almond brittle, cookies or brownies in air-tight containers and then slip them into gift bags tied with ribbon or raffia. Set them in a basket by your door so there will always be a treat waiting for guests to take home.

Candy Corn-Popcorn Balls

Grandma's
Chocolate Popcorn

Grandma's Chocolate Popcorn

Pop a batch of this tasty treat and your family will demand more...it's addictive!

14 c. popped popcorn
3 c. crispy rice cereal
Optional: 2 c. dry-roasted peanuts
1½ lbs. melting chocolate, chopped
3 T. creamy peanut butter

In a large bowl, combine popcorn, cereal and peanuts, if desired; set aside. Combine chocolate and peanut butter in a microwave-safe bowl. Microwave on high 2 to 3 minutes, or until melted, stirring after every minute. Pour over popcorn mixture, tossing to coat well. Spread onto a large greased non-stick baking sheet; cool completely. Break apart; store in an airtight container up to 5 days. Makes about 20 to 22 cups.

Jayne Kohler
Elkhart, IN

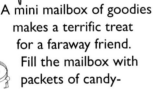

thoughtful surprise

A mini mailbox of goodies makes a terrific treat for a faraway friend. Fill the mailbox with packets of candy-striped stationery and envelopes, stamps, cookies, candies and gift mixes. Tuck in a phone card so you can catch up on holiday plans!

Caramel-Chocolate Pretzel Rods

Experiment with other toppings such as crushed cookies or multi-colored sprinkles...the kids will love to help!

14-oz. pkg. caramels
⅓ c. evaporated milk
10-oz. pkg. pretzel rods
12-oz. pkg. semi-sweet chocolate chips
Optional: 8-oz. pkg. chopped pecans

In a medium saucepan, combine caramels and evaporated milk. Cook over medium heat until caramels are melted, stirring constantly. Spoon caramel mixture over pretzel rods, one at a time, leaving about one inch uncovered. Lay pretzels on a wax paper-covered baking sheet until slightly hardened. Melt chocolate in another saucepan over medium heat, stirring constantly. Carefully pick up caramel-coated pretzels, one at a time, and spoon melted chocolate over them, leaving a small amount of caramel uncoated. Return pretzels to wax paper-covered baking sheet; sprinkle with pecans, if desired. Let cool completely. Store in an airtight container. Makes about ¾ pound.

Michele Carathers
Dalton, OH

"Line an empty coffee can or a new, unused paint can with colorful plastic wrap or wax paper, then fill with these treats. My co-workers loved them... you will too!" —Michele

White Chocolate Cookies 'n' Cream Fudge

1 c. sugar
¾ c. butter
5-oz. can evaporated milk
2 12-oz. pkgs. white chocolate chips
7-oz. jar marshmallow creme
25 chocolate sandwich cookies,
   coarsely crushed and divided
⅛ t. salt

Line a greased 9"x9" baking pan with aluminum foil, allowing 2 to 3 inches to extend over sides; set aside.

Combine first 3 ingredients in a medium saucepan. Cook over medium-high heat, stirring constantly, until mixture comes to a boil; cook 3 minutes, stirring constantly. Remove from heat; add white chocolate chips, marshmallow creme, 2 cups crushed cookies and salt. Stir until chips melt.

Pour fudge into prepared pan. Sprinkle remaining one cup cookies over fudge, gently pressing cookies into fudge. Cover and chill until firm (about one to 2 hours).

Lift uncut fudge in aluminum foil from pan; remove foil and cut fudge into squares. Makes 4 pounds.

White Chocolate
Cookies 'N Cream
Fudge

Sweet & Salty Mixed Nut Brittle

with a buttered large metal spoon. Let candy cool on pan. Break into pieces and store in an airtight container. Makes 2 pounds.

NOTE: *We tested this recipe in an 1100-watt microwave oven. If your oven is a different wattage, adjust times accordingly.*

---

cooking tip
Have the butter, baking soda and vanilla measured ahead of time, but don't combine them, so you can add them quickly. The candy will become a deep golden color after the baking soda is added.

Sweet & Salty Mixed Nut Brittle

Many are intimidated by making homemade candy, but we've made it easy...it's cooked in the microwave.

2 c. sugar
1 c. light corn syrup
11.5-oz. can lightly salted mixed nuts
2 T. butter, softened
1 T. baking soda
2 t. vanilla extract

Heavily butter a large baking sheet. Combine sugar and corn syrup in a 4-quart microwave-safe bowl, stirring well. Cover with plastic wrap, and microwave on high 4 minutes.

Carefully uncover, and microwave 8 to 9 minutes or until lightly golden in center. Stir in nuts. Microwave one minute or until mixture boils.

Using oven mitts, remove bowl from microwave. Quickly stir in butter, baking soda and vanilla. Mixture will foam. Quickly pour mixture onto prepared pan, spreading to edges of pan

Thinking-of-You Turtle Candies

A sweet way to let someone know they're missed.

36 mini baking cups
6 1-oz. sqs. bittersweet baking chocolate, chopped and melted
2¼-oz. pkg. pecan pieces, divided
6-oz. pkg. caramels
1 to 2 T. water

Arrange baking cups in a 15"x10" jelly-roll pan; set aside. Place ½ teaspoon chocolate in the center of each baking cup; sprinkle each with a few pecan pieces. Set aside until firm. Pour water to a depth of one inch into bottom of a double boiler over medium heat; bring to a boil. Reduce heat, and simmer; place caramels in top of double boiler over simmering water. Melt caramels, adding one to 2 tablespoons water to thin; cool slightly. Spoon ¼ teaspoon caramel over pecan pieces; set aside to harden. Top each with ½ teaspoon melted chocolate; set aside until firm. Drizzle with remaining melted caramel; set aside until firm. Makes 3 dozen.

Buttery Pistachio Brittle

Make on a breezy day with low to no humidity... better yet, turn up the air conditioner and pretend it's Christmas in July!

2 c. sugar
1 c. corn syrup
½ c. water
1 c. butter
2 c. salted shelled pistachios
1 t. baking soda
1 t. vanilla extract

Combine first 3 ingredients in a heavy 3-quart saucepan; heat over low heat until sugar dissolves and mixture comes to a rolling boil, stirring occasionally. Add butter; continue heating until mixture reaches the soft-crack stage, 270 to 290 degrees on a candy thermometer, stirring occasionally. Stir in pistachios; cook, stirring constantly, until mixture reaches hard-crack stage, 300 to 310 degrees on a candy thermometer. Remove from heat; carefully stir in baking soda and vanilla. Mixture will foam. Pour mixture onto 2 buttered 15"x10" jelly-roll pans; spread with forks until about ¼-inch thick. Cool completely; break into pieces and store in an airtight container. Makes about 2 pounds.

---

clever craft idea

Delivered in a clever container, Buttery Pistachio Brittle is a great way to say "I'm nuts about you!" Use decoupage lacquer or varnish to secure nuts and bolts to the flat lid of a jar; let dry. Use a clear epoxy coating, and following manufacturer's instructions to apply coating to lid. Allow to dry; attach to candy-filled jar.

Rocky Road Bars

Brownies with chocolate chips, marshmallows and peanuts...need we say more?

18.4-oz. pkg. brownie mix with
   chocolate syrup pouch
⅓ c. oil
¼ c. water
2 eggs, beaten
12-oz. pkg. semi-sweet chocolate chips,
   divided
1½ to 2 c. mini marshmallows
½ c. dry-roasted peanuts, chopped

Grease bottom only of a 13"x9" baking pan; set aside.
Combine brownie mix, syrup pouch, oil, water and eggs; stir until well blended. Mix in one cup chocolate chips; spread in baking pan. Bake at 350 degrees for 20 to 25 minutes or until a wooden pick inserted 2 inches from side of pan comes out clean. Immediately sprinkle with marshmallows, remaining one cup chocolate chips and peanuts. Cover pan with a baking sheet for 2 to 3 minutes; remove and cool completely. Cut into 4-inch by 2-inch bars; store tightly covered. Makes one dozen.

Dale-Harriet Rogovich
Madison, WI

Rocky Road Bars

Brownie Buttons

Brownie Buttons

16-oz. pkg. refrigerated mini brownie bites
  dough
11-oz. bag assorted mini peanut butter cup
  candies and chocolate-coated caramels

Spoon brownie dough evenly into paper-lined
mini muffin cups, filling almost full. Bake at
350 degrees for 19 to 20 minutes. Cool in pans
3 to 4 minutes; gently press a candy into each
baked brownie until top of candy is level with
top of brownie. Cool 10 minutes in pans. Gently
remove brownies from pan. Cool on a wire rack.
Makes 20.

Chocolate-Covered Cherry Bites

2 16-oz. pkgs. powdered sugar
14-oz. pkg. sweetened flaked coconut
16-oz. jar maraschino cherries, drained and
  chopped
½ c. chopped pecans
14-oz. can sweetened condensed milk
16-oz. pkg. melting chocolate, chopped

Combine powdered sugar, coconut, cherries
and pecans in a large bowl; mix well. Top with
condensed milk; mix well with hands until thoroughly combined and sugar is dissolved. Roll into
one-inch balls; place on wax paper-lined baking
sheets. Refrigerate overnight. Place chocolate
in a microwave-safe bowl; microwave on high
one to 1½ minutes or until melted and smooth,
stirring at 30-second intervals.

Using a toothpick or candy dipper, dip chilled
cherry balls into melted chocolate. Return to
prepared pans; refrigerate until set. Makes
about 4 dozen.

Kristie Rigo
Friedens, PA

Bite-Size Cheesecake Treats

*Blueberry or raspberry pie filling makes tasty mini
cheesecakes, too!*

12-oz. pkg. vanilla wafers, crushed
2 8-oz. pkgs. cream cheese, softened
¾ c. sugar
2 eggs
1 t. vanilla extract
21-oz. can cherry pie filling

Place ½ teaspoon crushed vanilla wafers
into 48 paper-lined mini muffin cups; set aside.
Beat cream cheese, sugar, eggs and vanilla at
medium speed with an electric mixer. Pour
mixture evenly into muffin cups, filling almost
full. Bake at 350 degrees for 15 minutes. Cool
completely. Top each with one teaspoonful of pie
filling. Makes 4 dozen.

Friendship Toffee Cookies in a Jar

1 c. toffee chips
½ c. chopped pecans, toasted and cooled
½ c. dark brown sugar, packed
2 c. buttermilk biscuit baking mix, divided
½ c. light brown sugar, packed
½ t. salt
½ c. semi-sweet chocolate chips

Layer first 3 ingredients in a one-quart wide-
mouth jar, packing tightly after each addition.
Layer one cup biscuit baking mix, brown sugar,
salt and remaining biscuit mix on top. Fill remaining space with chocolate chips; secure lid and
attach instructions.

Instructions: Combine mix, ½ cup melted
butter, one egg and one teaspoon vanilla extract in
a medium mixing bowl. Mix well. Shape dough
into one-inch balls; arrange on greased baking
sheets. Bake at 375 degrees until golden, about
10 to 12 minutes. Makes 2 to 3 dozen.

Chocolate-Mint Brownie Pops

½ c. butter
2 1-oz. sqs. unsweetened baking chocolate
10-oz. package crème de menthe
    chocolate chips, divided
1 c. sugar
2 eggs, beaten
1 t. vanilla extract
¾ c. all-purpose flour
¼ t. salt
2 T. shortening
5 2-oz. sqs. melting chocolate
31 4-inch white craft sticks
4 2-oz. sqs. white melting chocolate
crushed peppermint candies

Combine butter, baking chocolate and one cup chocolate chips in a medium saucepan. Cook over low heat, stirring constantly, until melted. Remove from heat; add sugar, eggs and vanilla, beating until smooth.

Combine flour and salt; stir into chocolate mixture until blended. Stir in remaining chips. Pour batter into a lightly greased 8"x8" baking pan. Bake at 350 degrees for 32 minutes. Cool completely in pan on a wire rack.

Using a 2-tablespoon scoop, scoop out balls from cooked brownie in pan. Gently reshape into smooth balls; place on a large baking sheet lined with parchment paper. Chill 30 minutes.

Place shortening and melting chocolate in a 2-cup glass measuring cup. Microwave on high one minute or until melted, stirring at 30-second intervals. Insert a craft stick into each brownie ball. Dip each ball into melted chocolate mixture, reheating as necessary to keep mixture liquid. Place dipped balls, top side down, on a large baking sheet lined with parchment paper. Let stand until firm.

Place white melting chocolate in a bowl. Microwave on high 40 seconds or until melted, stirring until smooth. Spoon into a large plastic zipping bag; seal bag. Snip a small hole (about ⅛-inch in diameter) in one corner of bag. Squeeze white chocolate onto dipped brownie balls to decorate as desired; sprinkle with crushed peppermint candies. Makes 31.

Peanut Butter Cup Cookie Mix

Peanut butter lovers won't be able to resist these.

20 mini peanut butter cups, chopped
1¾ c. all-purpose flour
¾ c. sugar
½ c. brown sugar, packed
1 t. baking powder
½ t. baking soda

Place peanut butter cups in a large plastic zipping bag. Combine remaining ingredients in another large plastic zipping bag. Attach instructions. Makes about 3 cups dry mix.

Instructions: Place dry mix in a large bowl. Add ½ cup softened butter, one slightly beaten egg and one teaspoon vanilla extract; stir until completely blended (mixture will be crumbly). Stir in peanut butter cups. Shape dough into 1½-inch balls and place on greased baking sheets. Bake at 375 degrees for 12 to 14 minutes; cool 5 minutes on pans; remove cookies to wire racks to cool completely. Makes 2 dozen.

Chocolate-Mint
Brownie Pops

Peanut Butter Cup
Cookie Mix

Lemon Delights

1 c. butter, softened
1 c. sugar
3-oz. pkg. cream cheese, softened
1 egg, separated
1 T. lemon juice
1 t. vanilla extract
1 t. lemon extract
¼ t. salt
2¼ c. all-purpose flour
2½ c. pecans, finely chopped

Combine butter, sugar, cream cheese, egg yolk, lemon juice, extracts and salt. Mix well with an electric mixer on medium speed; beat in flour. Wrap in plastic wrap; chill for at least one hour.

Form dough into one-inch balls. In a small bowl, lightly beat egg white. Dip balls into egg white; roll in pecans. Place 2 inches apart on ungreased baking sheets. Press thumb deeply into center of each cookie. Spoon Lemon Cheese Filling into indentations. Bake at 375 degrees for 8 to 10 minutes or until filling is set. Cool slightly; remove to a wire rack. Keep refrigerated in an airtight container. Makes 6 dozen.

Lemon Cheese Filling:
3-oz. pkg. cream cheese, softened
¼ c. sugar
1 egg yolk
1 T. lemon juice
1 t. lemon extract
1 drop yellow food coloring

Beat together all ingredients until smooth.

Tracey Varela
Thomasville, GA

Lemon Delights

Pfeffernuesse Cookie Mix in a Jar

Traditionally, these firm cookies were meant to be dunked and enjoyed during long visits and get-togethers. So why not make a batch ahead of time, brew a pot of tea and invite friends over to catch up?

4 c. all-purpose flour
½ c. sugar
½ t. nutmeg
1½ t. cinnamon
½ t. ground cloves
⅛ t. pepper

Combine all ingredients in a mixing bowl; mix well. Place in a one-quart, wide-mouth canning jar; press to pack and seal tightly. Attach instructions. Makes about 4 cups.

Instructions: Combine ¾ cup light molasses and ½ cup softened butter in a large saucepan. Heat and stir until butter melts; cool to room temperature. Stir in 2 eggs and cookie mix; mix well. Cover and chill several hours or overnight. Shape dough into walnut-size balls. Arrange 2 inches apart on greased baking sheets; bake at 350 degrees for 12 to 14 minutes. Cool on wire racks; roll in ⅓ cup powdered sugar. Makes 5 dozen.

Carol Lytle
Columbus, OH

---

gifts all year long

Wrap jar mixes with clever seasonal toppers...in fall, place a golden leaf over the lid and secure with kitchen string or jute. In summer, make it a bright green leaf! In spring a dainty handkerchief makes a pretty topper, while a glittery paper snowflake is perfect for winter.

Crispy Graham Delights

These are great for making when friends drop in or the family needs something yummy fast!

graham crackers
½ c. sugar
1 c. butter
½ c. chopped pecans or walnuts

Line bottom of an ungreased 15"x10" jelly-roll pan with one layer graham crackers; set aside. Place sugar and butter in a saucepan; bring to a boil for one minute. Pour over graham crackers; spread to cover evenly. Sprinkle with pecans or walnuts; bake at 325 degrees until golden and bubbly, about 5 to 9 minutes. Cool slightly; remove with spatula and set aside to cool completely. Gently break into squares; store in an airtight container. Makes 2 dozen.

Ginny Shaver
Avon, NY

Bavarian Mint Coffee Mix

¼ c. powdered non-dairy creamer
⅓ c. powdered sugar
¼ c. instant coffee granules
2 T. baking cocoa
3 peppermint hard candies

Combine all ingredients in a blender or food processor. Blend until candies are finely ground. Pour into a one-quart, wide-mouth canning jar; seal tightly and decorate as desired. Attach instructions. Makes about one cup.

Instructions: Pour 2 to 3 rounded tablespoonfuls of mix into a mug. Add one cup boiling water and stir to dissolve. Serves one.

Sherry Gordon
Arlington Heights, IL

menus for all occasions

Kid-Approved Dinner

Serves 8 to 10

Corn Dogs (page 87)

*Mom's Macaroni & Cheese (page 116)

green salad

Whoopie Pies (page 250)

Mother's Day Brunch

Serves 8

Citrus Mimosa (page 16)

Laura's Eggs Benedict (page 39)

Sugar Plum Bacon (page 51)

*Melon Salad with Honey Dressing
(page 195)

*double recipe

Easy Summertime Picnic

Serves 6

Tangy Deviled Eggs *(page 28)*

Yummy Blue Cheese Burgers *(page 177)*

Picnic Salad Skewers *(page 319)*

Fourth of July Beans *(page 313)*

brownies

Game Day Gathering

Serves 6 to 8

Caramelized Vidalia Onion Dip *(page 20)*

Barbecue Chicken Wings *(page 125)*

Ultimate Nachos *(page 26)*

Karen's Cayenne Pretzels *(page 35)*

Bite-Size Cheesecake Treats *(page 351)*

Christmas Treats Swap

Serves 8 to 10

Chocolate Mint Brownie Pops (page 352)

Everyone's Favorite Party Mix (page 35)

Blue Cheese Cut-Out Crackers (page 288)

Snowcap Cookies (page 250)

Peanut Butter Fudge (page 262)

Farmers' Market Veggie Supper

Serves 8

Fried Okra Salad (page 195)

Ripe Tomato Tart (page 316)

Squash & Zucchini Casserole (page 313)

Sour Cream Corn Muffins (page 311)

Fresh Peach Pie (page 231)

Holiday Feast
Serves 8 to 10

Tuscan Pork Loin (page 81)

Garlic Smashed Potatoes (page 183)

Caramelized Brussels Sprouts (page 192)

Chocolate-Cappuccino Cheesecake
(page 223)

Southern Fish Fry
Serves 6

Cornmeal Fried Catfish
& Fresh Tartar Sauce (page 89)

Waldorf Slaw (page 196)

Buttermilk Hushpuppies (page 287)

Girls' Night In

Serves 6

*Spinach & Cheese-Stuffed
Chicken Breasts (page 69)*

wild rice

Easy Fancy Broccoli (page 191)

Parmesan Bread Sticks (page 288)

*Grandma & Katie's Frozen Dessert
(page 324)*

Holiday Open House

Serves 12

Sonia's Holiday Sangria (page 16)

Mom's Sweet Potato Biscuits (page 286)

Festive Chicken Enchilada Dip (page 20)

Green Olive-Cheese Puffs (page 24)

Cranberry Cocktail Sausages (page 32)

Triple Chocolate–Nut Clusters (page 149)

Grilling Out with Dad

Serves 4

Firecracker Grilled Salmon (page 88)

*Roasted Asparagus with Feta
(page 195)*

grilled corn

tomato wedges and cucumbers

Parmesan-Garlic Bread (page 311)

Brown Bag Lunch

Serves 4

Turkey-Veggie Bagels (page 175)

Old-Fashioned Potato Salad (page 312)

apples and green grapes

Chocolate Chip Cookies (page 249)

METRIC EQUIVALENTS

The recipes that appear in this cookbook use the standard U.S. method for measuring liquid and dry or solid ingredients (teaspoons, tablespoons, and cups). The information in the following charts is provided to help cooks outside the United States successfully use these recipes. All equivalents are approximate.

METRIC EQUIVALENTS FOR DIFFERENT TYPES OF INGREDIENTS

A standard cup measure of a dry or solid ingredient will vary in weight depending on the type of ingredient.
A standard cup of liquid is the same volume for any type of liquid. Use the following chart when converting standard cup measures to grams (weight) or milliliters (volume).

Standard Cup	Fine Powder (ex. flour)	Grain (ex. rice)	Granular (ex. sugar)	Liquid Solids (ex. butter)	Liquid (ex. milk)
1	140 g	150 g	190 g	200 g	240 ml
¾	105 g	113 g	143 g	150 g	180 ml
⅔	93 g	100 g	125 g	133 g	160 ml
½	70 g	75 g	95 g	100 g	120 ml
⅓	47 g	50 g	63 g	67 g	80 ml
¼	35 g	38 g	48 g	50 g	60 ml
⅛	18 g	19 g	24 g	25 g	30 ml

USEFUL EQUIVALENTS FOR LIQUID INGREDIENTS BY VOLUME

¼ tsp	=							1 ml
½ tsp	=							2 ml
1 tsp	=							5 ml
3 tsp	=	1 tbls			=	½ fl oz	=	15 ml
		2 tbls	=	⅛ cup	=	1 fl oz	=	30 ml
		4 tbls	=	¼ cup	=	2 fl oz	=	60 ml
		5⅓ tbls	=	⅓ cup	=	3 fl oz	=	80 ml
		8 tbls	=	½ cup	=	4 fl oz	=	120 ml
		10⅔ tbls	=	⅔ cup	=	5 fl oz	=	160 ml
		12 tbls	=	¾ cup	=	6 fl oz	=	180 ml
		16 tbls	=	1 cup	=	8 fl oz	=	240 ml
		1 pt	=	2 cups	= 16 fl oz	=	480 ml
		1 qt	=	4 cups	= 32 fl oz	=	960 ml
					33 fl oz	=	1000 ml = 1 liter

USEFUL EQUIVALENTS FOR DRY INGREDIENTS BY WEIGHT

(To convert ounces to grams, multiply the number of ounces by 30.)

1 oz	=	¹⁄₁₆ lb	=	30 g
4 oz	=	¼ lb	=	120 g
8 oz	=	½ lb	=	240 g
12 oz	=	¾ lb	=	360 g
16 oz	=	1 lb	=	480 g

USEFUL EQUIVALENTS FOR LENGTH

(To convert inches to centimeters, multiply the number of inches by 2.5.)

1 in =		=	2.5 cm		
6 in =	½ ft	=	15 cm		
12 in =	1 ft	=	30 cm		
36 in =	3 ft	= 1 yd	=	90 cm	
40 in =		=	100 cm	=	1 meter

USEFUL EQUIVALENTS FOR COOKING/OVEN TEMPERATURES

	Fahrenheit	Celsius	Gas Mark
Freeze Water	32° F	0° C	
Room Temperature	68° F	20° C	
Boil Water	212° F	100° C	
Bake	325° F	160° C	3
	350° F	180° C	4
	375° F	190° C	5
	400° F	200° C	6
	425° F	220° C	7
	450° F	230° C	8
Broil			Grill

index

Pimento
Cheese Biscuits
(page 284)

breakfast & brunch dishes

Strawberry
Cheesecake
French Toast
(page 52)

cakes

candies & confections

Blackberry
Lemon Squares
(page 253)

mixes & concentrates

pies & pastries

Pasta Bake Florentine
(page 98)

Our Story

Back in 1984, we were next-door neighbors raising our families in the little town of Delaware, Ohio. Two moms with small children, we were looking for a way to do what we loved and stay home with the kids too. We had always shared a love of home cooking and making memories with family & friends and so, after many a conversation over the backyard fence, **Gooseberry Patch** was born.

We put together our first catalog at our kitchen tables, enlisting the help of our loved ones wherever we could. From that very first mailing, we found an immediate connection with many of our customers and it wasn't long before we began receiving letters, photos and recipes from these new friends. In 1992, we put together our very first cookbook, compiled from hundreds of these recipes and, the rest, as they say, is history.

Hard to believe it's been over 25 years since those kitchen-table days! From that original little Gooseberry Patch family, we've grown to include an amazing group of creative folks who love cooking, decorating and creating as much as we do. Today, we're best known for our homestyle, family-friendly cookbooks, now recognized as national bestsellers.

One thing's for sure, we couldn't have done it without our friends all across the country. Each year, we're honored to turn thousands of your recipes into our collectible cookbooks. Our hope is that each book captures the stories and heart of all of you who have shared with us. Whether you've been with us since the beginning or are just discovering us, welcome to the **Gooseberry Patch** family!

Your friends at Gooseberry Patch

We couldn't make our best-selling cookbooks without YOU!

Each of our books is filled with recipes from cooks just like you, gathered from kitchens all across the country.

Share your tried & true recipes with us on our website and you could be selected for an upcoming cookbook. If your recipe is included, you'll receive a FREE copy of the cookbook when it's published!

www.gooseberrypatch.com

We'd love to add YOU to our Circle of Friends!

Get free recipes, crafts, giveaways and so much more when you join our email club...join us online at all the spots below for even more goodies!